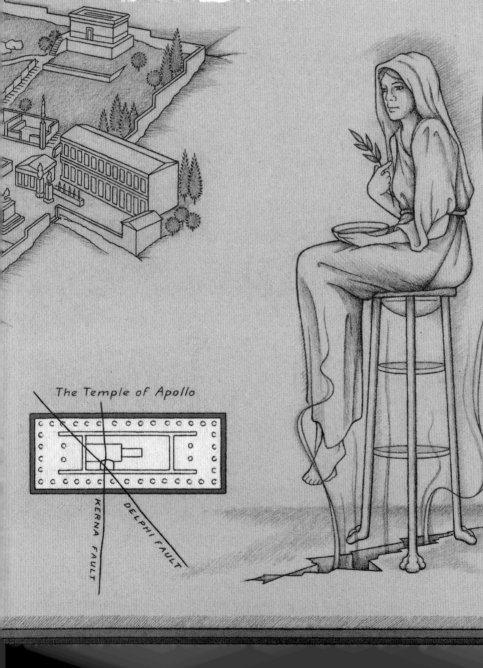

The Temple of Apollo

KERNA FAULT

DELPHI FAULT

THE
ORACLE

ALSO BY WILLIAM J. BROAD

Germs: Biological Weapons and America's Secret War
(with Judith Miller and Stephen Engelberg)

The Universe Below:
Discovering the Secrets of the Deep Sea

Teller's War: The Top-Secret Story Behind
the Star Wars Deception

Star Warriors: A Penetrating Look into the Lives of
the Young Scientists Behind Our Space Age Weaponry

Betrayers of the Truth: Fraud and Deceit in the
Halls of Science (with Nicholas Wade)

THE
ORACLE

THE LOST SECRETS

and

HIDDEN MESSAGE

of

ANCIENT DELPHI

William J. Broad

THE PENGUIN PRESS

NEW YORK

2006

THE PENGUIN PRESS
Published by the Penguin Group
Penguin Group (USA) Inc., 375 Hudson Street, New York, New York 10014, U.S.A. • Penguin Group (Canada),
90 Eglinton Avenue East, Suite 700, Toronto, Ontario, Canada M4P 2Y3 (a division of Pearson Penguin Canada Inc.) •
Penguin Books Ltd, 80 Strand, London WC2R 0RL, England • Penguin Ireland, 25 St. Stephen's Green, Dublin 2, Ireland
(a division of Penguin Books Ltd) • Penguin Books Australia Ltd, 250 Camberwell Road, Camberwell, Victoria 3124, Australia
(a division of Pearson Australia Group Pty Ltd) • Penguin Books India Pvt Ltd, 11 Community Centre, Panchsheel Park,
New Delhi – 110 017, India • Penguin Group (NZ), Cnr Airborn and Rosedale Roads, Albany, Auckland 1310,
New Zealand (a division of Pearson New Zealand Ltd) • Penguin Books (South Africa) (Pty) Ltd,
24 Sturdee Avenue, Rosebank, Johannesburg 2196, South Africa

Penguin Books Ltd, Registered Offices:
80 Strand, London WC2R 0RL, England

First published in 2006 by The Penguin Press, a member of Penguin Group (USA) Inc.

Copyright © William J. Broad, 2006
All rights reserved

Grateful acknowledgment is made for permission to reprint excerpts from the following copyrighted works:
"Ion" from *Euripides: Ten Plays*, translated by Paul Roche. Copyright © Paul Roche, 1998. Used by permission of Signet, an imprint of Pen-
guin Group (USA) Inc.
Plutarch: Volume V, Loeb Classical Library 306, translated by Frank C. Babbitt. Copyright 1936 by the President and Fellows of Harvard Col-
lege. Reprinted by permission of the publishers and the Trustees of the Loeb Classical Library, Harvard University Press, Cambridge,
Mass.
Letter from the Archeological Institute of America, May 11, 1889. Used by permission of the Archeological Institute of America,
Boston, Mass.

Illustration credits appear on page 321

LIBRARY OF CONGRESS CATALOGING IN PUBLICATION DATA

Broad, William J.
The Oracle : the lost secrets and hidden message of ancient Delphi/William J. Broad.
p.   cm.
Includes bibliographical references (p.) and index.
ISBN 1-59420-081-5
1. Delphian oracle. I. Title
DF261.D35B75 2006
292.3'2 2005055515

Printed in the United States of America
1 3 5 7 9 10 8 6 4 2

Designed by Stephanie Huntwork
Endpaper Map by Jackie Aher

Frontispiece Illustration:
The British artist John Collier (1850–1934) relied
on ancient Greek accounts to create his 1891 portrait of
the Oracle, *Priestess of Delphi*. He depicted vapors from
a rocky chasm transporting her to mystic heights.

For Tanya, my Oracle

Contents

List of Illustrations

"The greatest blessings come by way of madness, indeed of madness that is heaven-sent."

—Socrates on the Oracle of Delphi

Prologue

THIS BOOK IS ABOUT a voice from the remote past that has come back to question the metaphysical assumptions of our age, to urge us to look beyond the claims of science and reexamine our attitudes toward spirituality, mysticism, and the hidden powers of the mind. The Oracle of Delphi has prompted this kind of reassessment before, starting three millennia ago, and, as improbable as it seems, is doing so again. Her message challenges some of the most basic tenets of our day, suggesting that we have deluded ourselves into thinking we know more than we really do.

Her own life evoked high purpose and what appeared to be superhuman powers. The Oracle was no single person but a sisterhood of mystics that spoke on behalf of the god Apollo to answer questions, give advice, and make prophesies. Her voice carried far. From Athens to the Greek colonies scattered throughout the Mediterranean to the distant kingdoms of Lydia and Egypt, people credited her with godlike accomplishments, saying she could not only predict the future with remarkable precision but read minds and see events far away, even ones carefully hidden from view. Her reputation as a social catalyst was just as great. She set Socrates, arguably the most celebrated philosopher of all time, onto the path of his life's inquiry. And her moral influence helped the Greeks learn to revere oaths, human life, and the line between right and wrong.

The Oracle is back today because a team of American scientists managed to uncover one of her greatest secrets and, in the process, to restore her reputation and voice. It turns out that she got high.

The ancients alluded to this possibility, claiming that the Oracle regularly inhaled a sacred pneuma to prepare for communing with the gods and speaking on their behalf to mortals. But in modern times, armies of scholars could find no evidence of fumes or vapors and over the course of a century came to doubt the ancient claims and the honesty of the Oracle herself. Some ridiculed her as a fraud. Then the Americans took up the question. Carefully examining the ruins of the temple of Apollo at Delphi, analyzing rock and water, faults and landforms, working patiently for decades, the scientists discovered stark evidence that the Oracle had in fact inhaled a mist of intoxicating fumes, a mixture of potent gases that could promote trancelike states and aloof euphoria. It turned out that cracks in the bedrock had let powerful vapors rise into the temple, helping send the Oracle into her mystic ecstasies.

Getting high would seem to have little to do with illuminating the foundations of metaphysics or questioning the tenets of our age. But in this case it does. Moreover, the finding is not fleeting and ephemeral—not a drug mirage—but grounded in a serious examination of the methods of science and the nature of true knowledge. The Oracle's secret, it turns out, harbors what is possibly her ultimate gift.

This book tells that story, doing so in chronological order. The first chapter considers the Oracle in antiquity. The second tells of the rediscovery of the high priestess in the late nineteenth century and her eventual discrediting. The third through sixth chapters detail the detective story,

Michelangelo painted a pensive Oracle on the ceiling of the
Sistine Chapel. His chaste priestess contrasts with more
recent portrayals of her as sexually alluring.

telling how a team of four American scientists discovered the intoxicating
fumes and how their finding established the reality of the ancient claims,
bringing the Oracle back to life as a serious historical figure. And the last
chapter discusses how that discovery lays bare the metaphysical assumptions of our day.

The origins of this book go back to August 2001 when I read one of the
team's reports and first learned of the fume discovery. Back then, what
excited me was the scientific challenge to a century of scholarship, not the
Oracle. Of her I knew little. Only much later did I find out about her connection to Socrates and that Michelangelo had given her a place of honor
on the ceiling of the Sistine Chapel as one of the seers who foretold the
coming of Christ. Moreover, as a science writer and newspaperman
steeped in traditions of skepticism, I was inclined to dismiss reports of her
psychic abilities. The discovery of the fumes seemed to show that her

prophetic visions were no more real than the hallucinations of any drug addict, her acclaim no more significant than any example of group illusion or wishful thinking.

The first surprise came before I went to Greece, which I had long admired but never visited. As an undergraduate, I had studied ancient Greek philosophy and mythology as a complement to my science curriculum, and as a graduate student I had specialized in the history of science, reading the early Greek thinkers who pioneered what became the scientific view of the world. They were my heroes, these fierce rationalists. Now I learned that the Greeks also revered the occult, consulting hosts of sibyls and psychics, seers and augurs, diviners and soothsayers. This hubbub coincided with the rise of Eastern philosophies that stressed an acceptance of fate, of karma. Not the Greeks. They constantly sought to know the future, to outwit the gods, to wage war on destiny. Nothing had prepared me for the existence of this mystic industry and the vast competition it presented to the Oracle. The old, somewhat obscure literature describing it bristled with amazing facts. Aristotle himself, it turned out, had authored a theory of telepathy. It was like discovering that Einstein had moonlighted as an astrologer.

Libraries held more surprises. I learned that early modern science had embraced the Oracle as a psychic star. Distinguished men of research—even Nobel laureates—did many experiments to investigate how she might have read minds, seen faraway places, and glimpsed the future. Impressed by such experiments, Freud argued that extrasensory abilities arose in the dim past before the development of language when individuals communicated with one another via telepathy. To me, these forgotten theories and experiments seemed noteworthy, as science later disparaged the Oracle and generally turned its back on psychic claims.

The most interesting part of my journey began when I finally got to Delphi. It was a revelation. For centuries, writers have struggled to convey its grandeur, describing it as a place where primal forces have thrown open the secrets of the earth to human inquiry. You are enveloped by

mountains and canyons and cliffs and slopes that stretch out in a stagger-
ing array of hues and removes, some lush and intimate, some cool and
faraway, so that every time you walk around a little bit or turn your head,
you glimpse a hidden world or, across a wider expanse, a striking new
view. It's like having your favorite sights from a lifetime of hiking all gathered into one spot. Sound reinforces the splendor. Close your eyes intermittently and you can better appreciate the song of the wind, of crickets,
of water on rock, of sheep in pasture, of bees in almond blossoms. One day
while climbing the surrounding hills I came upon a herd of migrating
goats. Their bells captivated me with the syncopated clang of metal on
metal and the thump of wood on wood.

The Oracle spoke to the world from the temple of Apollo, the god of
prophecy and the sun. Appropriately enough, the temple's surviving
parts face eastward, so the dawn's rays can illuminate the entrance. One
day, as I gazed on the ruins, a scholar sitting next to me mentioned that,
well, no, the temple was not really all about Apollo. The side we faced, the
west, was actually dedicated to Dionysus—a god who in some ways was
the antithesis of bright Apollo, devoting himself to wine and animal impulse and demanding of his followers acts of worship that centered on orgiastic frenzies. The Dionysian side of the temple faced the setting sun,
welcoming the night.

Intrigued, I followed a rocky, seven-mile path that young Greek
women once tread in darkness, zigzagging my way up the cliffs behind the
sanctuary to a high cave where the Dionysian revelers engaged in wild rituals by the light of flickering torches. It was eerie. Animal bones lay scattered in the dirt and a number of rocky pillars rose up from the floor, the
women by all accounts worshipping them as divine phalli.

The big surprise came not as I stumbled on unexpected scenes around
the temple, but as I talked to the American scientists. Jelle de Boer, the
team's leader, especially interested me. As a boy, he had managed to survive a Japanese concentration camp during World War II, and he had gone
on to become a world-class geologist, teaching at Wesleyan University in

Connecticut and roaming the globe on projects that were intellectually bold and economically important. Personally, he projected an air of European charm and American drive.

We shared a love of geology. I had fallen for the subject after cramming myself into a tiny submersible, dropping to the bottom of the Pacific, and witnessing the birth of planetary crust. I wrote about the 1993 dive in a book, *The Universe Below,* and began doing articles for the *New York Times* on the earth's inner secrets. De Boer told me how he too had plunged into the deep on the submersible *Alvin.* We swapped stories and I like to think we bonded.

Toward the end of a weeklong visit to Delphi, de Boer made a comment that threw the fume discovery into a new light and recalled philosophic riddles I had studied long ago. The Oracle's secret, it turned out, held a hidden message. Very quickly, this book fell into place—with a crash. It shook old certainties about science and gave new credence to a range of otherworldly possibilities. In quiet conservations, de Boer would discuss whether people had the power to acquire information by means beyond the known senses.

The Oracle answered many questions in antiquity. Today, she asks them. Her new voice is one of inquiry and questioning, much like that of Socrates. The pluralism of her new voice stands in stark contrast to modern science. Its authority has grown so immense over the centuries that it now claims supremacy over all other forms of thought, with a continuing surge of technological wonders seeming to reinforce its sway. Recently, it has sought to subsume religion. Some analysts trace this development to Einstein and his flair for showing how science could outdo theology in answering life's overarching questions. The physicist's language, more metaphorical than reverential, nonetheless held out the vision of science as the great unraveler of ultimate mysteries. Today, a small industry of popular books, television shows, magazine articles, and conferences explains how science is either seizing religious ground or revealing insights that are profoundly religious in nature. Nobel laureates lead the way, as with Leon Lederman in *The God Particle* and Francis Crick in *The Astonishing Hypothesis*, which seeks a scientific explanation for the soul.

Science may be our religion. But the dirty little secret, reflected in the wisdom of the Oracle, is that it is more a loose collection of insights and slogans than a universal explanation for what is real.

Some people may see this book as an attack on science. It is not. I have devoted all my professional life to exploring its nuances and trying to convey its insights, as I attempt to do here with the story of the fume discovery. I see science as one of the supreme achievements of the human mind. It led us out of darkness and became the heart of humane civilization as well as the engine of astonishing material progress. In my career, however, I have sought to avoid scientific boosterism and to look as clearly as I can not only at the many triumphs of science but at some of its less appealing aspects, such as how research can result in unconventional arms that put civilians and whole societies at risk.

This book, rather than an attack, is ultimately an inquiry into the true breadth and depth of modern science. It examines the philosophic implications of the fume discovery and finds them indicating that science regularly overreaches in terms of explanatory power. Moreover, the cultural evidence of late suggests that such displays of hubris are abetting a popular backlash.

The new voice of the Oracle honors a more balanced approach. So does her past. How the Greeks laid the foundations of Western civilization is a familiar story. But it turns out that the Oracle, with her diverse talents and charms, Dionysian and otherwise, played a starring role.

ONE

Center of the Universe

WE KNOW LITTLE OF HOW the ancient Greeks viewed aspects of their world, even ones that seem important to us. Consider the Parthenon, lauded in modern verse, visited by Freud and mobs of other tourists, frolicked on by naked dancers, looted by collectors of antiquities, cried over by Lord Byron for its dismemberment, fought over by nations for generations, storied and photographed and sketched and plundered and itemized and memorialized and treasured. We have but one description of the Parthenon from the ancient world. It runs to a single paragraph.

The Oracle of Delphi was a different matter. She and her sacred jurisdiction on the slopes of Mount Parnassus in central Greece inspired not just a paragraph or a slim volume but a library. The literature began with Homer in the eighth century BCE and accumulated for twelve hundred years—the period of recorded history in which the Oracle advised multitudes of pilgrims, repeatedly, it was said, by foretelling the future and revealing the hidden present.

Her scores of admirers (and a few detractors) included Herodotus, Euripides, Sophocles, Plato, Aristotle, Pindar, Xenophon, Diodorus, Strabo, Plutarch, Livy, Justin, Ovid, Lucan, and Clement of Alexandria, men ranging from Greeks to Romans to early Christians. And, of course, missing from any list of authors are the remarks and monographs that disappeared along with vast amounts of other classical literature. What survived was what medieval scribes and their patrons chose to copy. It was that arbitrary.

Even so, just on the narrow issue of what the Oracle is said to have communicated on behalf of Apollo, we have received from the ancients a near riot of declarations and prophecies: 535 by one count, 615 by another. A much larger body of work described her origins, methods, reputation, history, and general role in the complex world of Greek life and religion.

Euripides in his play *Ion* cast all the action in and around the temple of Apollo and described the Oracle and her rituals in loving detail. Herodotus, the father of history, told how the Oracle's guidance helped lead the Greeks to victory in the Persian wars. The lyric poet Pindar wrote a dozen Delphic odes; his knowledge of the Oracle and the ways of the temple was so great that the priests there set up a throne for him that was cherished and exhibited after his death.

Such authors described how the priestess would go into ecstatic union with Apollo, the god of prophecy. Their imagery could throb. The Oracle's chest would heave and she would moan and wail as the god penetrated her depths, annihilating all other thoughts, impregnating her with visions of the future. Other accounts highlighted the union's otherworldly side. The prophetess, seized by divine rapture, soaring to heights beyond all human experience, at one with all time and space, would bring back glimpses of eternity to enlighten man.

The literature about the Oracle was extensive because of her importance in Greek life. It can be risky to make generalizations about an institution so enduring that its own guardians had a hard time comprehending its long history, and where today the evidence can be sketchy in places de-

A flailing Oracle enlivened an Athenian calendar of 1863. Such
portrayals drew on ancient Greek accounts that described the priestess
as locked in rapturous union with Apollo, the god of prophecy.
Socrates called it divine madness.

spite the wealth of ancient material. The record is nonetheless clear. No
seer or diviner stood higher. No voice, civil or religious, carried further.
No authority was more sought after or more influential. None. She quite
literally had the power to depose kings. The findings of history suggest
that by the golden age, during the fifth century BCE, the Greeks saw the
Oracle as a not-so-secret weapon that made them politically and militarily unassailable—able to defeat any foe, to win any battle.

In ancient Greece, priests tended to be symbolic intermediaries between the human and the divine. By contrast, the Oracle merged with the
most illustrious of the gods in a holy marriage. She became Apollo's
mouthpiece, and her words were the incarnation of his authority. Her
master, a youth of great physical beauty, ruled over not just prophecy but
the sun and music, medicine and poetry. He was light and enlightenment,
a god as well as the embodiment of goodness.

We have little hope of understanding the Greeks unless we understand the Oracle, her grip on the religious imagination, her reputation for accuracy, her sway, her preeminence. She moved effortlessly from the sacred to the mundane. The high priestess advised rulers, citizens, and philosophers on everything from their sex lives to affairs of state, most especially by forecasting the outcomes of wars and political actions. She did so thousands of times. The evidence suggests that her words repeatedly changed the course of history. Over a vast period—ages in which peoples came and went, empires rose and fell—the Oracle proved to be the most durable and compelling force in what was arguably the most important society that humans ever devised. She was the guide star of Greek civilization. We have no equivalent. No religious or secular figure, no pope or imam, no celebrity or scientist, commands the kind of respect that the Greeks accorded the Oracle of Delphi. Her sacred precinct on the flanks of Mount Parnassus was the spiritual heart of the Hellenic world.

So great was her authority that at times the Greeks happily credited her with bold prophecies that scholars judge she never made. For instance, she was widely believed to have foretold the fate of Oedipus, warning that he would kill his father and marry his mother. We view this as myth. But the Greeks saw Oedipus as a historical figure and the prophecy as a startling demonstration of the Oracle's powers. Sophocles, writing in the fifth century BCE, at the height of Athenian glory, has a speaker mount the stage near the end of *Oedipus Rex* to emphasize the Oracle's infallibility.

Such regard was extraordinary for anyone, much less a woman. Most of ancient Greece lived by a code of extreme male chauvinism, at times of misogyny. Philosophers taught that men were superior to women even as artists such as Euripides railed against the oppression of females. For the middle and upper classes of Athens, a woman's place tended to be in the home, working as a mother and a domestic manager, rarely allowed out except during festivals. Female babies were often victims of infanticide because of the economic drain of dowries. Men ruled public life. Some temples banned women and pigs. Some gods, such as Heracles Misogynous, sang the virtues of hating women. Even in the sacred environs of Delphi, woman petitioners seldom if ever had the authority to question the Oracle directly but instead had to put their questions through male intermediaries. Yet the jarring contradiction—suitable for any number of psychoanalytic studies—is that the greatest authority of ancient Greece was a woman.

Actually, of course, it was women, plural. The Oracles of Delphi were a succession of mystics who cloaked many of their operations in secrecy and apparently passed down the cult methods from woman to woman for generations. Plutarch, a Greek philosopher who at one stage in his life presided over Delphi as high priest, seems to have known little of their inner workings. However, we do know from Plutarch that three Oracles operated in unison at Delphi's height, two on call and one as a backup or an assistant. The job, while taxing at times of peak demand, clearly had its benefits. As a rule (which doubtless had its exceptions), the women worked only on the seventh day of the month, seven being Apollo's lucky number.

We tend to see the ancient Greeks as icons of rationality. Their reputation is for clear thinking, for being simple and lucid, for doing pioneering work in mathematics and the sciences, politics and philosophy. But their genius had another side, one of occult impulses and procedures far removed from the world of reason. Even dedicated rationalists gave the gods and omens their due.

Relatively few modern scholars have looked into the mystic side of Greek life, which explains our somewhat lopsided, sanitized view of the Hellenes, which is what the Greeks called themselves. Scholars who have resisted the rationalist pressures have found that the transcendental impulse played an important role in Greek society because its citizens lacked other means of divine communication—means that perhaps seem more natural to us given our history. Greek religion had no founding prophets, no formal set of religious laws, no sacred scriptures, no documents of revelation, no formal institutions of priests, and, of course, no single god. It was a fluid, pragmatic, polytheistic faith based on sacred rituals and beliefs that found legitimacy by providing comfort and strength from generation to generation. Communicating with the gods, be it through mediums or entrails, was a main way that individuals could get spiritual guidance and reassurance of their virtue. Thus, it became a foundation of piety, fusing the practical wish to know (and at times control) the future with the imperative of learning the will of gods who could influence every breeze that blew, every human act. As Walter Burkert, a historian of Greek religion, has put it, any Greek who doubted the arts of divination fell under suspicion of godlessness.

The diverse nature of this communion made Greek religion quite egalitarian. The authorities, though vitally interested in the enterprise, could never exert monopolistic control, could never prevent an individual from communicating directly with the gods. The character of the sacrament meant religious power was distributed widely.

The Oracle's lofty status was all the more surprising given the democratic nature of Greek religion. In the spiritual free-for-all, she managed to establish her own kind of monopoly.

Apollo had competition in the Greek pantheon from Hermes, Mercury, Pan, Athena, and Zeus himself—all of whom were credited with certain visionary gifts they would occasionally share with mortals. The common assumption was that the gods would secrete their superior vision into hidden signs, inspired utterances, and subtle rearrangements of the natural world in order to help earnest supplicants.

So too, the Oracle had many earthly rivals, making her standing all the more remarkable. Many sanctuaries beyond Delphi set up oracles because the priests found that the presence of such visionaries drew pilgrims, adding to a shrine's wealth and popularity.

More widely, the competitors included hordes of sibyls, psychics, priests, soothsayers, and astrologers, who left little unexamined in the effort to see what lay beyond ordinary human understanding. Looking for omens, priests studied curls of smoke from sacred fires as well as the con-

dition of sacrificial animals, examining the behavior of the doomed creatures when alive and the condition of their internal organs when dead.
Livers got special attention. Their shape and color were deemed important, with a healthy red hue considered a good sign and a missing lobe the
herald of disaster. Also analyzed were dreams, moles, dice, trances, and in
time the motions of the planets.

Virtually no one abstained. Kings and city leaders sought divine guidance. Military units went nowhere without resident mystics and fought
no war without first making careful inquiries into the signs. Opposing
forces would sometimes camp in sight of one another, waiting patiently
until the portents turned auspicious for one side or the other.

Embarrassing errors of divination, if not necessarily frequent (who
knows how many went unreported), were accepted as real and at times
were quite famous. But the Greeks tended to dismiss these blunders as
failures of interpretation—not as an indication that the foundations of
the enterprise were flawed. When the Athenians in 414 BCE laid siege to
the city of Syracuse in Sicily, the attack failed and the dejected men prepared to leave. Suddenly, the full moon went dark, a grave omen. When
the diviners ruled that the eclipse meant the expedition had to delay its
retreat until the next full moon, and the commander agreed, the Syracu-
sans proceeded to pummel, slay, and enslave the weary Athenians. Later,
it was easy to assign blame. The military unit's best seer, Stilbides, had
died, forcing the commander to rely on second-rate advice.

The common man was no less superstitious than the generals and civic
leaders. Shepherds watched the night sky for portents. Servants and workers saw harbingers in a clap of thunder and a flight of birds. A sneeze, twitch,
or shudder could be a sign, since involuntary movements were often attributed to divine influence. People used simple methods of divination all the
time, such as alphabet oracles. From a bag or box, questioners would pull
stones painted with letters. Each had specific portents—for instance, alpha
might foreshadow success, zeta danger, and omega difficulties ahead.

The spiritual elite claimed not only special gifts of interpretation but godlike powers. One account described how the priests at Claros in Anatolia would inquire about the names of clients, retire to a sacred grotto, and reply to unspoken questions.

The ancient Greeks had no special words for telepathy and clairvoyance. But they firmly believed that pious individuals could achieve feats of extrasensory perception, as well as precognition in the form of prophecy and divination. Indeed, philosophers sought out likely mechanisms for the transfer of psychic energy. Democritus, known for his atomic theory of matter, taught that all living things emitted invisible rays that sensitive individuals could discern. Aristotle developed a similar idea based on a wave theory. The Stoics held that a man could not raise a finger without its effect being felt throughout the universe.

The Oracle of Delphi stood at the apex of this sprawling, chaotic, feverish, metaphysical industry. Remarkably, she won her celebrity despite (or perhaps because of) a history of cryptic ambiguities, occasional outright errors, and even episodes where it seemed possible to bribe the priestess, or at least one of her functionaries. The odor of corruption wafted about the Oracle when at times she seemed ready to please whoever held power. Even so, on balance, the Greeks saw her as delivering the prophetic truth and doing so more reliably than anyone else. They trusted her. She prevailed even into the worldly, skeptical days of the fifth and fourth centuries BCE, when the Athenians shook free of much religion and most of the interventionist gods.

Respect for the Oracle and her divine patron translated into monumental wealth that must have staggered even the most resolute cynics. It was the custom for thankful supplicants to send back riches. These and other gifts and tithes accumulated over the centuries to the point that Delphi became one of the wealthiest places on Earth, filled with gold and silver and marble and brilliant works of art by the most famous artists of the day. Literally thousands of statues and paintings and high reliefs crowded the sacred district, as did treasuries. For a supplicant to walk the switchbacks of the Sacred Way up the slope toward the temple of

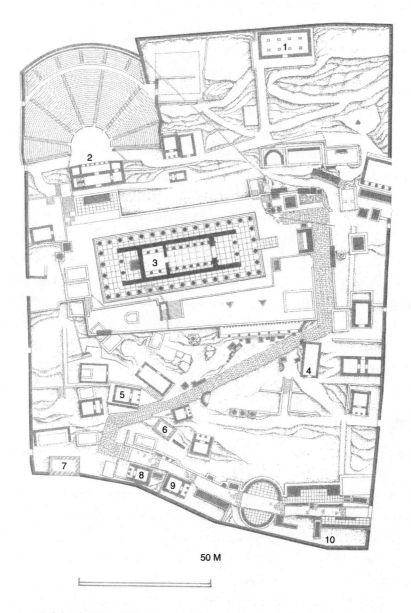

At ancient Delphi, the Sacred Way zigzagged through the crowded sanctuary of Apollo up to the temple, where the Oracle gave advice and foretold the future. 1) Clubhouse. 2) Theater. 3) Temple of Apollo. 4) Corinthian treasury. 5) Athenian treasury. 6) Syracusan treasury. 7) Theban treasury. 8) Siphnian treasury. 9) Sicyonian treasury. 10) Trojan Horse.

Apollo—past riches and war memorials and statues of gods and goddesses, heroes and kings—was to be awed and dazzled. First-time visitors surely gazed about in reverential silence. Some probably wept. Scores of statues of Apollo greeted pilgrims, one looking down from a height of nearly sixty feet. Made of bronze, it could gleam in the clear mountain air, not unlike the god of the sun himself.

The immediate setting for the temple was nothing short of spectacular. Behind it rose twin limestone cliffs known as the Phaedriades, "the Bright Ones" or "the Shining Rocks." Their intersection formed a hollow in the southern flank of Parnassus that made the perfect backdrop for Delphi's religious epics, the cliffs often golden as the sun rose and set.

The temple itself was a Doric gem. A bit smaller than the Parthenon, it arose in the fourth century BCE during Greece's classical age and represented the culminating edifice of a series of temples that were increasingly large and stately. Its entrance bore such inscriptions as "Know Thyself" and "Avoid Extremes" lest visitors doubt their arrival at the epicenter of wisdom. Its layout differed from that of other temples. Meant not only for worship but for divination, it housed countless precious objects and toward the back opened to an area that led down to the Oracle's chamber.

Many modern-day scholars dismiss her supposed powers as rooted in luck, self-deception, political manipulation, or the kind of calculated ambiguity that shifted responsibility onto the shoulders of interpreters, as often happens in the world of prophecy. Our language honors this interpretation. *Delphic* is a synonym for an utterance that is ambiguous or obscure in meaning. Even so, a few analysts hold that the Oracle's more spectacular predictions support the findings of psychic research and confirm the existence of a realm of natural law beyond the current understandings of science.

Given the fierce competition that the Oracle faced from armies of seers, gods, and intermediaries to the divine, a basic question that arises in any examination of her world is why she was so influential. How did she come to dominate Greece? What explains her centrality?

Her perceived accuracy was certainly a factor, as was her antiquity. Delphi had a long history with Apollo—from the ninth century BCE and possibly much earlier, the beginnings lost in time. Another factor was surely the popularity of Apollo, a god the Greeks saw as wise and generous and understanding and generally superior to members of the Greek pantheon, renowned for violence, fickleness, and immorality. Apollo was sympathetic. He stood apart from the rough gang of deities quick to display anger or shake with reckless laughter. Scholars call Apollo the most Greek of the Greek gods. Perhaps most important, his prophetic abilities made him a huge draw, a god judged to be not only indulgent but omniscient. As Pindar put it: Apollo "knows the end supreme of all things, and all the ways that lead thereto; the number of the leaves that the earth putteth forth in spring; the number of the sands that in the sea and the rivers are driven before the waves and the rushing winds; that which is to be, and whence it is to come."

Even so, pilgrims who sought Apollo's wisdom had many sanctuaries from which to choose other than Delphi. His temples could be found at Corinth and Bassae in the Peloponnese, at Delos and Aegina in the Aegean, and at Segesta in Sicily. At Didyma on the coast of Asia Minor, the Greeks built a stupendous temple of Apollo where priests ran a thriving business in prophecy. Apollo could be consulted in so many places that the Greeks called him the wandering god. Interestingly, Apollo's temples as a rule used men as oracles. Only at Delphi did women speak on his behalf.

In analyzing what made the Oracle so influential, scholars zeroed in on one of the temple's unique attributes that ancient authors often noted— a mystic pneuma said to rise from a cleft in the floor of the *adyton,* the shrine's holy of holies, the inner sanctum in the basement of the temple where the Oracle communed with Apollo. Pilgrims sitting nearby in an anteroom were said to occasionally get whiffs of a strange, sweet odor, like the fragrance of an exotic perfume.

Adyton in ancient Greek means "do not enter" or "inaccessible," and pilgrims of the day knew little about such areas other than their reputations as the hearts of places of worship. *Pneuma* means "spirit" or "soul," "wind" or "breath," much as the Sanskrit *prana* refers to both breath and vital spirit. At Delphi, the mysterious substance was said to be a gift of the god that inspired the Oracle's divine madness, though the accounts varied and tended to be vague about its nature, whether material or spiritual or a combination of the two.

In her need to breathe the pneuma, the Oracle functioned differently from sibyls or prophets, who were seen as requiring no external stimulation because they possessed special powers of their own. Such was the reputation of Cassandra, the mythical daughter of the king of Troy, endowed with the gift of prophecy but fated never to be believed. By contrast, the Oracle was said to be an unremarkable person in normal life. It was only when she went through a number of rituals of purification and descended into the *adyton* and breathed the holy pneuma that Apollo possessed her. Some scholars reasoned that the pneuma, like a drug, was the source not only of the Oracle's inspiration and authority but perhaps of her reputation for moodiness and unpredictability. It was said that when the Oracle answered questions, she was always in a trance, at times in a frenzy, and occasionally foaming at the mouth.

For a long time, ancient literary sources provided scholars with their only direct clues about the Oracle and her methods, most especially about the chasm and the question of whether any material substance aided her divine inspiration. But then, starting in 1892, French archaeologists put the whole thing under the light of science by traveling to Delphi and unearthing the buried temple itself. Their guide was the ancient literature. It proved remarkably accurate, with one glaring, baffling exception—the excavators could find no hint of a chasm beneath the temple, no evidence that the rocky ground had ever brought forth vapors of any kind.

Disappointment echoed through modern judgments about the Oracle for nearly a century, a time when scholars were eager to be seen as swimming in the sea of science and were looking for reasons to downplay the mystic side of Greek life. If the vapors were a mirage, so too, perhaps, were other aspects of the sanctuary's operations. Maybe it was all a lie, a sham meant to defraud a gullible public. Maybe the gods were laughing yet again.

ANCIENT DESCRIPTIONS of Delphi's founding tell of a cleft in the side of Mount Parnassus where goats suddenly began crying and leaping about in a frenzy. Herdsmen marveled at the sight. They approached the fissure and had the same experience. Goats and men acted like beings possessed. Some goatherds reported visions. Others foretold future events. A growing number of visitors came, and all, it was said, had convulsive ravings or fell into inspirational trances. The experience could be risky as well. Frenzied experimenters were said to disappear occasionally into the cleft, apparently overcome. Residents of the region, awed by the phenomenon and perhaps eager to set themselves apart from neighbors, decided that the vapors put mortals in contact with the gods. They built a shrine. To limit the dangers, and perhaps to keep out of harm's way themselves, the local authorities designated one woman as the exclusive conduit for the divine madness. For her own safety, they made a tripod on which she could sit, physically supported if she should become light-headed or faint. Soon, the Oracle began to speak from the shrine on behalf of the gods.

Exactly when all this occurred is lost to history. Moreover, it is quite possible that the sketchy accounts are apocryphal or half truths, though the reports of Diodorus and Plutarch are detailed enough to give the name of the goatherd who allegedly made the discovery, a man named Coretas. Archaeological evidence indicates that people had begun to worship at the rugged site by 1600 BCE, the late Bronze Age. At the time, Troy was a boomtown and Babylonian astronomers were charting the heavens. Nomadic tribesmen had recently seized control of Egypt, an ancient empire full of architectural wonders.

From the topography of Mount Parnassus, it is clear that the early temple, like later ones, sat in a cleft, a natural theater surrounded on three sides by the mountain's flanks. Indeed, the name Delphi is said to derive from *delph,* Greek for "hollow," or alternately from *delphis,* an old Greek word for "womb."

Crystalline springs, from which people and animals could refresh themselves, added to the site's allure. The Greeks deified springs. Cool waters that bubbled up out of nowhere amid the dry landscape, by their very existence and value in quenching thirst, especially on a hot summer day, seemed to shimmer and pulsate with a magic luminosity all their own. Greek mythology personified this vitality in the naiads, nymphs who presided over brooks, springs, and fountains. Worshipped as distant offspring of Tethys, a goddess of the sea, the naiads were depicted in ancient Greek art as beautiful women and young girls, in essence female sex symbols. They were notorious for seducing lustful deities as well as men.

The bounty of Delphi's pools and springs boded well for the institution of prophecy because the Greeks saw enchanted waters as able to cure disease, inspire poetry, and—most especially—induce raptures conductive to augury. Basic to life, full of constantly changing forms and patterns, often flashing with light, moving water seemed to mimic the infinities and help inspire those individuals who sought to comprehend what lay ahead. A drink from a sacred spring was often considered a prerequisite to prophetic rites.

Another gift of nature favored religion. The rocky slopes of Parnassus abounded in limestone, a soft rock easily cut into blocks for temples. But therein also lay a drawback—the rocky incline. To set up a temple, builders would first have to create a semblance of level ground by moving around rocks and fill to make terraces. Even with such leveling, however, the area was still prone to landslides and earthquakes that could quickly undo any structure. More generally, it was barren. The stony locale would never support thriving agriculture, only goatherds. It was clear that religious authorities would have to find other means of support.

The answer lay at their feet. The mountainous cleft sat astride the main east-west route through central Greece, bringing a steady flow of travelers and caravans. The glade beckoned even without a temple. Visitors could pause not only to refresh themselves at Delphi's bountiful springs but to feel the unique atmosphere of the place lift their spirits. The experience came on suddenly. The surrounding hills and mountains keep the cleft hidden from view until the last minute, giving Delphi a sense of seclusion. From the east, the road passes close to a mountain face before a passerby can see into the cleft. The sense of surprise is even greater from the west, where a high ridge forms a protective wall. Weary travelers coming into the cleft would find themselves in a stunning retreat where they could refresh not only their bodies but, with the establishment of a temple, their souls.

Mainland Greece in the Bronze Age pulsed with its first great civilization, the Mycenaean, which was centered in the Peloponnese, the large peninsula to the south that formed the Greek heartland. It was characterized by city-states such as Corinth and, most powerful, Mycenae. Warriors ruled. They built palaces atop hills and surrounded them with massive walls that were easy to defend. They filled their tombs with swords, daggers, and spears.

Religion for the Mycenaeans centered on ritual sacrifices to gods that foreshadowed the Olympians—Zeus, Hera, and so on, as well as less familiar deities. The Olympians took their name from Mount Olympus, the highest mountain in Greece, the home of Zeus's family of immortals. It was a natural choice. The peak, often covered in snow, its whiteness a symbol of otherworldliness, was the largest single object that the Greeks could see on land and was easily perceived as a divine abode. Often lost in clouds, it was too lofty for mortal footfall. (Its highest peak remained unscaled until 1913.) It was also in Greece's remote north, its distance reinforcing the notion of sacred precincts.

Mount Parnassus was more familiar, if still a towering mass of rock often cloaked in clouds. It lay near the Gulf of Corinth, a busy waterway, and on the main overland trade route. Some one hundred miles over the mountains from Athens, it was also close to the Peloponnese and its rich farmlands and cities. Even so, Parnassus was still in the woods, so to speak. No big cities, palaces, or teeming markets lay nearby. The sprawling mountain, as its debut in history suggests, was a place of rocks and boulders, glades and springs, goats and goatherds.

It was natural, then, to attribute the mystic powers at Mount Parnassus not to one of the Olympians but to Ge, also known as Gaia, the female goddess of fertility and the earth. Along with water, the Greeks considered earth the mother of all living things and the primordial source of all divination. Gaia's roots were ancient, going back to the creation myths of early times. According to Hesiod, an early Greek poet, Gaia sprang from Chaos, who also sired Eros and Night. These primal gods had more to do with things that filled rural people with wonder—sky and rain, soil and fertility—than with the urbane, all-too-human rivalries of the Olympian sophisticates. At Mount Parnassus, the productions of the earth itself brought about the inspiration of the Oracle, and a spontaneous response seems to have been the worship of Gaia, the earth mother.

Little is known of what the Oracle communicated during this distant era, perhaps forecasts on when to sow and reap and so on. In time, other patron deities came and went, including Themis, a goddess daughter of Gaia, and Poseidon, not yet the god of the sea but of springs, subterranean waters, and earthquakes, as suggested by his epithet at the time, the earth-shaker. All spoke through the Oracle, the ancients reported, but none had much cultural impact.

Delphi's rise to a global hot spot with not only a major sanctuary but pools, gyms, athletic games, music festivals, merchants, guides, food vendors, poets, art displays, hawkers of religious souvenirs, a theater for thousands of spectators, and all the other aspects of a thriving religious enterprise coincided with the arrival of an impressive new god, Apollo.

Just when he descended from Mount Olympus is unclear because our knowledge of that era is so limited. The period from roughly 1100 BCE to 900 BCE was a time of decline, Greece's so-called dark age. Foreign trade dwindled. Farming dropped to subsistence levels. Scribes no longer cut tablets with Linear B, an early script. Simple geometric designs replaced pictorial art. It was a time of invasion and migration.

Things picked up by the eighth century, when written Greek debuted. The earliest inscriptions have been dated to around 750 BCE, and were followed by the first Greek literature, the poems of Hesiod and the epics of Homer. Gold, silver, and other signs of wealth began to reappear, both in commerce and personal life. Coins debuted in the seventh century BCE, speeding commerce.

At Delphi, the Oracle and her new divine partner wielded growing influence and renown. Apollo had a wonderful billing: the god of light and order, reason and prophecy. He was always portrayed as young, a god the ancient Greeks came to revere as the greatest of all next to Zeus and who in turn came to symbolize the best of the Greek spirit. A symbol of hope and vitality, he was the antithesis of the dark age.

In legend, young Apollo, armed with bow and arrow, set out from Mount Olympus looking for his own home from which to guide men. At Delphi, he found the perfect spot, "a hollow, rugged glade," said the Homeric *Hymn to Apollo,* rich in fresh water and boasting a magnificent view. Apollo's declaratory aims were both immodest and improbable—in other words, perfectly godlike.

> In this place I am minded to build a glorious temple to be an Oracle for men, and here they will always bring perfect hecatombs [a sacrifice to the gods, consisting originally of a hundred oxen], both they who dwell in rich Peloponnesus and the men of Europe and from all the wave-washed isles, coming to question me. And I will deliver to them all counsel that cannot fail, answering them in my rich temple.

In Greek mythology, a monster ruled Delphi before Apollo killed the beast with bow and arrow and seized control of the oracular site, symbolized by the tripod on this ancient Greek coin.

Apollo on the Delphic tripod, the seat of the Oracle during prophetic sessions. The image symbolized how the god of prophecy spoke through the priestess. The tripod, an icon of ancient Greek art, signified not only divine revelation but earthly power and status, with tripod trophies often given as athletic prizes.

But the idyll already had a resident, a huge snake or dragon that ancient writers called Python. Every god has an adversary. Apollo fought the
monster and seized control of the shrine. The defeat of the snake came to
symbolize the god's victory over the powers of darkness. For instance, the
Homeric *Hymn* describes the beast as hostile to the nearby people, killing
them and their sheep, and says that during its death throes Apollo proclaimed himself the liberator of humanity.

Python's slaying, in addition to providing a dramatic narrative for
Apollo's new sanctuary, gave Delphi its other name—Pytho, from the
Greek word for "to rot," a reference to the decay of the snake's body.
Pytho came to refer to the sacred region at the foot of Parnassus, while the
name Delphi applied only to the sanctuary and, in time, the nearby town.
The Oracle herself came to be known as the Pythia.

The earliest reference to the Oracle is found in Homer, whose epics were
recorded around the eighth century BCE and drew upon an oral tradition
that was much older, dating back to the dark ages and the Mycenaean era.
In the *Odyssey,* he tells how Agamemnon, the king of Mycenae, consulted
the Oracle "in sacred Pytho" and heard her prophesize about the disasters
that would befall his enemy, the Trojans. Already—even in Homer's day—
the Oracle's successes in prognostication and earthly rewards were seen as
so great that Delphi had become synonymous with extravagant wealth. In
the *Iliad,* Achilles sings of "the treasures in rocky Pytho."

Early riches came from thankful supplicants who had set up colonies
overseas and sent back tithes and gifts as their settlements prospered. The
colonists also helped spread the Oracle's fame throughout the wider
Greek world. The greatest period of migration, from the eighth to sixth
centuries BCE, sent waves of settlers to Italy, Sicily, the Black Sea, North
Africa, France, and eventually Spain. Such ventures, while rooted in political and financial ambitions, were deeply religious in character. The
colonists sought Apollo's advice on choosing the best sites as well as his
blessing for the settlements because the construction of new temples and
sanctuaries would be among their first acts.

We have several tales of colonization in which the Oracle is depicted as playing a visionary role in picking choice locations for colonists or in helping them defeat local adversaries. These are among the oldest accounts of her influence, and scholars usually evaluate them as spurious or of questionable authenticity, mainly as myths.

All the while Delphi grew richer, creating a growing atmosphere of prophetic accomplishment. Cyrene in Libya, the most successful Greek city in Africa, sent Delphi a statue of a chariot with the goddess Cyrene at the reins. Colonists in the Lipari Islands just north of Sicily sent twenty statues of Apollo—one for each victory the god had granted them over twenty enemy warships.

After the dark ages, as the colonies prospered and the Oracle's fame grew at home and abroad, the Greeks increasingly viewed Delphi as central to their rebirth, not only spiritually but physically. After all, the shrine's geographic setting made it roughly equidistant among the flourishing outposts.

It was during these early days that the Greeks began honoring Delphi as the center of the world, marking the site with a large conical stone, the *omphalos,* meaning "navel" or "center." Most accounts put the omphalos in the *adyton,* near the Oracle. By legend, the centrality of Delphi was established by no less an authority than Zeus himself. He was said to have sent out two eagles that flew from the edges of the world, meeting at the sanctuary. Physical truth lurked behind this myth. Early maps showed Delphi as located in the exact center of the Greek world, midway not only among the mainland states but the distant colonies in Italy and Asia. Moreover, holding title as the terrestrial hub meant being at the center of the wider universe as well, since Greek cosmology pictured the stars, planets, and celestial bodies as rotating around the earth. The one sanctuary ruled them all.

At Delphi, two solid gold eagles stood on either side of the omphalos, memorializing the divine tribute to the sanctuary's centrality. The arrangement became an icon of Greek art. A striking fifth-century relief found at

A venerated stone known as the *omphalos* (Greek for "navel") marked the sanctuary of Apollo at Delphi as the center of the world. Replicas, like this one of marble, were placed around the sanctuary as a reminder of Delphi's centrality and holiness. Its patterned surface mimicked a net placed over the real omphalos, which was kept in the Oracle's chamber.

Ancient coins often represented Apollo as sitting on the omphalos, symbolizing the god's presence at Delphi, the spiritual heart of the Greek world.

Piraeus, the harbor at Athens, shows Apollo seated on the tripod and at his feet the omphalos flanked by the two eagles.

The growing prominence of the shrine was no small feat for a rocky cleft in the side of Parnassus that had begun life as a spiritual backwater. Now, Delphi was fast becoming one of the unifying elements in a part of the ancient world famous for fractious city-states and uncivil wars.

WHO WAS the Oracle? What kind of woman gave herself to the gods? How was she chosen? In most cases, we have only hints of answers to such questions. No single account presents an overview of how the Pythia was selected and the nature of her procedures. But pieces of the puzzle lie scattered throughout the ancient literature and when gathered together give a fairly complete portrait.

At least initially, the Oracle appears to have been an innocent girl, probably naive and unquestioning and chaste. The priestess, as the mistress of Apollo, was to save herself for the god alone and have no intimate relations with men. Originally, the emphasis on purity was so great that the person chosen to be the Oracle was invariably a young virgin, clad appropriately for her role. But then came a man from Thessaly, a northern region of Greece known for its rough inhabitants. Fake money was called Thessalian coin and untrue action Thessalian deceit. Diodorus, an ancient historian, recounts the infamy.

> People say that Echecrates the Thessalian, having arrived at the shrine and beheld the virgin who uttered the Oracle, became enamored of her because of her beauty, carried her away with him and violated her; and that the Delphians because of this deplorable occurrence passed a law that in the future a virgin should no longer prophesy but that an elderly woman of fifty would declare the Oracles and that she would be dressed in the costume of a virgin, as a sort of reminder of the prophetess of olden times.

The image of the Oracle as lithe and young, almost swooning, ready for divine communion, became a cliché. Modern painters often conjured up a priestess who was quite seductive. Some portrayals showed her with fleshy lips and breasts that were bare or lightly covered. At least one rendering showed her naked.

But the reality was surely otherwise, as Diodorus suggests. Over time, the tradition of innocence gave way to one in which Oracles tended to be older and more learned, usually woman over fifty who had put aside their marital and family duties. Still, it could do no harm for the Pythia to have a comely face and a good reputation. An unwritten rule seems to have made sure that the Oracle had no physical defects, which would have been perceived as an insult to the gods.

Usually, the women came not from Athens or Corinth or some other big city but from Delphi itself, which, if not a pinnacle of culture, was a place steeped in the ways of prophecy. The Pythia that Euripides depicts in *Ion* declares that she is "the chosen one from all the women of Delphi."

Euripides, who wrote during the fifth century BCE, set the play in the temple of Apollo and clearly knew its minutiae. His Oracle is crowned with laurel and a chaplet of ribbons and wears a long white alb reaching down to her ankles. Even so, despite the presence in the historical record of such rich detail, the ancient writers divulged little about how the priestess was selected. Perhaps it was wrapped in cult secrecy. H. W. Parke and D. E. W. Wormell, fellows of Trinity College, Dublin, who wrote one of the best histories of the Delphic Oracle, published in 1956 in two volumes, gave a plausible theory. They suggested that the sanctuary had a guild of mature women whose main responsibility was to keep the eternal fire burning in the temple's central hearth. Like the Pythia, the women had to have led a pure life and to have ceased from marital relations. This guild, the scholars suggest, provided a natural recruiting ground for the oracular post.

The livelihood, despite its dangers, must have had great appeal for women who craved upward mobility in a society that otherwise offered little. Priests and priestesses were the keepers of the temples and the only individuals allowed to go into a deity's inner sanctum, a sign of their high status. Moreover, the job of priestess, one of the few public careers available to a Greek woman, tended to be rich in worldly benefits. Scholars say adult priestesses enjoyed freedom from taxation as well as the right to own land and view public contests. At the theater, they were often given seats in the front row. In addition, the state paid them salaries and usually gave them housing. At Delphi, the Pythia had her own official residence. The priestesses of some cults had wide duties, levying fines, granting loans, signing documents, appointing aides, and disciplining the sacrilegious. Special distinctions bestowed upon important priestesses included edicts for exemplary service and statues set up in their honor. Some priestesses were awarded gold crowns. Being an oracle—or better yet, the Oracle of Delphi, in effect the high priestess of the land—was a chance to be extraordinary, to achieve exalted social, spiritual, and financial status, to win wide respect and recognition for nurturing a vigorous, just society. By definition, the Oracle lived in a lofty world where she enjoyed a unique independence from men and the often grim realities of life for most Greek women.

It took centuries for the more elevated persona of the Delphic Oracle to emerge. But by the fifth and fourth centuries BCE, the height of classic Greek civilization, the sophistication of the institution was such that her position appears to have been routinely if not always held by women of high social standing, cultivated and discerning. In *Ion,* her demeanor outside the *adyton* is portrayed as solemn and wise, her words precise. "You are sinning too by ruthlessness," she admonishes Ion, the play's protagonist.

Plutarch, the Greek philosopher and high priest of Delphi, father of four sons and one daughter, had much to say about the Oracle and much reason to be heeded. Born in Greece not far from Delphi, he was a man of great charm and erudition, widely knowledgeable of the Mediterranean world because of his travels and hugely popular because of his gift for explaining complex things to general audiences. He wrote biographies of famous men as well as dissertations on history, antiquities, religion, and social life, such as *The Amorous Man* and his charming *Advice to the Bride and Groom.*

Plutarch seems to have regarded many of the Oracles as quite cultured and intelligent, drawing on personal knowledge. He dedicated his collection of essays *Isis and Osiris,* about the Egyptian gods, as well as his collection of stories *The Bravery of Women,* to Clea, a high priestess of Delphi or, as he puts it affectionately, "head of the inspired maidens." Clea was plainly a good friend of the learned Plutarch, a woman he respected and probably admired.

But this image of the latter-day Oracles as smart and accomplished had its exceptions, especially in Delphi's later days, as Plutarch took pains to note. In one essay, he described how the current medium of the holy tripod was a commoner with no special knowledge.

It is impossible for the unlettered man who has never read verse to talk like a poet. Even so the maiden who now serves the god here was born of as lawful and honourable wedlock as anyone, and her life has been in all respects proper; but, having been brought up in the home of poor peasants, she brings nothing with her as the result of technical skill or of any other expertness or faculty, as she goes down into the shrine. On the contrary, just as Xenophon believes that a bride should have seen as little and heard as little as possible before she proceeds to her husband's house, so this girl, inexperienced and uninformed about practically everything, a pure, virgin soul, becomes the associate of the god.

Here Plutarch, the high priest of Delphi and a prominent defender of its values, is perhaps acting more as a promoter of Apollo than as a historian. It made no difference if the Oracle was a simple country girl or a wealthy sophisticate, he seems to be saying. His message was that it was ultimately the god, not the medium, who radiated wisdom and insight. The Oracle was simply a lamp awaiting divine illumination.

Around 440 BCE, an Athenian potter decorated a large cup with a portrait of the Delphic Oracle in the midst of a prophetic session. It turns out to be the only surviving image that we have of the Pythia from her own day. The illustration shows neither a rustic maid nor a youthful seductress. Rather, it portrays a woman in her prime, with full breasts and supple gracefulness, her long alb coming down to her ankles. She sits on the tripod, her bare feet dangling off the floor, her body slumped, not quite herself, thoughtful, her eyes gazing down, looking into a small dish, presumably filled with water from a sacred spring, perhaps fragrant with a sweet aroma. In her right hand she holds a sprig of laurel, Apollo's holy plant. The ceiling of her oracular chamber is low, and beneath her feet, below the floor, the artist has depicted a void.

ONCE A MONTH (or more on special occasions), the Pythia and her retinue of assistants and priests would go through an intricate series of rituals to purify the priestess for union with the god. The preparations are

Ancient Greek artists usually depicted Apollo rather than the Oracle since the god was considered more important than his mortal representative. This exception—done by an Athenian potter around 440 BCE, as the Parthenon neared completion—shows the Oracle while prophesizing. Her contemplative air contrasts with depictions of divine frenzy.

said to have included fasting. But the real work began at dawn on Apollo's special day, the seventh of the month.

Euripides paints a rich portrait of the ceremony, starting with a young priest, Ion, paying homage to the sun's early rays dancing on the peaks of Parnassus. The scent of incense drifts through the temple as Ion goes about his duties: chasing away flocks of birds, sweeping the temple with sprays of bay and sacred laurel, sprinkling the floor with holy water, advising the day's first pilgrims on how to perform sacrifices.

The main ceremony began as the Oracle purified herself in nearby waters named Castalia, after the naiad daughter of a river god. The cool spring waters flowed down a mountain gorge a half mile east of the temple's grounds. The ravine, unlike much of the arid region, bristled with trees and, in summer, cool shade. Ion sang of the visit of the Oracle, as well as separate groups of male priests who also purified themselves in the holy waters.

> But come, you Delphians, Apollo's devout,
> Go to Castalia's silver springs
> And dip yourselves in its crystal dews.
> Then enter the shrine with lips all purged
> Of hurtful converse. Set your tongues
> As paragons of gracious speech
> To those who would consult the god.

Freshly bathed, the Oracle and her group would proceed to even holier waters. Walking up the hillside, moving through the sanctuary's terraced compound, they drew close to the temple itself where the Kassotis flowed clear and cool. Like any spring in ancient Greece, it was seen as the home of a naiad who possessed magical powers. In this case, the power was that of prophetic inspiration, according to Pausanias, a travel writer. The spring emerged in the sanctuary and ran into a basin protected by a wall just above the temple. Apparently, the Oracle drank its sacred waters.

From the Kassotis spring, the Oracle would go through the temple and descend into her chamber. There she had access to all her essential aids: the tripod, the omphalos, the laurel branches. The authority of Zeus was invoked not only by the presence of the omphalos but, on either side of the rounded stone, by the two eagles made of gold. The ancient authorities tell us that the divine pneuma wafted up amid all this paraphernalia, enveloping the Oracle and bringing her and the god into spiritual union.

Outside the temple, petitioners would have gathered and the priests would have had them draw lots to determine their order of admission into the Oracle's presence (but not her area in the sacred *adyton*). In special

Modern guesswork on the layout of the *adyton*, the Oracle's inner sanctum at the temple of Apollo. Though here depicted as uncovered, it probably had a roof or a low ceiling. 1) Waiting room for pilgrims. 2) Omphalos with gold eagles. 3) Statue of Apollo. 4) Grave of Dionysus. 5) Oracle on tripod. 6) Sacred laurel. 7) Temple hearth. This view sets the *adyton* at the rear of the temple, whereas the French excavators pictured it at the side.

cases, an esteemed visitor representing an important city-state would be granted precedence in consultation.

No visitor could gain admission without first paying a nominal fee and without sacrificing an animal to Apollo. The animal victim had to exhibit favorable signs. Goats held a special place of honor among the sacrificial animals because of their alleged role in the site's discovery. In the temple's forecourt, the priests doused the animal with sacred water and watched to make sure that it trembled in just the right way, from the hooves up; otherwise they judged the omens inauspicious and called off the session. Apparently, the goat's shaking was meant to foreshadow the Oracle's divine tremor. When the omens were favorable, the priests would sacrifice the animal at a large stone altar just outside the temple's front entrance. If all the preliminaries were completed successfully, a priest would lead the petitioner down toward the Oracle's chamber, where more senior officials would take over. As Ion told a pilgrim asking about who represented the Oracle: "Outside the temple, I do; inside, the duty falls on others; those, sir, who are seated around the tripod—the noblest citizens of Delphi, chosen by lot." Apparently, the visitors sat in an anteroom just outside the Oracle's area but could go no farther. Only priests or the Oracle herself could enter the inner sanctum.

Disaster could strike if the sacrificial ritual was defiled. Plutarch told of one session in which the priests hosting an important foreign delegation tried to rush the process. The animal exhibited none of the requisite trembling when sprinkled with holy water. It was only after the creature "had been subjected to a deluge and nearly drowned" that it at last shuddered all over, Plutarch wrote. The omen was bad. But the priests nonetheless pushed ahead—with fatal results.

> She went down into the Oracle unwillingly, they say, and half heartedly; and at her first responses it was at once plain from the harshness of her voice that she was not responding properly; she was like a laboring ship and was filled with a mighty and baleful spirit. Finally she be-

came hysterical and with a frightful shriek rushed towards the exit and threw herself down, with the result that not only the members of the deputation fled, but also the Oracle-interpreter Nicander and those holy men that were present. However, after a little, they went in and took her up, still conscious; and she lived on for a few days.

The extreme vulnerability of the Oracle during her state of divine intoxication, Plutarch added, was why the authorities at Delphi had to pay special attention to protecting her virtue.

In favorable times, when all the rituals worked properly, the Oracle and the petitioner would engage one another at some remove, with the pilgrim in the anteroom. Legend has it that the Pythia in ancient times would read a petitioner's mind and respond while the question was still unspoken. But later, when the Pythia was more famous and many writers detailed her responses, the authors recounted no such telepathy. The petitioner could ask one question, and only one. It appears that a priest would put the question forward. The Pythia, presiding over the *adyton*, rapturous in her divine intoxication, would turn inward, reflect on the question, shake a laurel branch as the spirit of Apollo swept through her, and utter the god's response. As the Pythia spoke, the priest recorded her words. Some writers suggest that the Oracle herself may have remembered little or nothing of the session.

Over the centuries, the form of the recorded answer changed. Early relics were often written in hexameter verse—the same Homer used in his poetry. Many centuries later, when the institution of the Oracle was in decline, the pronouncements were usually rendered in prose. Some of the recorded Oracles have come down to us in both verse and prose. Peter Hoyle, a Delphi scholar in Britain, has argued that the variations tended to be a measure of the enthusiasm and diligence of the priests, and that they must have had a good deal to do with the versification of the Oracle's responses.

Delphi scholars have battled for decades over who actually took the prophetic lead, the Pythia or the priests. With notable exceptions, men have tended to see the Oracles as incoherent babblers and mere mouthpieces of the priests. In contrast, women have lately argued that the priestesses actually said what they were reported to have said, at least in the case of genuine pronouncements. The evidence would seem to support the latter view, with every ancient source saying it was the Pythias who actually delivered the answers.

It seems that on days of the month when no Oracle was available for consultations, pilgrims could still get divine guidance on simple questions. A stone inscription unearthed during the excavations suggests that a petitioner did this by throwing beans, with one color giving the answer "yes" and another "no." We have little insight into the exact method or popularity of this form of prophecy. But at least in theory, it kept the flow of patrons and their largesse coming to the shrine even when the Oracles were unavailable.

THE ORACLE SPOKE only nine months of the year. In wintertime, from November through February, when blizzards and high winds could blow across Parnassus, when springs could freeze, Apollo left Delphi and the Pythia no longer made proclamations on his behalf. The god was said to be traveling up north, and his mediums, too, took a break from their duties.

Instead, in one of antiquity's most psychologically arresting twists, Apollo's rowdy young brother, Dionysus, took control of Delphi, and his devotees joined him in orgiastic rites. Exactly when such worship began is unclear. But certainly by the time of Clea, Plutarch's friend, Dionysus had held sway at Delphi for at least a half dozen centuries. His coming meant the spiritual refuge now had two very different masters, one representing light and reason and life, the other darkness and ecstasy and rebirth. Apollo was the god of order, the spiritual force who helped forge the bonds of civilization. Dionysus loosened them. The differing times of day in which devotees communed with the two gods highlighted their differences. Followers of Apollo tended to worship during the day, and those of Dionysus at night.

The coexistence of the two deities was seen as unusually powerful, both in ancient and modern times. Euripides in *The Bacchae* told a horror story of what happens if Apollonian restraint and rationality deny the primal urges of human nature, as represented by Dionysus. And Nietzsche, in his first book, *The Birth of Tragedy,* traced the rise of Greek civilization to tension between the two gods.

Although the cult of Dionysus spread widely in Greece, Delphi was one of the few sanctuaries where the two gods cohabited. It was a special place of sacred dissimilarities. Recently, archaeologists studying Delphi's iconography have concluded that the ancient Greeks actually saw Dionysus as Apollo's alter ego, his second self. The two gods were one.

At Delphi, young women honored Dionysus in an orgy of singing and dancing and drinking. (The rite was not only spiritually uplifting but surely a relief from the male agenda of everyday life.) The orgiastic frenzy of the women supposedly revealed the god's presence.

In the chill night air, often under the stars, accompanied by torches and a beating drum, led by a double flute and a youth playing the role of Dionysus, the worshippers would dance their way up the cliffs behind the temple and climb seven miles to the Korykian cave, where their rites continued amid the large stalagmites that were easily seen in flickering light as divine phalli. Little is known of what occurred there because the rite was part of a mystery cult whose initiates pledged to keep their activities secret. It appears that the orgy could include sexual liberties in which the women might swiftly embrace their male companions, though scholars say the god did not demand such tribute. His rapturous devotees were free to act, or not, amid the surrender of the human spirit to the will of the god. The frenzied women were known as maenads, after the Greek verb meaning to be mad or furious. Sophocles in *Antigone* conjured up the women's idyll:

Up there in the snow and winter darkness Dionysus rules in the long night, while troops of Maenads swarm around him, himself the choir-leader for the dance of the stars and quick of hearing for every sound in the waste of night.

A Greek amphora of the sixth century BCE depicts maenads and other revelers dancing around Dionysus. Some of the celebrants hold wine cups and pitchers. The maenads are clothed in festive attire, but the satyrs (male followers of Dionysus), close behind the women, are naked. Plutarch tells us that the rites culminated in screams and shouts and heads thrown back. Carl Kerényi, a religious historian, called them celebrations of living fire on the cold mountainside.

The rituals occasionally ended in chaos. Once, the parade of worshippers on the icy flanks of Parnassus got lost and ended up in a nearby town, where they collapsed in the marketplace. On another occasion, the revelers got snowed in atop the mountain and a party of volunteers had to be sent out to rescue them.

The extent to which the Delphic Oracle participated in the wintertime rites is unclear. No ancient author made a firm link between the Pythia's rituals and those of the maenads, nor did the latter have any apparent tie to Apollo's institution of divine prophecy.

But throughout the year at Delphi, not just in wintertime, worship of the two gods nonetheless became deeply entwined. Apollo's most scared area, the *adyton,* where he and the Oracle communed, also held a monument regarded as the grave of Dionysus. Moreover, the Oracle in her utterances often recommended the adoration of Dionysus, calling on pilgrims to establish his cults and make images of him. Scholars have concluded that the authority of Delphi was largely responsible for the growth of Dionysian worship throughout the ancient Greek world.

Finally, at Delphi, in at least in one case, the two cults seem to have shared a common mistress. Plutarch in an essay notes that Clea, his friend, was not only a high priestess of Apollo but leader of the Dionysian rites as well. Unfortunately, he gave no details of this provocative tie between light and darkness. "Let us," Plutarch said of the cult's secrets, "leave undisturbed what may not be told."

THROUGHOUT ANCIENT Greece and its outposts, the questions that pilgrims brought to armies of oracles and seers could be quite personal and often bordered on the frivolous. Even sanctuaries that were venerable did a thriving business in divining gossip and coming up with visionary answers to base curiosity. At Dodona, where Zeus spoke to pilgrims through the rustling of oak leaves, tablets recovered by archaeologists reveal that the questions were typically mundane:

"Should I assume guardianship of the child?"

"Would it be better for Onasimos to get married now, or should he avoid it?"

"Why have I not had any children from my wife Meniska?"

"May I hear something further concerning Mrs. N?"

In contrast to this emphasis on private affairs, the questions that supplicants brought to Delphi in the early centuries of its recorded history tended to deal with the most serious matters of state: war and peace, law codes and land allotment, duty and leadership, crime and punishment, famine and colonization. Her reputation was that good. In time, many a childless man went to Delphi for advice, and many an individual sought help on such issues as whom to marry, how to deal with inheritances, or whether to leave land untilled. But, especially in the early days, the questions tended toward the momentous.

This air of gravity set the Oracle apart from the competition and kept her reputation spotless even as divination and prophecy eventually fell into a boisterous industry riddled with fakes and con artists, and even as urban sophisticates grew skeptical of mystic revelation. The playwright Aristophanes satirized most every form of soothsaying and made fun of oracles and their conflicting visions. But, like all Greeks, he treated the prophetess of Delphi with respect.

The seriousness of the Oracle's petitioners is exemplified by how they sought advice on framing constitutions, especially for a polis that became synonymous with social order and iron discipline. Sparta, located in a valley in the southern Peloponnese and separated from Delphi not only by high mountains but by the Gulf of Corinth, nonetheless developed a close relationship with the Pythia. Spartan kings employed special envoys, the Pythioi, whose duty was to visit Delphi when the occasion arose and write down the Pythia's visionary responses. As Herodotus tells us, their services were considered so valuable that the Pythioi took their meals with the kings at public expense.

At first, as Sparta grew in size, so did crises and social instability, especially as it won new territories and faced new burdens of administration. The Spartans repeatedly went to Delphi to seek help in establishing laws to better rule their expanding state, most famously in the constitution attributed to Lycurgus. This constitution set Sparta apart from all other Greek poleis and contributed much to its rise, scholars agree. It laid the foundations for a complex system of governance that was part monarchy (with two kings), part oligarchy, and part democracy. At least four Delphic prophecies bear on Sparta's constitution and early laws. One, according to Aristotle, foretold that the polis would achieve greatness if the Spartans held periodic meetings at which the people would put forward proposals and vote on them. Others were full of vague moralizing. In one, Lycurgus reportedly asked the Pythia what constitutional rules would give the greatest benefit to Sparta. According to Diodorus, she replied:

There are two roads, most distant from each other: the one leading to the honorable house of freedom, the other to the house of slavery, which mortals must shun. It is possible to traverse the one through manliness and lovely concord; so lead your people on this path. The other they reach through hateful strife and cowardly destruction; so shun it most of all.

In contrast to such sermonizing, one prophecy dealt with a very specific issue involving Sparta's early crises and class conflicts. This was a developing taste for luxury. After the dark age, Sparta became quite wealthy and sophisticated, with little of the austere, militaristic focus that came to mark the latter phases of its evolution. By the seventh century BCE, its nobles lived in comfort and prided themselves on such refinements as the appreciation of music and lyric poetry. The state imported ivory, amber, and scarabs made of gold and silver. Its craftsmen rivaled the best in Greece. Amid this rush for opulence, according to Diodorus, the cold, mystic, unearthly voice of the Pythia issued a stern warning: "Love of money and nothing else will ruin Sparta."

Whether because of the Oracle's prophecy or some other reason (the dating of her utterance is uncertain), the Spartans took steps to curb their lifestyle, most significantly by rejecting the silver coinage that was beginning to circulate in Greece. Instead, the polis retained archaic iron bars as currency and prohibited the use of gold and silver. This step coincided with a gradual loss of material refinements and the emergence of the lean, militaristic edge that was destined to make Sparta so famous.

Eventually, when Sparta grew large on the world stage and reached for empire, the gold and silver and slaves that its warriors sent home became the basis for much political unrest and the eventual breakdown of Sparta's economic system. It was a denouement that the gods surely loved.

Athens, too, looked to the Oracle for guidance on how to frame a constitution. By the early sixth century BCE, the polis was riven by social and class tensions, with the poor clamoring for the redistribution of land. The city gave Solon, an Athenian statesman, sweeping powers to reform the city's economy and laws, and he took a number of bold steps to weaken the aristocracy and strengthen the foundations of Athenian democracy.

Plutarch tells us that when Solon went to Delphi, the Pythia foresaw that a policy of compromise would bring the best results. "Sit in the middle of the ship, guiding straight the helmsman's task," she said. "Many of the Athenians will be your helpers."

Such moderation became the watchword of Solon's legislation. He canceled all debts and freed those who had been forced into slavery because of their unrepaid loans. But he resisted calls for revolutionary steps against the wealthy. Most important, Solon made sweeping changes to the machinery of government. The new criterion for office, he ruled, would be material success rather than noble birth. Solon also established a people's court as a protection against abuses of power.

Solon's respect for Delphi was such that he wove deference to Apollo into the body of his reforms. Upon entering office, the archons, the chief magistrates of Athens, had to promise that if they broke the laws they would dedicate a golden statue at Delphi. In addition, he singled out the Pythia for an important post, putting her in charge of selecting (from a short list) three officials who acted as interpreters of sacred law and ritual. So it was that the Oracle aided the rise of what would become Greece's two leading city-states, and did so by encouraging democratic ideals. Her consultations on these matters were very public acts of political nurturing that were retold and honored from generation to generation. Increasingly, the Oracle was seen as a universal touchstone, aiding not only the misty realm of spirituality but the hard realities of governance—what would become one of the foremost achievements of ancient Greece.

A celestial rite that the Spartans observed for many centuries illustrates her continuing influence. Once every eight years, the ephors, the senior officials who guarded the rights of the people against the conduct of kings, would choose a clear and moonless night to sit in silence gazing up at the heavens. If a shooting star lit the sky in a certain prescribed way, they judged it an ill omen and would put the kings on trial, charging them with offending the gods. If the ephors so desired, they would then ask the Oracle, speaking on behalf of Apollo, to confirm or refute the charge. Thus was she able to determine the fate of kings.

THE GREEK WORLD came to recognize the Delphic Oracle and her priests as teachers of an enlightened morality, an early manifestation of what we might call humanism. From the *adyton,* she called for such social innovations as reverence for oaths, respect for human life, and the importance of developing an inner sense of right and wrong. The radical nature of her agenda is hard to appreciate today. But for the ancient world, it was a reformulation of the unwritten codes of human affairs, seeking to improve all kinds of behavior outside the bounds of state law and local custom.

The tradition of bloodguilt, for instance, held that any killing— malicious or accidental—was reprehensible and demanded recompense, often in kind. Athenian lawgivers spent much time struggling with religious and judicial questions arising from accidental killings, if only because the extreme form of retribution encouraged blood feuds and revenge slayings in endless cycles. The issue was considered so serious that the playwright Aeschylus devoted a trilogy of grim tragedies to a royal family's bloody chain of murder and revenge. In general, ancient Greek custom was to consider any person who killed another, by accident or design, unclean.

The Pythia taught otherwise. She emphasized the importance of intention and making inner evaluations of guilt and innocence, of what came to be known as conscience. A tale of uncertain date illustrated her point and became much repeated over the centuries. Bandits fell on three young men traveling to consult the Oracle. One ran toward Delphi. The two other men stayed to fight, one drawing out a sword. In the melee that followed, he accidentally stabbed his friend, killing him. When the two survivors reached Delphi, the Pythia curtly expelled the one who had fled, saying he had abandoned his friends in time of need. The other she praised as not only absolved of any guilt but actually elevated: "The blood has not stained you," she said. "You are now purer in hands than you were before."

Her message was exceptional for the day even though it conforms to modern ideas of morality. It ignored the outward act, however shocking, and focused instead on good intentions and the struggle to do right.

A similar preoccupation with inner goodness marked the Oracle's attitude toward personal riches. She chose to respect honest poverty and disdain garish pomposity. According to Theopompus, a Greek historian, the Oracle once rebuked a wealthy pilgrim. She faulted his offering as pretentious and declared Apollo's preference for the poor but pious supplicant who humbly offered a simple cake. As Parke and Wormell point out, the Oracle's preference for the lowly may have echoed the feelings of the Delphians, a modest people compared to some of their neighbors.

Another of the Oracle's moral imperatives had to do with the dignity of human life, no matter how unimportant the person in terms of social status. She proclaimed that anyone who shed a slave's blood was a murderer and had to undergo purification (unless, of course, the killing was accidental). True to her ideals, she and her colleagues used the power of Apollo to free hundreds and perhaps thousands of slaves. Today at Delphi, visitors who look closely at the foundations of the temple see that they are covered top to bottom with many hundreds of inscriptions. All refer to acts of manumission—the legal release of a person from slavery. And at least once in the historical record, perhaps apocryphally, the Oracle made herself available to a slave that was seeking advice. What, he asked, should I do to please my master? Seek and you will find, she replied, anticipating the Gospel of Matthew.

The Oracle and her god, over centuries of consultations on matters of morality, showed a clear tendency to avoid stridency and dogmatism in favor of forgiveness and liberality. The conservative side of the Oracle had a clear preference for ancestral rites, but, surprisingly, she indulged the ceremonial differences of other cults and religions. Xenophon, a famous general and historian, told how the Oracle, when asked how to please the gods, always replied that the most pious approach was to follow the local customs of the pilgrim's state and nation, honoring the local spirits and deities. It was a remarkable stand for the representative of a god whose family was famous for envy, jealously, and distrust.

$\mathcal{B}$Y THE SIXTH century BCE, the sanctuary and its mistress had become so influential that their administration was judged too important to be left to the Delphians alone. The site's emerging national character led to the founding of a large committee to oversee its operations. Known as the amphictyony, the league eventually comprised twenty-four representatives from twelve Greek cities. Its advent, as well as the continuing arrival of treasures from abroad, attested to the role Apollo and his mouthpiece played in forging a Greek national identity.

The sanctuary's authority was reinforced when the amphictyony issued Delphi coins. A silver one showed Apollo holding a lyre while seated on the omphalos. In effect, it advertised the sanctuary's status as the center of the universe.

Around 595 BCE, the league threw itself into a war on Delphi's behalf. The problem was Crisa, a town down the slope that acted like a tollbooth to impose duties on pilgrims and deprive the sanctuary of income. The god, speaking through the Pythia, blessed the war and urged caution lest the Crisaeans steal the holy tripod during the conflict and become unassailable. It was a remarkable claim. In effect, the Oracle was proclaiming herself and her prophetic apparatus as able to make a people indomitable, as predestined to military victory. She was to be the ultimate talisman. But Apollo's representative, moving quickly beyond claims of miraculous intercession through such means as clairvoyance and divination, urged a focus on worldly fury as well. According to Aeschines, an Athenian orator, she told the amphictyony to battle the people of Crisa "all days and all nights and lay waste their land and their city." Moreover, she ordered that the victors let Crisa's lands, which extended in a fertile valley down to the Gulf of Corinth, lie fallow and "perpetually uncultivated," dedicated not to man but to Apollo.

It was a bold gamble. If the war succeeded, Delphi could have maintained itself with income from the lands. But the Oracle renounced that option, instead choosing a purely religious way of life and reliance on the generosity of strangers.

The action lasted five years, until 590 BCE. The victory of the league brought a rush of energy, visitors, construction, and money to Delphi, as the Oracle had seemingly anticipated. Most important, Delphi was formally declared a center of pan-Hellenic worship. Nearby cities such as Corinth, Thebes, and Athens—and farther away, ones such as Siphnos (an island in the Aegean today known as Sifnos), Cyrene (a Greek colony in North Africa today known as Shahat, Libya), and Massalia (today known as Marseilles, France)—built treasuries there to house their most valuable offerings and riches. City-states vied to outdo one another.

In 582 BCE, the sanctuary broadened its appeal by instituting the Pythian Games, which were held every four years at the end of the summer and soon rivaled those of Olympia. The prizes were crowns of laurel. Pausanias tells us that the races included running in full armor, riding foals, and driving chariots pulled by up to four horses. In addition, contestants vied for honors in singing and music, their instruments including flutes and harps.

At their peak, the games and allied festivals attracted huge crowds. Scholars estimate that thousands of people could disembark in a single day at the docks of Kira, the nearest port on the Gulf of Corinth. From there, pilgrims, spectators, families, and athletes would slowly climb the foothills of Parnassus to reach Delphi, paying no duties on the way.

The state of peacefulness that now existed around the sanctuary helped forge the Greek identity, scholars agree. Distant tribes and peoples would meet, compete, talk over their differences, remember their common heritage, and perhaps feel greater goodwill toward one another in the future. The games—if not a recipe for lasting fellowship, as suggested by the quickness with which contestants could take up arms against one another when they went back to their cities—undoubtedly reinforced the sense of Greek distinctiveness.

The amphictyony not only ran Apollo's sanctuary and defended it and the surrounding territory from unholy acts and incursions but, in the middle of the sixth century, led the rebuilding effort after the temple burned down. (Wooden beams and roofs often topped the massive stonework of Greek temples, and over time the timber became dry kindling that could explode in flame.) In an apparent first, it solicited funds from the whole Greek world. As Herodotus tells us, the citizens of Delphi eagerly took the lead in soliciting help for the restoration project, going from city to city, near and far, seeking donations. In Egypt, the Delphians won large contributions from not only Greeks living along the Nile but also Amasis, the king of the Egyptians. Such was Delphi's stature.

ONE OF THE sanctuary's most famous tales, involving yet another distant ruler, spoke to the Oracle's soaring prominence. Croesus ascended to the throne of the kingdom of Lydia around 560 BCE and proceeded to rule in grandiose style. His rugged land in western Anatolia (modern-day Turkey minus the European part west of the Bosporus) sparkled with natural wealth that filled his coffers with gold and silver. From his opulent court at Sardis, he conquered most of the cities along the coastline, including the Greek ones. The king had a fairly good relationship with these Asiatic Greeks, mainly because he left them to their own business. They had to pay tribute but were free to pursue trade and their own customs, flourishing under his rule. The fame and wealth of Croesus attracted many foreign visitors, including distinguished teachers from mainland Greece who lived under his patronage. The king gave Aesop, the famous writer of fables, a court appointment. Another visitor was Solon, the Athenian lawgiver and admirer of the Delphic Oracle.

After Croesus had ruled Lydia for about a decade, he initiated a test to discover which was the world's most accurate oracle. Delphi was at or near the top of his list. But Croesus had many others from which to choose. As Herodotus tells us, Croesus chose seven he judged to be most reliable. Three were oracles of Apollo: the one at Delphi, one at Abae fairly close to Delphi (of which we know little because it fell into oblivion after invaders twice leveled it), and one at Didyma a hundred miles southwest of Sardis on the Aegean coastline. Oracles there were a hereditary line of male priests known as Branchidae, and their temple was so large that it could easily swallow the Parthenon.

Two other sites were oracles of Zeus: one at mountainous Dodona in northwestern Greece, where sibyls interpreted the rustling of oak leaves, and one at the oasis of Siwa in the Libyan Desert, where the cult of priestesses of Ammon foretold the future. The final two were popular oracles of demigods, both located in mainland Greece. Just north of Athens at Oropus, supplicants sought guidance from Amphiaraus, a diviner who reportedly predicted his own death and by some accounts was a son of Apollo. His oracles came by way of dreams. The busy site had inns, a theater, and many other amenities.

The last oracle was the spookiest: the cave of Trophonius at Lebadea, located in a gorge twenty miles east of Delphi and the beneficiary of periodic overflows from its famous neighbor. Trophonius was said to be a son of Apollo who killed his brother and fled to a cave, where he died and his devotees eventually set up his oracle. Pausanias, who went there, reported that the visionary sessions could leave clients so "paralyzed with terror" that they had to be carried away.

Croesus gave his emissaries one hundred days to travel to these seven oracles and pose, on the appointed day, this simple question: what was the king doing at that very moment? The answers had to be written down so Croesus could later compare them. When the emissaries returned with the answers, the king proclaimed the Oracle of Delphi the winner, with

Amphiaraus taking a distant second. Of the various replies to the king's question, Herodotus quotes only that of the Pythia:

> I count the grains of sand on the beach and measure the sea; I under-
> stand the speech of the dumb and hear the voiceless. The smell has
> come to my sense of a hard-shelled tortoise boiling and bubbling with
> lamb's flesh in a bronze pot: The cauldron underneath is of bronze,
> and of bronze the lid.

It was a most unkingly activity for Croesus to be cooking up a lamb-and-tortoise stew. But that is what he was said to be doing that day, and in exactly the manner that the Pythia had described. Delighted at her precision, Croesus showered gifts on Delphi: 117 ingots of gold, the image of a lion made of gold, huge bowls of gold and silver, a gold statue, casks of silver, sprinklers of gold and silver for lustral waters, necklaces belonging to the queen, and more.

The reason for the oracular test and the king's generous response became clear as the Lydians who brought the treasures to Delphi asked the king's follow-up question: should he attack Persia? This was like a bird considering war on a cat. But the Persian hordes under Cyrus the Great were pressing Lydia's borders, and Croesus felt he had to take action.

The Pythia gave what is arguably the most famous of her many replies: if he marched against Persia, he would destroy a mighty empire. Overjoyed, Croesus showered yet more treasures on Delphi, sending two gold ornaments to every man in the city. The Delphians in return granted Croesus and the people of Lydia the right of citizenship for any who wished, as well as priority in consulting the Oracle.

The unhappy end came as Croesus attacked Persia and fell in utter defeat. Amazed, the Lydians sent envoys to Delphi to ask how it was that the Oracle's prophecy could have been so wrong. Was Apollo always so accustomed to betraying his patrons? The Delphians replied that the prophecy had been fulfilled and that it was the interpretation that Croesus got wrong. A great empire had indeed been destroyed—his own. Herodotus tells us that Croesus lived to see his error. But some historians believe the king died promptly at the hands of the Persians, bringing his ancient line to an end.

Did the test actually occur? By most accounts, the treasure that rained on Delphi was real. Indeed, part of the hoard was uncovered accidentally in 1940 as workmen sought to fix a sanctuary road. But a few scholars argue that the trove was part of a Lydian plan meant to buy the loyalty of the Greek world against Persia. By this logic, the oracular test was a fiction that the Delphic priests told Herodotus as a way to enhance Apollo's credibility and, not insignificantly, their own. Whether the test was real or imaginary, the Oracle's advice about destroying a mighty empire proved to be a huge embarrassment that the Delphic authorities had a hard time explaining away despite their efforts at rationalization.

Catherine Morgan, a historian at the University of London, has argued that the Oracle's responses during the first centuries of her recorded history tended to be simple and straightforward, and that latter ones became increasingly vague and ambiguous. If so, the Lydian episode was probably a turning point. In its aftermath, the authorities at Delphi had every reason to take extraordinary pains, perhaps unconsciously, to give themselves as much interpretive leeway as possible. After all, they wanted to avoid criticism that would arise if the Oracle's prophecies turned out to be wrong or otherwise inappropriate.

Morgan noted that Delphic ambiguity and equivocation, though undermining the idea of miraculous oracular powers, at times proved quite beneficial to the rise of Greek civilization by forcing consultant states to rehash their questions and debate possible outcomes and courses of action. Oracular vagueness, as it were, worked to foster a Delphic agenda that at times sought to encourage democracy.

The most famous example of such deliberations is how the Greeks responded to the Oracle's warnings concerning the advancing Persians, as Herodotus also detailed. Scholars say the father of history, an admirer of the Pythia, shaded the tale to her benefit. Nonetheless, the epic is worth recounting as one of the best illustrations of the Greek's high regard for the Oracle as well as a study in her importance to world history. It details how the outnumbered Greeks saved Europe in one of the earliest victories of freedom over tyranny.

$\mathcal{A}$FTER A HALF century of war and conquest, Persia by the fifth century BCE had expanded to rule most of the eastern world—Lydia, Thrace, Macedonia, Egypt, Ionia, Mesopotamia, and many other lands stretching from the Balkans to the Himalayas. It was the first real empire in Western

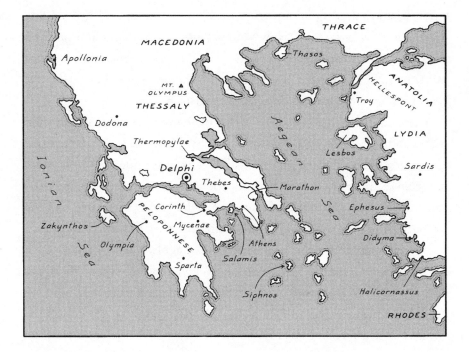

history. Persia wanted to grow westward but Greece stood in the way. For a decade, a loose federation of Greek states had put aside their differences to resist the invaders, most famously at the battle of Marathon. Then, in 480 BCE, the Persians returned, stronger than ever under their new king, Xerxes. He wanted not only to take Greece but to avenge his father, whom the Greeks had defeated and humiliated at Marathon.

For Athens, the situation was particularly dicey. The Persians would target Greece's most powerful city-state for early destruction to protect their supply lines. Moreover, its location on the Aegean coastline made it the closest large city to the likely invasion routes, so it expected to face Xerxes and his men soon.

The Athenians sent a delegation over the mountains to consult the Oracle of Delphi. Surely she would reassure them that the gods still found the Greeks worthy of protection. Her sharp words proved alarming. The Oracle insulted the delegation, calling it worthless, and foresaw cruel butchery and suffering for anyone foolish enough to defend Athens. She urged the Greeks to flee. "Now your statues are standing and pouring sweat," she warned eerily. "They shiver with dread. The black blood drips from the highest rooftops. They have seen the necessity of evil. Get out, get out of my sanctum and drown your spirits in woe!"

Stunned, the Athenians were at first overcome with despair but then rallied and turned to the locals for help. What did it mean? The Oracle was famous for her obscure pronouncements. That was understandable, since no ordinary mortal could withstand the direct communications of the gods, most especially those of radiant Apollo. Only the Oracle had the strength. And only she could put the blinding truth in ways that mortals could understand. But this prophecy seemed as black as night, with even cold marble twitching in apprehension over what was to come. There was no vagueness, no ambiguity. It seemed like a blunt prophecy of doom.

A distinguished man of Delphi told the delegation to go back to the Oracle but as unpretentious suppliants holding olive branches. They did so. This time, the Oracle again foresaw the destruction of Athens, but she added new information: the possibility of a partial reprieve.

The priestess told how the goddess Athena, the namesake and protector of Athens, had appealed to her father, Zeus, on behalf of the city and won an important concession, if grudgingly. According to Herodotus, the Oracle foresaw that Zeus would grant Athena "a wall of wood to be alone uncaptured, a boon to you and to your children." Still, despite this promised aid, she again advised the Athenians to flee:

Await not in quiet the coming horses, the marching feet, the armed host upon the land. Slip away. Turn your back. You will meet in battle anyway. O holy Salamis [an island off the coast of Attica, the area around Athens], you will be the death of many a woman's son between the seedtime and the harvest of the grain!

This prophecy was clearly better than the first and gave the delegation reason for hope. But, more typically, it was enigmatic. What was the wall of wood? Why flee if it would save them? And what did Salamis have to do with the looming battle?

The delegation hurried back to Athens. A great debate ensued. One group interpreted the wall of wood as meaning that the Acropolis (literally the extreme city) would survive. After all, its commanding heights had withstood many a siege in the past and had provided sanctuary for soldiers and citizens alike. More important in terms of the prophecy, many of its buildings were made of wood, and the city fathers could add more timbers to reinforce its ramparts.

Another faction argued that the wall of wood must refer to ships and urged the construction of more for a naval battle. But the official Oracle interpreters apparently faulted this idea. Drawing on their experience and authority, they argued that the Oracle actually meant that if the Athenians prepared to confront the Persians at sea, their forces would suffer defeat at Salamis, an island near Athens in the Saronic Gulf. There, many sons of Greece would die.

Into this dispute came Themistocles, a prominent Athenian states-man. For years, fearful of Persia's growing might, sure the Greeks could never match it in sheer manpower, he had argued and pleaded and schemed to turn Athens into a naval power, all in the face of great doubt and opposition. Surprisingly, he had prevailed. When a rich vein of silver had been discovered south of Athens, he had persuaded the city's assem-bly to apply the windfall to building new ships rather than distributing the fortune among the citizens. By the time of Xerxes' approach, Athens possessed a fleet of nearly two hundred triremes—warships with three tiers of oars, up to two hundred rowers, and a bronze ram at the prow for sinking enemy ships. In addition, each trireme could carry about twenty soldiers (up to forty in special circumstances) who could leap aboard a foe's vessel to wage hand-to-hand combat. To a degree, the city had sacri-ficed its army and treasure to become a naval power.

Themistocles criticized the official interpretation of the Oracle's an-swer and argued that her reference to massive death at Salamis indicated the slaughter of foreigners rather than Greeks. Otherwise, he said, the Oracle would have spoken of "O cruel Salamis" rather than "O holy Salamis." Athens, he argued, had been forewarned to prepare for a great naval battle: only a wall of wooden ships would save them.

His arguments won the day. The Athenians found his opinion far preferable to that of the official interpreters, who basically wanted to abandon Greece and find somewhere else to live. So the citizens and war-riors of Athens readied as many ships as possible and prepared to resist the Persians at sea. An added benefit of such a strategy, they reasoned, was that a naval victory would end the Persian fleet's ability to resupply the Persian army, draining the troops of fighting energy.

As the Athenians readied for a naval battle, the Spartans, possessing the best land force in Greece, made their own pilgrimage to Delphi. For them, too, the news was grim. According to Herodotus, the Oracle foresaw the destruction of either their city or their king. "The strength of bulls and lions cannot stop the foe," she warned. "No, he will not leave off, I say, until he tears the city or king limb from limb." Unsettled, the Spartans retreated to discuss their fate. Which would be the lesser evil, losing their city or king?

Troubled by these portents, dreading for themselves and the rest of Greece, the people of Delphi consulted the Oracle on their own. This time she foresaw a new break in the dark clouds, as if Athena had once again gone to her father and won yet more concessions. As Herodotus tells the story, the Oracle told the Delphians to pray to the winds because they would be great allies. The news quickly spread. Any Greek who wanted to remain free had better pray with heartfelt zeal. The Delphians set up a new altar and made sacrifices to the winds.

In the late summer of 480 BCE, the years and months and weeks of maneuvering ended. The Persian fleet had sailed from the Hellespont into the Aegean and approached Greece along its Magnesia coast, a northerly, rugged area near a strait leading through the Greek archipelago to Athens. The fleet moored just outside the strait. So numerous were the ships (more than one thousand, historians estimate) that only some could land, and the rest anchored in rows parallel to the coast.

The night was clear and calm, Herodotus tells us. But just before dawn, the sea began to boil and a violent storm hit the Persian fleet with fearsome gusts, blowing hard toward shore. The gale lasted three days. Some ships managed to land safely amid the crashing waves. But the wind carried many others away or smashed them to pieces on the rocks, the wrecks scattered up and down the coast.

Lookouts on the bluffs raced inland to report the disaster. Rejoicing, the Greeks said prayers of thanks and offered libations to the gods.

Meanwhile, the Persian army marched south along the strait and met a Greek force stationed at Thermopylae, a narrow pass in northern Greece between high mountains and an arm of the Aegean. There the Greeks had set up a defensive line. Three hundred Spartans and a thousand other troops put up fierce resistance, battling the Persian legions day after day and holding firm. But the Persians learned about a path through the mountains from a local and circled around behind the Greeks. They prepared to strike front and back.

Leonidas, king of the Spartans, upon learning of the betrayal, sent away most of his allies. But he and his men stayed behind. They fought until their spears broke and then engaged the Persians with swords and daggers. Eventually, they fell. Leonidas lay dead. But his death, if the Oracle's prophecy was right, perhaps meant the gods would spare Sparta.

The advancing Persians marched on Delphi, eager for its gold and silver, Herodotus tells us. But a violent thunderstorm with blinding flashes of light, as well as rocks crashing down from Mount Parnassus, terrified the superstitious men and caused them to turn back.

For the Athenians, the situation looked dire. Upon learning of the Greek defeat at Thermopylae, they evacuated the city and fled, some south to the isle of Salamis. The Persians marched into Athens unopposed, plundering and burning. Temples went up in flames. High on the Acropolis, with its temple to the goddess Athena, a small band of defenders had dug in and, around its periphery, built a barricade of logs and doors. Herodotus tells us that they believed the wooden barrier would save them. Instead, the Persians seized the high ground and killed its defenders. They then looted Athena's temple and set the Acropolis ablaze.

The refugees on Salamis, a few miles to the south, could see their beautiful city going up in flames. The Greek fleet had sailed into the waters around Salamis, ready to defend the evacuees and face the Persian armada. The Greeks now possessed more than three hundred triremes. That force was half the size of the Persians' (still mighty despite the storm's destruction) but big enough to put up a good fight.

However, when the naval commanders heard what the Persians had done to the Acropolis, some panicked and wanted to flee. The Greek leaders held a council of war. They took a vote and decided to retreat to the narrow isthmus leading to the Peloponnese, the Greek heartland. The army was building a wall there meant to run from the Gulf of Corinth in the north to the Saronic Gulf in the south, creating a new line of defense. The fleet, the leaders reasoned, could stay in close touch with the army and maneuver and fight the Persians near the isthmus and, in case of defeat, fall back to the Peloponnese.

Themistocles would have none of it. The man who had argued and begged and cajoled the Athenians into acquiring a navy now pleaded for reason. It made no sense, he said, to lead the Persian army into the Peloponnese, nor to fight its navy in the open waters of the Saronic Gulf. There, the Persians with their fast, light ships and superior numbers would outmaneuver the Greeks. Better, he said, to fight them in the familiar, narrow waters of the Salamis channel. The Oracle at Delphi, Themistocles stressed, had foretold that the Greeks at Salamis would prevail over the Persians.

A man demurred. He was a leader of Corinth, a city behind the wall being erected across the isthmus. He argued that Themistocles was now, with the fall of Athens, a man without a state and should have no vote.

Infuriated, Themistocles threatened to withdraw the whole of the Athenian fleet, which made up more than half the Greek force, and move every Athenian man, woman, and child to Italy. The Corinthian backed down. The Greeks decided to stay at Salamis and fight.

Xerxes, confident of victory, had his throne moved to a commanding height south of Athens from which he could view the action. The Persian ships positioned themselves around Salamis, bottling up the Greek fleet inside. The Persians moved forward.

The channel proved so narrow that they had to break formation, exposing an open flank that the Greeks attacked again and again. The Greek ships rammed and tore with their bronze prows as armed troops leaped onto the enemy vessels to fight in close combat. The carnage grew as the lead Persian ships tried to flee but ran into ones from the rear, which, conscious of the watchful eye of the Persian king, kept trying to move forward.

After a long day of losses and setbacks, Xerxes and his forces withdrew—eventually back to Persia.

. . .

*A*T DELPHI, the thankful Greeks erected a column that rose forty feet, or twelve meters, and crowned it with a golden tripod. The setting was prominent—high atop the Sacred Way in front of the temple of Apollo, perhaps the most conspicuous spot in all of Greece. Nassos Papalexandrou, a historian, argues that the war memorial not only symbolized how the Oracle's supposed gift of divination had contributed to the Greek victory but also represented the Greek acceptance and celebration of one of the Oracle's boldest claims—that she, speaking on behalf of Apollo, had the power to make them unassailable. The proof seemed obvious. They had prevailed against overwhelming odds.

*A*THENS HAD TO be rebuilt. It was a time of hardship and adversity, of doubt and indecision, and of a deep yearning for spiritual guidance. The Oracle forecast the city's renewed greatness. She reassured the weary Athenians, Aristides tells us, that their struggles and reconstruction efforts would prove successful. "Blessed city of Athena," the Pythia said in a message to the populace, "when you have seen much and endured much and toiled and suffered much, you will become an eagle among the clouds for all time."

The truth of her prediction became apparent over the ensuing decades and centuries as Athens rose to heights unparalleled in history, enjoying a golden age that produced generations of remarkable statesmen and playwrights, artists and historians, scientists and architects, orators and philosophers. The Athenians rebuilt their city more beautifully than ever, erecting such triumphs as the Parthenon. Even after the polis eventually suffered military defeats and saw its political influence wane, Athens for centuries remained the cultural and educational heart of the Mediterranean, an inspiration to all who went there, an eagle in the clouds.

. . .

$\mathcal{T}$HE INFLUENCE of the Oracle extended far beyond states and cities, kings and slaves. Three of the most famous men of Athens—Socrates, Plato, and Aristotle—all found themselves linked with Delphi and the Oracle. In general, the attitude of the philosophers seems to have been one of respect and even reverence.

The Oracle had her biggest impact on Socrates. A native of Athens born a decade after the Persian wars, he became the most celebrated thinker of antiquity because of his uncompromising inquiries into ethics and moral philosophy. The Pythia's relationship with him was beguiling in its simplicity. On a visit to Delphi, one of his students asked if any man was wiser. None, she replied. This declaration became a turning point that guided his inquiries. At the end of his life, at his trial for corrupting Athenian youth, Socrates testified that his pursuit of wisdom grew out of his puzzlement over this prophecy. Deeply aware of his own ignorance, and seeking to understand Apollo's claim, Socrates said he began a life-long search to interview men of high repute for wisdom but always came away unimpressed. Even as his constant questioning made him poor and unpopular, religious duty kept him asking and searching, trying to understand the Oracle's meaning. In the end, he decided it meant that real wisdom is the exclusive property of the gods and Apollo's reference to him was "as if he would say to us, The wisest of you men is he who has realized, like Socrates, that in respect of wisdom he is really worthless."

Socrates would frequently cite the Oracle and Delphic lore, for instance, asking pupils if they were familiar with the injunction "Know thyself." Xenophon, a student, tells us that the philosopher's query would typically begin an examination into the meaning of self-knowledge.

In his teachings, Socrates declared that the Oracle was an essential guide to personal and state development, doing so even as his probing mind dissected her method. "The greatest blessings come by way of madness," he said in *Phaedrus.* But the star of Western rationalism was quick to qualify the point, escaping the paradox that it is better to be mad than sane. The insanity, he said, had to be heaven-sent from Apollo and not a medical condition that left men babbling incoherently. When imbued with divine madness, the prophetesses of Delphi "achieved so much for which both states and individuals in Greece are thankful."

But the converse was also true. Socrates held that the Delphic Oracles, when their rituals failed to produce the requisite state of mania and left them sane, "did little or nothing." He thus rooted their effectiveness in the depth of their sacred madness. By the definition of Socrates, the preeminent states of ecstatic prophecy required the complete loss of human control, the total abandonment of self to a higher power.

His student, Plato, seems to have had an experience of the Pythia that was more characteristic of the day, but he too, perhaps swayed by his master's piety, gave the priestess leading roles in his political utopias. In his *Laws* and *Republic,* Plato describes a model commonwealth, laying out its legal structure in enormous detail and repeatedly assigning the Oracle a place of honor and responsibility. It was she, as the mouthpiece of Apollo, who was to exercise authority over making regulations for temples and sacrifices. It was she who was to direct the methods of burial and to organize the cult of the dead. It was she who was to preside over the disbursement of found treasure. It was she who was to select officials for a panel meant to interpret sacred rules and principles. "Religious law universally should be fetched from Delphi," Plato remarked, "and this must be adhered to." Plato's reliance on the Oracle is all the more remarkable because his idealized polis rejected so much of what was old and venerable in Hellenic culture. Nonetheless, he made the ancient, superhuman wisdom of the Oracle the guardian of Greek legislation and religious life.

His loyalty was rewarded. After his death, the Oracle directed that the Greeks set up at Delphi a stela to the philosopher among the statues of the gods, indicating that pilgrims should regard him as a semidivine figure. "You are right to honor Plato, master of a divine doctrine," she said.

It appears that Aristotle, Plato's student and the most scientific of the three men, had the least emotional resonance with the Oracle in terms of his life's work but the most direct contact with Delphi. He set up a monument there to an early patron. Later, the authorities asked him and his nephew to draw up a list of victors at the Pythian Games from their earliest days, a major undertaking that organized more than two centuries' worth of athletic history. Their work covered four great stone tablets. In gratitude for their service, the Delphians awarded the two men grants of honor, setting up a stone inscription to them in the crowded sanctuary.

Apollo and his Delphic Oracle appear to have had little or no role in Aristotle's world of belief and teaching. The philosopher's passion was for understanding nature rather than the mechanisms of divine madness. Even so, we see in his extant writings hints of his fascination with the kinds of superhuman powers attributed to the Oracle, as demonstrated by his wave theory of telepathy.

$\mathcal{B}$Y THE TIME Aristotle died in 322 BCE, both Greece and Delphi were falling into decline, shattered by civil wars, softened by affluence, infested by plague, haunted by a sense of loss. The golden age was over. Amid doubt and cynicism, Apollo nonetheless held his own, the one god that the Greeks seemed to find still worthy of veneration. But even his influence failed to save Delphi. A great earthquake destroyed the temple in 373 BCE. Over the decades, it was eventually rebuilt, and the *adyton* was restored to a semblance of glory, but invaders repeatedly seized the holy city. In 356, war erupted over the sanctuary, with soldiers melting down some of its greatest treasures. Eventually, the exhausted states left a vacuum that the Macedonians filled, first under Philip and then his son, Alexander the Great.

Highly educated (by no less a tutor than Aristotle), Alexander conquered most of the Eastern world, spreading Greek culture to distant lands and diluting it by encouraging intermarriage and concord with the proud cultures of antiquity. The death of Alexander in 323 BCE marked the end of classical Greece and the start of a new, cosmopolitan era.

Through much of the turbulent fourth century BCE, the Oracle continued to dispense advice and predictions. But she was no longer consulted on major questions of policy. Instead, as was the case at Dodona, the queries tended toward the personal and practical. The Delians asked for a cure for plague, the Achaeans for how to capture the town of Phana, Callistratus of Athens on whether to return from exile. In general, personal questions were easier to answer than those of a state seeking knowledge of the future so as to better manage a political crisis or the uncertainties of war.

The sudden downward spiral of Greece continued, reaching a nadir in 279 BCE with a massive Celt invasion. The fierce warriors, eager for plunder, marched on Delphi. "Care for these things falls on me," the Oracle reassured the anxious Delphians. By various accounts, the invaders met earthquakes, rocks hurtling down from high cliffs, and a heavy snowstorm. The Celts retreated.

The Romans proved more durable. They had expanded their empire in the West as Alexander enlarged his in the East. Now, they came in force. In 146 BCE, to set an example, Rome attacked Corinth with great energy, killing the men, selling the women and children into slavery, and sacking the city. It proceeded to tighten its grip on Greece. The Romans at first treated Delphi with reverence, but over the decades some of them showed less deference and plundered its riches under various pretexts. In 86 BCE, Sulla, a Roman general in command of Greece who soon became the empire's dictator, emptied the treasuries. Cicero, perhaps fearful of Sulla's reign, visited Greece and gave voice to what had become one of the standard questions at Delphi, asking the Oracle what he should do to attain the highest fame. The prophetess replied with characteristic advice: he should make his own nature, not the opinion of others, his guide in life. Cicero went on to become a great orator.

Starting in Roman times, writers began to do what Greek chroniclers had seldom done—detail the methods of the Pythia as well as her history. No one violated any rules to do so. The Oracle's rites, while secretive, had no official veil like those of mystery cults where initiates were formally sworn to secrecy. Instead, her rituals were widely known. We can only speculate why the Romans (or Greeks writing for Roman audiences) began to describe the methods. One factor was probably the general appetite of Rome to better understand its vast new holdings, including the most famous of the oracles. It had no tradition of ecstatic prophecy. The Greeks, on the other hand, had grown up with the Oracle and had known her well and to some extent had taken her procedures for granted. What she did in general was common knowledge and therefore no one bothered to describe her particulars. The Greek writers focused on her effects as the mouthpiece of Apollo, not particularly on her. But as the Romans and the diverse peoples of the empire looked upon the priestess with fresh eyes, they found her new and mysterious and worthy of description.

Diodorus told how goats on Mount Parnassus fell into spasms. Strabo said a craggy opening beneath the temple of Apollo emits a pneuma that "inspires a divine frenzy." Lucan wrote a melodrama that had the Oracle's bosom heaving, lips foaming, and laurel wreath dislodged as she whirled through the temple, scattering tripods, burning with divine fire. "All the centuries crowd her breast," he wrote. "All the future struggles to the light."

*F*OR A WHILE, in the late first and early second centuries CE, Delphi enjoyed something of a renaissance under Roman emperors who admired Greece and favored the pagan gods. Domitian, who became emperor in 81 CE, aided the restoration of the temple. Hadrian furthered the revival.

It was during this period that Delphi received into service one of its most learned and eloquent admirers—Plutarch, who arrived at the sanctuary around 90 CE and served as high priest for decades. In his religious essays, he not only defended the integrity of Apollo's preeminent sanctuary but described the Oracle's origin, character, and methods, especially the workings of the prophetic vapors.

Of importance to later analysts, he clarified how water flowed down the mountainous hillside in the sacred domain, noting that the spring located just above the temple reappeared just below. The authorities at Delphi, he said, used the lower waters for libations and lustrations. Plutarch's writings on Delphi addressed several aspects of what at first glance appeared to be the Oracle's social decline: her pronouncements were no longer given in verse, she was again often untutored, and questions put to her tended toward the personal and the superficial. But in general on such issues, Plutarch found benign explanations. For instance, he attributed the change in questioning not to the Oracle's deterioration or her inability to handle tough inquiries but to Pax Romana.

> There is, in fact, profound peace and tranquility; war has ceased, there are no wanderings of peoples, no civil strifes, no despotisms, nor other maladies and ills in Greece requiring many unusual remedial forces. Where there is nothing complicated or secret or terrible, but the interrogations are on slight and commonplace matters, like the hypothetical questions in school: if one ought to marry, or to start on a voyage, or to make a loan; and the most important consultations on the part of the States concern the yield from crops, the increase of herds, and public health—to clothe such things in verse, to devise circumlocutions, and to foist strange words upon inquiries that call for a simple short answer is the thing done by an ambitious pedant embellishing an oracle to enhance his repute. But the prophetic priestess has herself also nobility of character, and whenever she descends into that place and finds herself in the presence of the god, she cares more for fulfilling her function than for that kind of repute or for men's praise or blame.

It was in his long essay *The Obsolescence of Oracles* that Plutarch broke from this vein of optimistic analysis and speculated on physical mechanisms for the Oracle's decline. He noted that the earth discharged many kinds of mists and vapors, some producing derangements and diseases or death. Others were quite beneficial. Greatest of all, he said, was the pneuma. "The prophetic current and breath is most divine and holy," he said, "whether it issue by itself through the air or come in the company of running waters."

His allusion to vaporous waters seemed to embrace the possibility that spring and cleft coexisted at the same location, a new suggestion for Delphi. Near the end of the essay, Plutarch discussed the likelihood that the strength of the vapors had waxed and waned over the centuries, laying out a potential explanation for inspirational fluctuations. And he implied that visitors to the *adyton* could discern such changes. All they had to do was sniff the air in the anteroom just outside of the Oracle's chamber. He said many foreigners and all the officials and servants of the shrine had noticed the coming and going of the fragrant odor, which he likened to "the most exquisite and costly perfumes."

In the *adyton,* Plutarch wrote, the pneuma laid hold of the Oracle's body and filtered into her soul. He warned that her surrender to the god should never occur when she was in a state of high emotion and instability, lest the divine intoxication and her heightened sensitivity leave her vulnerable to harm. Plutarch ended the essay by throwing open a possible explanation for the variable performance of the Oracles over the centuries.

The power of the spirit does not affect all persons nor the same persons always in the same way, but it only supplies an enkindling and an inception, as has been said, for them that are in a proper state to be affected and to undergo the change. The power comes from the gods and demigods, but, for all that, it is not unfailing nor imperishable nor ageless.

.   .   .

_A_FTER PLUTARCH, little came into the historical record that matched his depth of curiosity or analysis. But devotion to the Oracle and her divine master long endured.

The cult of Jesus would have none of it. By the second century, Christian bishops and writers were rising to prominence throughout the empire and were working hard to discredit the pagan gods and practices, especially at Delphi, which they considered a headquarters of heathen belief. They did not dismiss the Oracle's powers as trickery or delusion, and expressed no doubts about the Pythia entering a superhuman frenzy in which she worked miracles. Instead, they argued that the real inspiration behind her prophetic outpourings was the devil. The powers of darkness had adopted the guise of pagan deities. Apollo was really Satan. He had bamboozled his followers with confusing prophecies and at times had given out real glimpses of the future, but only to further his demonic ends, only to distract men from the one true God. Worse, Christian writers suggested that Satan not only kept the Oracle under his spell but physically violated her as she sat on the tripod.

It was the coming of Christ, his apologists said, that brought an end to these demonic rites. "The fountain of Castalia is silent," Clement of Alexandria wrote in a somewhat premature declaration of victory.

By the early fourth century, the emperor Constantine had converted to Christianity and moved the vast bureaucracy of the Roman state toward adopting it as the official religion, as did his sons. In 361 CE, however, Julian the Apostate became emperor and sought to reestablish the pagan gods. As a youth he had fallen in love with Greek life and philosophy, as Gore Vidal evokes beautifully in his novel _Julian._ As emperor, Julian disavowed the doctrines of Christianity, offered solemn sacrifices to the ancient gods, and sought to reinstate them as the foundations of official Roman religion. He also tried to revive the Oracle at Delphi.

Julian made the impoverished Delphians exempt from taxation and assured the priests of his protection. But it was too late. His reign lasted two short years, and that brief moment of imperial favor was insufficient to stop the rise of the church or reverse the ages of slow decline that had reduced Delphi to broken marble and lost splendor. When the emperor sent an emissary to question the Pythia, her gloomy response is the last we hear from a voice that for many centuries had guided the ancient world. The end was all the more remarkable because of its mutuality. The last Roman reached out to the last Oracle but learned nothing to comfort him, nothing to inspire, nothing to suggest that the gods foresaw a bright future. Instead, her reply began a long silence.

Tell the king, the fair-wrought house has fallen.
No shelter has Apollo, nor sacred laurel leaves;
The fountains now are silent; the voice is stilled.

TWO

Doubters

FIFTEEN CENTURIES WOULD PASS before a country exhibited the kind of occult enthusiasm that seized ancient Greece and made the Oracle such a celebrity. Surprisingly, the state was staunchly Christian. Moreover, it had distinguished itself as a founder of the scientific and industrial revolutions, acquiring vast wealth and power, not to mention a global empire rooted in fierce discipline and levelheadedness.

Even so, the Victorian world of late nineteenth-century England fairly seethed with mind reading, ghost chasing, and other spiritualist ado often conducted in darkened parlors and drawing rooms, especially among the elite of London and the university towns. Even Queen Victoria attended a séance. Participants often sought to communicate with the dead and reported that spirits would respond by tilting tables, lifting objects, and materializing in shadowy forms. At times, the departed would speak out, causing the sessions to crackle with emotion. "My boy," "My darling," sobbed a woman to her lost son. Other times, the darkened rooms had a frivolous or even wanton air. One frequently reported ghost was Henry Morgan, a rakish pirate with a deep voice who seemed to cast a spell on ladies. At some séances participants would chant or hold hands or join their wrists by silk threads. The relaxed air gained a reputation as a fertile ground for flirtation and the start of more intimate relationships.

The movement gained popularity as a counterpoint to the suppressed emotions and energies of the Victorian era. It also filled a growing spiritual void, a sense of emptiness and doubt that could make life seem meaningless despite England's rising prosperity. Scientific advance was calling religious truths into question, and materialism threatened to snuff out the spiritual. By contrast, the world of spiritualism offered direct contact with things supernatural and perhaps divine. To some people, it offered proof that man possessed an immortal soul.

The explosion of interest prompted the world's first scientific studies of occult phenomena. Most notably, in 1882, a group of Cambridge dons founded the Society for Psychical Research, which became world famous. Its aim was to investigate this shadowy world and document rare human abilities. The society's founders—sure the whirl of activity hid frauds and charlatans, as well as sincere individuals mired in delusion—nonetheless presumed that at least some of the spectacle was real.

The society's membership included Lewis Carroll, Sir Arthur Conan Doyle, Alfred Lord Tennyson, and other nobles and notables, artists and eccentrics. Though sometimes derided as the "spook society," it in fact had excellent social, scientific, and intellectual credentials. Over time, its presidents included Arthur James Balfour, the British prime minister; William James, the American psychologist and brother of Henry James; and Lord Rayleigh, the British physicist and Nobel laureate. Many society members were staunch naturalists who believed that science had so far simply failed to account for the complexity of the universe. In time, they believed, it would uncover new domains of natural law to explain a rich variety of remarkable phenomena.

From the start, the Society for Psychical Research showed a fascination with the Oracle of Delphi. Her actions and reputation in the dim past seemed to demonstrate the continuity of psychic abilities from age to age. Many of its founders read Greek and had little difficulty seeing the parallels. More than any other historic figure, the Oracle seemed to embody otherworldly prowess and offer concrete evidence that the society's aspirations were likely to bear fruit. Writing in the first volume of the society's journal, a member called for a detailed examination of "the ancient oracles, especially of Delphi" as a way to help prove the reality of occult phenomena.

The Oracle exerted an especially strong influence on Frederic W. H. Myers, a principal founder of the society and a star of British scholarship who possessed a restless mind and a deep knowledge of the ancient world. While a student at Trinity College, Cambridge, Myers had studied classics under Henry Sidgwick (later a moral philosopher there), and both took to the idea of putting the spiritualist claims to the test. Sidgwick was the society's first president. Myers, a lecturer in classics at Trinity and later a fellow, became a brilliant man of letters, translating ancient texts, publishing poems and essays, writing a biography of Wordsworth, exploring the new science of psychology, and introducing the British public to the works of Freud. All the while he devoted himself to promoting the society and its agenda.

Myers acted as its guiding hand, strengthening the society's reputation for integrity by steering a middle ground between the extreme skeptics and the avid spiritualists. He also had a gift for linguistic precision that produced much of today's extrasensory vocabulary. Disdaining the term *thought transference* as misleading, Myers instead coined the term *telepathy,* literally "far-feeling"—the communication of impressions from one mind to another. Because he felt that centuries of Christianity had unfairly put occult phenomena into the realm of the supernatural—literally beyond nature—he coined the term *supernormal* (later replaced by *paranormal*) to drag them back into the world of human investigation. For the perception of distant places and things, he favored the term *clairvoyance,* literally "clear-seeing," now known as *remote viewing.* He and his colleagues also felt the word *prophecy* carried too much baggage and instead favored the terms *precognition* or *foreknowledge.*

In 1883, when the society was a year old, Myers published a collection of essays on a variety of classical topics, including the oracles of ancient Greece. With delicacy and a wealth of footnotes, he sought to trace their origin and assess their significance. Myers dwelled on Delphi. Sensitive to the parallels between the Oracle and contemporary spiritualism, he zeroed in on what the ancients regarded as one of her greatest feats: the test of Croesus, in which the Oracle had correctly identified the king as cooking a lamb-and-tortoise stew.

In the preface to his book, Myers expressed optimism that science would one day learn the reality behind such ancient claims and develop "a true comprehension" of the Oracles. "I am not without hope," he said, that "research conducted on a wider and sounder basis than heretofore" will shed light on the ancient mysteries and that scientific law will "extend itself farther over that shadowy land." His wish seemed to come true. When his book was reissued five years later, in 1888, Myers noted that psychic investigators had made a number of breakthroughs in understanding the basis for the Oracle's powers. He pointed to issues of the *Proceedings of the Society for Psychical Research* that focused on experimental proof of extrasensory perception. Nine years later, in the edition of 1897, his excitement was palpable. The revelations detailed in the society's journal had become "indispensable," Myers declared, for the comprehension of psychic truths old and new.

It turned out that the enthusiasm of Myers and friends eager to reconcile ancient Delphi with modern science was short-lived. The problem was not weakening interest in the occult or faltering diligence on the part of the society. If anything, they both grew stronger.

Rather, the blow came from a competing line of inquiry that cast doubt on the truthfulness of the Delphic enterprise and the veracity of the ancient lore and accounts. Quite suddenly, almost overnight, many centuries of oracular feats seemed to wither and lose credibility. Paradoxically, the blow came not from scientific skeptics or wary historians but from archaeologists who had no intention of discrediting the Oracle but rather of establishing her greatness for all time.

Aᴄᴛᴇʀ ᴛʜᴇ ᴘʀᴏᴘʜᴇᴛᴇꜱꜱ fell into silence in the fourth century CE, Delphi was pillaged, destroyed, and then forgotten. Christian fanatics tore apart the pagan monuments and fashioned the remains into humble churches, doing their part to speed the sanctuary's disintegration. So did centuries of neglect on a sloping terrace prone to earthquakes, rockfalls, avalanches, mudslides, and sudden torrents of rushing water. In time, a humble Greek village arose atop the ancient ruins. The Christian villagers, living in primitive conditions, had little or no idea what lay beneath their homes and no memory of the site's extraordinary past. Nor did they recognize the name Delphi. Instead, they called their village Kastri.

In 1436, Cyriac of Ancona, a scholar of the Italian Renaissance sometimes known as the father of classical archaeology, traveled to Greece to look for ancient sites, climbed Mount Parnassus, and found the village. He also discovered a spring and gradually realized the place was Delphi. The itinerant scholar located some of its ancient inscriptions and transcribed them into his travel diaries.

Soon after, Greece came under Ottoman rule, and investigation of the site all but ended. Delphi nonetheless grew in Western consciousness as people increasingly read translations of ancient Greek and Roman authors. Michelangelo painted the Oracle on the ceiling of the Sistine Chapel between 1508 and 1512. But it was not until the late seventeenth century that modern explorers returned to Delphi and reidentified the site, largely by relying on detailed descriptions of the sanctuary from Pausanias, the ancient travel writer. Inscribed on one slab, they found the word *D E L F O I*—six letters that conjured up a lost world. Little happened for two more centuries. The main activity was experts arriving every so often to inspect the cellars of village homes, looking for ancient walls. In time, archaeologists from Britain, Germany, France, Denmark, the United States, and other nations trekked to the drowsy village and searched in vain for remnants of the ancient temple.

Greece fought a war of independence from Turkey between 1821 and 1829. The exhausted state, though extraordinarily proud of its past, had no energy for classical investigations. The foreign archaeologists did, however, and eventually sought help abroad. France came on particularly strong amid rising competition for the celebrated site. In 1862, while trying to buy land around Delphi, the French sent a fleet of warships to cruise nearby in the Gulf of Corinth in a show of force. The stakes for scholarship were seen as nothing less than gargantuan, as was the challenge for archaeology. Early studies suggested that the whole village of Kastri would have to be removed and resettled.

Over the years, the French adopted a more conciliatory approach to the Greeks that sought to win over the fledgling kingdom, which was distrustful of foreigners after the long war of independence and many centuries of brutal occupation. Trade picked up and then flourished. In the 1880s, after disease killed many vines, the French began to import hundreds of thousands of barrels of Greek grapes. Eventually, the amity extended beyond trade. In 1886, France sided with Greece when Britain, Austria, Germany, Italy, and Russia tried to blockade Greek ports to prevent a new war with Turkey.

Slowly, such acts influenced the cautious Greeks, who came to see France as an ally. But for assistance in the new field of archaeology, it was the wealthy and confident United States that beckoned. The Greek government, impoverished after the long occupation and war, needed money more than anything else. So early in 1889, Athens offered the excavation rights to the American School of Classical Studies at Athens. The

Americans considered the proffer a coup, given the decades of international rivalry, the likely rewards, and the national prestige that would follow from the resurrection of Delphi. To secure the concession, all they had to do was to raise the funds needed to buy and resettle the village, which consisted of fewer than one hundred homes. The requisite sum was seen as eighty thousand dollars.

In Boston, excitement rose at the Archaeological Institute of America, the nation's foremost group for the scientific exploration of humanity's past, newly founded and full of youthful vigor. Its membership included not only academics but millionaires and industry barons, including Cornelius Vanderbilt, the railroad magnate, and James Loeb, a banker and eventual founder of the Loeb Classical Library, a series of English translations of ancient Greek and Latin texts. The group's treasurer was Percival Lowell, a famous astronomer from a wealthy New England family, and its president was Charles Norton, the equally famous art historian at Harvard.

Wary of competition from abroad, Norton urged immediate action. "Any considerable delay" in raising the requisite funds, he cautioned a colleague, "is likely to spoil our chance."

Four months later, in May 1889, the group's council met in New York City and resolved to take the financial lead on behalf of the American school in Athens. It would raise eighty thousand dollars to buy out Kastri and, for five years, devote five thousand dollars a year to excavating Delphi—a considerable sum in those days. A formal letter went out to members urging them to contribute according to their means and to consider the excavation a unique opportunity that "should not be allowed to escape." It continued:

The investigation of the remains at Delphi is the most interesting and important work now remaining to be accomplished in the field of classical archaeology. The part which Delphi played in the history of Greece is too well known to need recounting. The imagination of every man who recognizes what modern civilization owes to ancient Greece is stirred by the name of Delphi as by no other name except that of Athens. The centre of Greek religion for centuries, the site of its most famous oracle, the meeting place of its greatest council, the locality adorned by man of the noblest works of the incomparable genius of the Greeks, and crowned with poetic as well as with historic associations throughout the whole periods of the glory of Greece,— Delphi will be forever one of the most sacred seats of the life of the human race. To recover what may now be recovered of the remains of its ancient greatness, to ascertain all that may now be ascertained concerning the character of its famous buildings, to collect the fragments of the works of art which lie buried in the soil, to gather the inscriptions with which its walls were covered, to gain all possible knowledge concerning it,—is a task of the highest honor to those who may accomplish it, and one which Americans may well be proud and glad to undertake.

Despite Norton's warning about the danger of delay, the cognoscenti of Boston and New York got off to a slow start in collecting the needed funds. By April 1890, nearly a year after the institute's council had taken on the responsibility, it had managed to raise just twenty-five thousand dollars, roughly a third of what was needed. Moreover, it failed to get the federal government interested in taking on a role in the endeavor or making a financial contribution. At the time, the administration of Benjamin Harrison, a Republican, was under fire for spending so immoderately from the federal purse that a treasury surplus had rapidly turned into a deficit.

As a result of the lackluster progress, the institute redoubled its focus on individual patrons. New urgency echoed in the editorials of local papers, which called for greater generosity and sowed visions of vast treasures just waiting to be unearthed. "It would be strange indeed," said the *New York Times,* if some of the immense riches bequeathed to Delphi over the ages "were not 'cached' in the earth from time to time and the memory of their whereabouts lost." The editorial suggested that even the Pythia's tripod might come to light, and that proceeds from the sale of reproductions of recovered artifacts might be so great that the team that won the right to excavate ancient Delphi would actually turn a profit.

The French despaired. The plum seemed to be slipping from their hands. But then, in late 1890, while the Americans were still raising funds and congratulating themselves on the honors to come, a new man arrived from Paris to make a last bid for Delphi. Théophile Homolle was a worldly man despite his given name, a distinguished scholar from the Collège de France. Forty-two years of age, he had a flair for administration and political intrigue as well as the day's fondness for slight beards and long mustaches. His speech was as lively as his style. He called Delphi "full of mystery, grandeur and divine terror." He wanted it, badly.

A tenacious negotiator, Homolle convinced Paris to offer a half million francs (later raised to a million) for the town's resettlement and Delphi's excavation. The French offer, equal to nearly one hundred thousand dollars, made the American pledge of eighty thousand dollars seem not only provisional but insubstantial.

In early 1891, with the deal all but signed, Homolle learned to his horror that the French Ministry of State Education had dragged its feet, shelving the Delphi proposal instead of studying it sufficiently to pass judgment. Nothing would happen without its blessing, and the minister expressed doubts about the wisdom of devoting such large sums of public money to so unpredictable a venture. Was it really necessary? he asked Homolle.

Exasperated, the archaeologist threw himself into a campaign to educate the education ministry, doing the rounds in Paris and redoubling his efforts to build a wide constituency. At stake, he felt, were the glory of France, the advancement of science, and the honor of the French school in Athens. Homolle's whirlwind paid off. In Paris, the votes were taken, the deal was approved, and the money was sent on its way. The culmination came in April 1891, when the Greek government awarded France the monopoly to excavate Delphi. In Paris and Athens, toasts and celebrations marked the new alliance.

The Americans felt cheated. Athens, the *Times* grumbled, "played America against France very neatly." A newspaper story from London fixed the blame on Washington, citing its "indifference and lack of energy," not to mention its decision to forgo any financial contribution.

The job that lay before the giddy French differed from most other excavations that had been done over the decades. Around the world, many digs in the fledgling science of archaeology had sought to reveal the secrets of anonymous peoples. Others, especially in Greece, had sought to preserve the remains of ancient glory, such as those of the Acropolis in Athens. But at Delphi, nothing was visible. All had been destroyed and buried, at times under meters of rocky soil. It was arguably the most challenging archaeological site in Greece, if not Europe.

Homolle and his colleagues held out little hope of making truly surprising finds or of recovering great treasures. Rather, the general goal was to reveal the course of history, add fresh detail to the ancient depictions, gain subtle insights into a place that had proved so influential, and—if at all possible—deepen modern understanding of how the Oracle had gained her renown and held sway for so many centuries.

THE WORLD OF ARTS and letters shivered with anticipation. And the public—even the bruised American public—responded with enthusiasm. Ancient Greece had been wildly popular in Europe and America throughout much of the nineteenth century, its ways studied as a model of democracy, its language part of any serious curriculum, its architecture reflected in stately, pillared homes and public buildings, many of which boasted details reminiscent of the Parthenon. Workmen readying the Columbia Exposition in Chicago applied tons of glossy white paint to make wood look like polished marble. They created a metropolis of imitation Greek temples, topping many columns with carvings of acanthus leaves, a common motif in ancient Greece.

Now, one of the triumphs of that vanished world was finally going to come to light. Eager anticipation over the lost splendors of Delphi fit the mood of the 1890s, the Gay Nineties, an age of bumper harvests and clanging trolley cars, of red plush and ten-course dinners. In worldly Vienna, home of Mozart and Freud, a burlesque opera debuted—*Apollo; or, The Oracle of Delphi.* After a run of three months, it moved to New York City and opened in May 1891 at the Casino, the first American theater built specifically for musicals, located at Broadway and Thirty-ninth Street, in the heart of the theater district. The Casino was the undisputed home of comic opera in the United States, and *Apollo* was one of its great hits. Night after night, gentlemen in proper evening attire and ladies displaying the latest Paris fashions crowded into the ornate house.

The story centers on a beautiful young maiden who serves as the Oracle. In the temple's archive, Dioskuros, an aide, has discovered an old law warning that if the Pythia should ever allow herself to be kissed, the gods will visit wrath upon the offenders and demolish the temple. The sanctuary's high priest, informed of the ancient prohibition, flies into a panic when the Oracle returns to Delphi after a tour of Greek cities and brings with her a handsome young Athenian she has met, Helios. The two, it develops, have fallen in love and are planning to elope.

Frantic, the temple authorities hatch ridiculous plots to separate the lovers, with deceptions and impostors and finally the imprisoning of the young Pythia inside the temple. Out of love for Helios, she decides to resign her post, but hesitates after a friend warns her of the threat of divine fury. Helios, defying Apollo's wrath, barges in and kisses her. Nothing happens. Encouraged by Helios, the Pythia renounces Apollo. Meanwhile, outside the temple, devout pilgrims who have been waiting patiently for oracular consultations grow angry at the delays and turn into a riotous mob. Dioskuros, emboldened by the lack of punishment for the stolen kiss, announces to the crowd that the temple will close, and reopen soon as an amusement palace devoted to free entertainments.

"It is, of course, a light and airy plot," the *Times* sniffed, adding that such productions "are meant to give amusement, not to provoke thought."

People loved it. Lillian Russell, the queen of American musical theater, bejeweled and flamboyant and famous for her affair with Diamond Jim Brady, starred as the Oracle. It was an appropriate role given how popular culture hung on her every word. At the Casino, a chorus of eighty voices produced a thunderous backdrop for Russell, and the elaborate sets helped transport the audience to a remote era. The first act took place in a mock-up of the Castalian gorge, with a cascade of real water plunging into a pool near center stage. The second act took place in the temple's interior, dominated by a statue of Apollo.

The designers took special care with the Pythia's inner sanctum. It featured a sacred pool. At key points in the story, clouds of vapor rose from the water through colored lights. The final scene took place on the temple's grounds, dominated by massive stone steps, columns, and statues.

Russell, perhaps inspired by her character's independence of spirit, decided to tear up her contract after the run and negotiated a tough new agreement that became a turning point in her career. Thereafter, she grew not only immensely famous but comfortably rich.

However, in the whirl of Delphic anticipations, the comic opera tended to be the exception. Most of the observances were sincere, some reverential. In London, one of the most sought-after painters of the day took it upon himself to do a portrait of the Oracle that was richly sensual and evocative of the Victorian era's spiritualist mood. John Collier, an aristocrat of forty-one, the younger son of Lord Monkswell, had a successful career doing landscapes and society portraits, including dour statesmen and self-assured captains of industry. He often exhibited at the Royal Academy. His sitters included Rudyard Kipling, Charles Darwin, T. H. Huxley (his father-in-law and president of the Royal Society), and the Dukes of York and Cornwall. He was known for a strong sense of color that could create a surprising realism of mood and appearance. His lighter side found expression in the theatricality of the pre-Raphaelites; these romantic paintings were marked by great beauty, intricate realism, and a fondness for willowy, exotic women. Collier's study of the Delphic Oracle, done in 1891, nearly life-size at more than five feet tall, gave this very proper late Victorian gentleman an opportunity to indulge himself.

He draped her in red against a dark background that deepened into a midnight absence of color, as if the Oracle stood between the viewer and infinity. Educated at Eton, Collier knew his classics and for inspiration clearly drew upon the fifth-century Athenian image of the Oracle in a prophetic state. That had been done in profile. Collier had the good sense to turn the Oracle ninety degrees so that she faced the viewer. Striving for a mystic air, Collier departed from the original to close her eyes and put her in a state of deep concentration, as if her mind was moving through all time and space. His Oracle was young and attractive, perhaps in her twenties, in contrast to the more mature priestess of the Athenian original. Moreover, her dress was diaphanous, her skin luminous, her shoulder bare. Still, as in the early rendering, Collier gave his Oracle an air of modesty, her head veiled, her breasts covered. And he faithfully showed her sitting astride the tripod, her feet limp, dangling off the floor.

It was the floor where Collier made the biggest change, relying on the writers of late antiquity to add new detail. Instead of a black void, he depicted a rugged chasm a few inches wide running between the legs of the tripod. Faint mists rose from the cleft, enveloping the Oracle in clouds of vapor, helping carry her off to divine ecstasy.

BACK IN Greece at Delphi itself, the scene bore no resemblance to the happy swirl engulfing the world of culture. Just as the French arrived, a huge mudslide rushed down from the cliffs, ripping through the town and killing several people.

Over the centuries, the humble Greek village of Kastri grew atop the ruins of
the sanctuary of Apollo at Delphi. Eager for knowledge and glory, French
archaeologists in 1892 began relocating the town in preparation for
unearthing the lost epicenter of the ancient Greek world.

Workmen pitched the first spadeful of dirt in October 1892, inaugurat-
ing the mammoth undertaking. Angry villagers proceeded to attack workers and destroy tools. The military was called in and work resumed under a
show of rifles. As things settled down, the French set up lorries to haul away
dirt, rock, and demolished homes. Soon, tracks crisscrossed the site. Workers filled woven baskets with debris and emptied them into cars that they
pushed by hand or pulled with horses to nearby dumping grounds. A new
town was set up a mile away to house the villagers. Photographers with
large box cameras clambered about, documenting the chaotic dig.

Homolle and his team zeroed in on the central sanctuary. Following
the detailed account of its layout by Pausanias, the ancient travel writer,
the men started low on the rocky slope, beginning at what they judged to
be the start of the Sacred Way, the main thoroughfare. Soon, empty treas-

86

uries of the city-states came to light, as well as a few broken pieces of art-work that had escaped looting and destruction. Twin marble statues, dated to the sixth century BCE, showed young, naked, beardless men of athletic build, their heads raised and fists clenched at their sides.

Near the buried temple, workmen found a marble statue of Antinous, a favorite of the emperor Hadrian who in 130 CE had drowned in the Nile while still very young. It was larger than life, its surface polished to a brilliance like that of porcelain, the face ringed by curls. A photograph of its unearthing shows the statue surrounded by swarthy workmen, the backdrop a tableau of dirt and broken rock.

Such outstanding finds, coming from Delphi's earliest and final days, seemed to bode well. The French excavators threw themselves into the dig with renewed vigor. Who knew what else they would uncover? Maybe the site did in fact harbor treasures hidden over the ages, not only gold and silver but statues of great artistry and temple reliefs that would surpass those the British had removed from the Acropolis.

The archaeologists bore down on the temple itself with a nervous mix of fervor and trepidation. After all, they knew all too well of Delphi's inglorious end. Now, fifteen centuries later, the moment had come to see the actual damage. Waves of picks and spades tore into rocky ground. Soon enough, the answer was clear—the ancient wrecking crew had been extraordinarily thorough. All that was left of the magnificent fourth-century BCE temple was a jumble of foundation blocks and some column drums.

Homolle felt betrayed. "The temple, on which so much hope had rested, has been a great deception," he confided in 1894, two years after the excavation's start.

It got worse. After unearthing what remained of the temple, the French turned their attention to digging into its foundations at a spot they judged to be the holy of holies. But it proved to be especially jumbled, perhaps because of earthquakes and landslides, or perhaps because the Christian fanatics had focused their fury on the *adyton*. For whatever reason, neither its location nor its form could be discerned with any certainty.

The French leaders of Delphi's excavation in 1893, a year after the dig began. At the center is Théophile Homolle, who called the sanctuary "full of mystery, grandeur and divine terror."

In 1894, workmen at Delphi unearthed a statue of Antinous, a favorite of
Roman emperor Hadrian. At its peak, the sanctuary held thousands of
statues, votives, monuments, reliefs, and treasuries. Invaders eventually
seized the riches that were most easily appropriated.

So the excavation of what was arguably the most hallowed site of ancient Greece proved to be a demoralizing anticlimax. "We were greatly disappointed," Émile Bourguet, one of the main excavators, recalled. "Several times as we pressed ahead with the work with the utmost care and with a growing sense of disquietude one idea began to force itself upon us more and more insistently: that all we should find would be the result of systematic destruction."

Then came the final, painful insult. The French dug deeper into the area of the temple's foundations judged to be the *adyton* and found that its depths bore no resemblance to what the ancient writers had depicted. There was no cave, no fissure, no vaporous cleft, no bottomless abyss from which gases could rise, no obvious means for production of the mystic pneuma. Yes, water did well up as the workers dug, suggesting that Pausanias had been right in asserting that a sacred spring arose within the holy of holies. But that proved nothing. Springs flowed down many parts of the rocky hillside, though no worker or archaeologist who came in contact with the waters ever seemed to experience anything that could be described as sacred intoxication or divine madness.

Disenchantment ran deep. Was it all a ruse? What had the Oracle and her retinue been up to? Maybe it was all a farce, a wholesale deception meant to cheat the pious. After all, the authorities at Delphi had made a good living at divine prophecy, a very good living by the day's standards. For the women especially, presiding over the holy rites had been lucrative and elevating. Homolle and his aides kept their feelings private. The stakes were too high for public displays of embarrassment or frustration, especially after the long competition with the Americans.

The Frenchmen expanded their search away from the temple to focus on other sanctuary areas, finding more relics and many hundreds of weathered inscriptions. In 1898, the men found a monument to Aristotle and his nephew, the stone erected in gratitude for their compiling the list of victors in the Pythian Games. It was ancient history come to life. While news of such finds circulated quickly and widely, Homolle and his men treated the big letdowns and overall analyses as state secrets. They published so little that foreign critics, especially the Germans—who had unearthed ancient Olympia in the Peloponnese and felt superior to the French after their victory in the Franco-Prussian War—began to berate them publicly, with some barbs quite sharp. Even so, it would be decades before the French gave ground and began to publicly detail their findings.

*T*HE FIRST comprehensive description of the Oracle's sanctum came in a roundabout way, not from the French but from a young English scholar who had toured Delphi and met Homolle and his men. It was his disclosure that began a process of Oracle deconstruction that lasted much of the twentieth century. The outcome of this academic offensive reduced her standing, undercut her mystic allure, gave spiritualists pause, discredited the ancient authors, and in general killed the public's interest in Delphi. The torrent of popular appreciations all but dried up.

If the French had struck gold, they would have publicized their breakthrough from the rooftops, doing so with government ministers from Paris and Athens at their sides. Instead, they entrusted the announcement to a minor foreign scholar, albeit one of French descent. Adolph Paul Oppé was a young historian, not yet thirty, who had just taken a job lecturing on ancient history at Edinburgh, Scotland's most prestigious university. In 1904, he published "The Chasm at Delphi" in the *Journal of Hellenic Studies,* a leading forum.

Oppé praised the French for their "industry and care" at Delphi and heaped ridicule on ancient and modern authors. Excavations of the temple ruins, he said, had revealed that its foundations bore no *adyton,* no fissure, and no possible means for the production of fumes. "The French excavators have failed to find a trace of it," he said of the famous chasm. The inspirational mist was a fiction that the ancient sources had passed down through the ages. They were wrong. He boasted that his own investigations of the mistakes and inconsistencies of the ancient literature backed up the French discoveries.

Boldly, Oppé ventured outside his own field to propose, on geologic grounds, the impossibility of a vaporous cleft. Delphi in general and the temple in particular, he argued, sat on the wrong kind of bedrock for the production of fumes. The right land for such emissions was volcanic, and no volcanoes or volcanism marked Delphi or its surrounding region. Ancient and modern authors, he wrote, had mistakenly ascribed to Delphi the kind of volcanic fumes that surrounded the sibyl of the temple of Apollo at Cumae (in Italy near Mount Vesuvius). But Delphi had nothing in common with Cumae, Oppé wrote. Nor in all likelihood did it possess more subtle geological features such as rocky cracks that might serve as conduits for underlying gases and fumes, least of all a crack that "stood immediately under the temple." Finally, he argued that, even if Delphi had produced vapors, they would have caused the Oracle to gag and choke, as did all such emissions from the earth. "They could never have inspired the Pythia."

Oppé's analysis reverberated through the scholarly world for several reasons. Most important, it challenged many centuries of conventional wisdom, an accomplishment few scholars could claim. And it argued forcefully with few qualifiers and caveats. Finally, it offered not only negative reasons to doubt the Oracle's vaporous ecstasy—no *adyton,* no fissure, no mist, no consistent story in the literature—but a positive one as well: the region's geology was wrong for the production of vapors. His point carried the kind of intellectual heft that could stifle challenges and rejoinders. In short, he had scored an academic triumph.

Despite his bravado, however, Oppé had made a serious error in describing the sanctuary's physical makeup. On the basis of geology, he claimed that the temple region had no spring—contrary to Pausanias and contrary to what the French excavators had actually discovered. In a way, his mistake was understandable for a person who had acquired only a superficial knowledge of what the French had uncovered. But in time it would prove embarrassing, obscuring as it did an aspect of Delphi that would prove central to solving the mystery of the pneuma.

Other scholars, eager to learn firsthand what the French were up to, also made the pilgrimage to Delphi. A more seasoned one than Oppé was Frederick Poulsen, a Danish scholar who specialized in classical art. He toured the dig in 1907, three years after Oppé's paper appeared. The result was his monumental *Delphi,* a handsome book rich in photographs and detailed illustrations that laid out what had come to light so far and how it fit the historical record.

Poulsen accepted the no-vapor thesis but went further, speculating on what, if not mystic fumes, had inspired the Oracle. He advised colleagues to look to the new science of psychology rather than physical factors. "The French excavations have not exposed any bottomless abyss from which strong and stupefying gases could be supposed to rise," he wrote. "One does well to reject the physical and hold fast to mental causes, hysterical affections, which in every religion make women serviceable media."

After this remarkable injunction, Poulsen sought to reconcile at least part of the ancient lore with the modern discoveries. He focused on water. Unlike Oppé, he asserted that a spring had in fact been found to well up under the holy of holies, enhancing, if not causing, the Pythia's state of intoxication. The cold vapors, he said, "increased the ecstasy of the priestesses." That was it. He named no particular substance that might have arisen in the cool mist and no particular mechanism by which the exhalations would have helped drive the Oracle into a rapturous frenzy. Still, if faint in force, his point helped correct Oppé's mistake.

SCHOLARSHIP, no less than fashion, can undergo changes that in hindsight seem arbitrary and driven by nothing more substantial than a thirst for newness. It had now been a quarter century since the French had started to unearth the ancient site, and much of the academic world had come to accept the lack of a vaporous cleft. Still, new interpretations began to circulate that, unlike Oppé's and Poulsen's, tried to find ways to make the absence of a fissure comport with the ancient literature. Perhaps, some analysts argued, the chasm had existed in antiquity but vanished over the centuries. For believers in the old accounts, this explanation marked an optimistic new turn.

It also marked the start of a pattern that reoccurred in decades of debate over Delphi's authenticity: If the prophetic mechanism was a hoax, so too the Oracle's powers. If not, then her mystic side seemed to gain credibility. Maybe she really could read minds, see faraway places, and glimpse the future. The new phase began in 1918, as World War I drew to a close. The Reverend T. Dempsey, headmaster of Saint Joseph's College, in Ballinasloe, Ireland, laid out his analyses in *The Delphic Oracle.* Though the French had found no trace of the famous crevice, cave, or subterranean chamber, he wrote, the reason was not necessarily ancient dishonesty but rather the violent nature of the Delphic region. The land's frequent earthquakes could easily have closed up any void, he reasoned, echoing Plutarch. Given the ancient claims and modern clues regarding the landscape, he concluded that the presence of a small cleft or crack in the floor of the temple was "highly probable."

Having found support for the presumed honesty of the old accounts, Dempsey went on to dismiss the idea that the Oracle was "a mere sham, a conscious fraud" trading on the credulity of a superstitious age. All the evidence, ancient and modern, he wrote, suggested otherwise. Emboldened, the good reverend went on to embrace the possibility that at least some of the Oracles had psychic powers. He cited the test of Croesus and concluded, like Myers, that it may have involved extrasensory perception.

Dempsey had distinguished company. The Society for Psychical Research, shaking off the disappointments of Delphic archaeology, was busy revisiting the question of ancient mental powers. Indeed, Gilbert Murray,

the Regius Professor of Greek at Oxford University and the most prominent classical scholar of the day, had taken up the group's presidency and
become deeply immersed in telepathic experiments.

One of Murray's students, Eric R. Dodds, soon to follow him as Regius
Professor and eventually as the society's president, published a paper that
reviewed the evidence for psychic powers in classical antiquity and focused on the Oracle, citing the test of Croesus. While doubting that the
ancient evidence *proved* the existence of psychic communication, Dodds
nonetheless found it quite significant. "If a particular supernormal phenomenon, alleged to occur spontaneously among civilized people in recent times, is not attested at other times and places of which we have
adequate knowledge, the presumption is thereby increased that it does
not occur as alleged," he wrote. The converse, Dodds added, was equally
true. He noted that feats of the past could demonstrate the continuity of
psychic abilities from age to age, adding that such considerations had
prompted his own examination of the ancient psychic claims.

Eventually, after doing his own experiments in mind reading, Dodds
came to accept ancient and modern telepathy as indisputable facts of life.

THE BIG ADVANCE of the day had nothing to do with renewed sympathy
for the Oracle's mystic side. It was more concrete. The French, breaking
their long silence, finally described their discoveries at Delphi. Moreover,
in so doing they ceded significant ground in the overall debate.

Fernand Courby, a young colleague of Homolle's, had taken up the
challenge of compiling the overall findings and publishing them in the
official records of the dig, *Fouilles de Delphes* (*The Excavations of Delphi*). With
their usual public reluctance, the French waited until the second volume—
published in installments from 1920 to 1927, more than three decades after the excavation's start—to describe formally the main discoveries and

The dig's main goal—unearthing the temple of Apollo—
initially produced a confusing puzzle. But over the years,
excavators found that its surviving parts fell slowly into
place, including traces of the Oracle's inner sanctum.
This man stands near that spot.

conclusions. But the delay paid off. Rather than presenting early, inchoate
evidence, Courby, the volume's editor, was able to report a major find: the
adyton, the most sacred spot in ancient Greece.

The French found that the holy of holies had simply been lost initially
amid the jumble of temple blocks and broken remains. Careful investigation, however, had laid its outlines bare. Courby described two areas—
one for consultants, one for the Oracle. They stood to the temple's
southwest side, he said, an arrangement that interrupted a row of interior

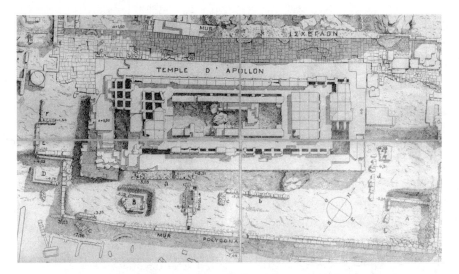

A French drawing of 1927 details the extant foundations of the temple, its layout
typical of Greek shrines except for the opening to the southwest for the Oracle's
sanctum. The L-shaped blocks mark its left side. In the sanctum's depths,
the French found no trace of a vaporous crack or fissure.

columns and broke the normal rules of temple symmetry. Overall, the
adyton measured just nine feet wide and sixteen feet long. It was from this
modest room that the Oracle had inspired poets, decided the fate of nations, and acted like a magnet to draw religious pilgrims from around the
world. The deeper excavations, Courby added, revealed no "mysterious
fissure." It was quite an anticlimax, given more than two decades of scholarly discussion about the missing feature.

In a poignant foreword, Courby expressed publicly what the archaeologists had long said among themselves: uncovering the temple had proved a
disappointment. For the French, the admission had to have been humiliat-
ing, given their long maneuvering for possession of the famous site and the
contest with the Americans. But Courby carried it off with dignity and grace.

When I began the architectural study of the Delphic sanctuary, perhaps I had not sufficiently realized the weight of the honor offered to

me. Perhaps I was wrong to start, but I was unable to resist the very powerful attraction that these prestigious ruins exercised on me. Had I foreseen all the effort that the task demanded, and the poor satisfaction the results were to give me, I think I would have left to others the task of coming to a greater understanding.

The report gave new credibility to the old accounts—and not only about the holy of holies. Courby also reported the discovery of what the French judged to be the omphalos, the conical stone that marked Delphi as the center of the universe. It was a curious find, however. The stone was fairly small (about a foot high) and bore an inch-wide hole that penetrated its center from top to bottom. The hole's purpose was a mystery.

Many gaps of understanding remained after decades of labor. But the temple of Apollo was slowly—more slowly and painfully than the French or Americans had ever imagined—giving up its secrets.

At the same time, it was increasingly clear to everyone that the debunking of Delphi had faltered. Oppé started with simple clarity, demolishing what he called a series of ancient myths. Little by little, however, some of the alleged falsehoods were turning out to be true. The spring under the temple was real, as was the *adyton.* And the theory of the fissure had won new adherents.

THE REVISIONIST mood set some scholars looking for ways to reconcile the new discoveries with one of the pervasive beliefs of antiquity and one of the main areas of modern doubt: the Pythia's inhalation of a pneuma that prepared her for spiritual union with Apollo. The Americans proposed a physical mechanism for such euphoria, and the French abjured. The old antagonism still had life.

The debate centered on an intriguing block that the French had found amid the jumble. By a process of elimination, Courby deduced that it originally lay in the *adyton*. The limestone block, three feet wide and four and a half feet long, had clearly found no use in routine construction or flooring, as suggested by its unusual appearance. One side bore a square hole six inches wide that penetrated all the way through. Tapered, it widened to nine inches at the bottom.

Courby decided the block was part of an altar and that the hole acted as a drain for the blood of sacrificial animals. American scholars doubted this. In 1929, Walter Miller, a classics scholar at the University of Missouri and translator of Greek texts for the Loeb Classical Library, offered an alternative explanation. For Miller, the unearthing of the limestone block added up to the discovery of perhaps the holiest site of ancient Greece—the seat of the Oracle, the place from which her voice had carried forth to inspire the ancient world.

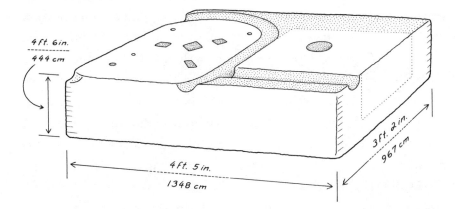

Amid the ruins of the Oracle's chamber, the French discovered an intriguing block. American archaeologists of the early twentieth century theorized that it once formed part of the sanctum's floor and that its shallow holes (to the left) anchored the Oracle's tripod. Another scenario proposed that a furtive den under the floor piped intoxicating smoke through the block's penetrating hole (right) into the inner sanctum.

Miller focused on the area of the block opposite the hole, where a shallow trough circled three gouges arranged in the form of a triangle. These hollows, he reasoned, once held the tripod's legs. Elaborating, Miller argued that the trough had acted as a conduit for the sacred waters of the temple spring, sending the flow around the Pythia. Visual evidence seemed to back him up. A heavy deposit of travertine, the rocky coating that makes caves so interesting and at times so beautiful, encrusted the block's periphery as well as the circular trough and an artery leading off of it. The deposit gave mute testimony to long flows of lime-rich water. Miller offered no theory on how the "mystic waters" might have intoxicated the Pythia and made no mention of Poulsen's cold vapors. With a beguiling mix of intellectual modesty and confidence, he simply stated that the holy spring under the temple flowed around the Oracle to "help in some way in the prophetic spell."

Miller's explanation caught the eye of several American scholars, most especially Leicester B. Holland, an archaeologist from the University of Pennsylvania who directed the fine arts division of the Library of Congress. A former Philadelphia architect, he prided himself on his physical intuition. Holland turned it on Delphi in a long article of 1933 that went far beyond the Miller thesis. Meditating on the whole limestone block—including the arrangement of the hole and the tripod mounting—he proposed a conclusion that was nothing short of startling. Holland argued that the Pythia, conspiring with temple authorities, had found a stealthy way to generate clouds of powerful, drug-laden smoke that the priestess inhaled deeply to prepare herself for glimpses of eternity.

His idea relied on a leap of imagination. He proposed that the putative omphalos sat atop the limestone block to form what amounted to a small smokestack at the Oracle's feet. That in itself might have been considered far-fetched. Even so, his evidence was intriguing. Holland noted that the area around the block's hole had no crust of travertine but instead bore a smooth region that was square in shape, suggesting that it once held a stone base, shielding that part of the block from mineralized water. This lost base, Holland argued, had also been penetrated by a hole that aligned with ones in the block and omphalos to make a continuous channel. As evidence, he reproduced a picture of an ancient Greek relief that showed the omphalos sitting on just such a square base (with eagles on either side, memorializing Zeus's blessing of Delphi's centrality).

And where did the smoke come from? Holland argued that the temple authorities had dug a subbasement below the *adyton* that they could enter unobtrusively through a narrow passage. Down there, by the spring waters, the priestess would light a fire and throw on the psychoactive ingredients. The hemp plant, *Cannabis sativa,* and its seeds, Holland wrote, might have produced the desired effect. He noted that the Scythians, an ancient nomadic people who lived north of the Greeks, had used hemp in various rites. Hemp, too, had a pungent, sweet odor, perhaps not unlike the intermittent fragrance that Plutarch had reported.

The Oracle's routine had been designed to fool pilgrims, Holland argued. Ostensibly, she went into the subbasement simply to get the spring waters for a libation, a liquid offering to the gods that she poured around the tripod. But in a subterfuge, while down low, she also "actually lit a brazier there, and then coming up again and mounting upon the tripod, inhaled the fumes piped through the floor beneath her feet."

Unlike Miller's elegant if sketchy idea, Holland's strung together many what-ifs into a debatable whole: what if the omphalos sat atop the large block, what if the Oracle poured many libations, what if a subbasement existed, what if the Oracle burned hemp, what if temple authorities engaged in a complicated scheme. The whole thing teetered on the brink of implausibility. Still, Holland had achieved what seemed like a brilliant stroke in visualizing the arrangement of the artifacts to make a hollow channel. It bespoke an ease with problems of three-dimensional geometry that only an architect might possess. But he was severely limited in visualizing the potential uses of the novel assemblage because he subscribed to Oppé's theory about the absence of volcanic activity ruling out natural fumes. So it was that Holland came up with the idea of hallucinogenic smoke and gave no weight to natural alternatives, to simpler ideas.

His reach for an improbable explanation was rooted in a false assumption that another scholar decades later would be sure to avoid.

Modern visualizations of the Oracle had now come full circle, back to the phase before the French excavations, back to the days of Collier's moody Victorian rendering. Once again, the priestess was intoxicated, but now as a reefer maniac. Holland's theory, if unconfirmed and unconvincing, was so detailed and lively that by midcentury it inspired a new round of artistry that once again set the Oracle before the public.

The priestess starred in a National Geographic Society book called *Everyday Life in Ancient Times,* which found its way into many American homes. It was lavishly illustrated in color, with one beautiful rendering after another. The portrayal of the Oracle's vault drew heavily on Holland, showing the omphalos on a square block and its hole spewing fumes like a runaway locomotive. True to tradition, it placed golden eagles on either side of the omphalos. However, the painting's mood bore no resemblance to the reverential quietude of Collier, or the atmosphere of dark sobriety that probably existed in antiquity. Instead, it showed a brightly lit hall with a half dozen priests and male consultants fixated on the Oracle—understandably so.

The book's priestess was fully clothed but her face was contorted into something approaching a snarl, her mouth agape as if shrieking. Her body had none of the languid suppleness of the Athenian original or Collier's interpretation. Instead, the portrayal showed her as tense, her arms flailing, her hands clutching a laurel branch and libation dish. She had one foot hitched up on a rung of the tripod, as if ready to bolt. Her state seemed to be one of deranged frenzy.

"No one could understand her incoherent ravings," the book said, "but the priests professed to do so."

. . .

IT WAS too much. The French—the serious, sober, painstaking, subdued French—mustered their best authority and let loose a corrective blast. Released in 1950, *La Mantique Apolliniene à Delphes* (*The Apollonian Soothsayer at Delphi*) drew on more than a half century of indignation and frustration that the French had amassed during the swirl of scholarly and public reactions to their labors. Its author was Pierre Amandry, a Delphi expert destined to become director of the French School of Archaeology at Athens. From the start, the book was unusual by American standards. It started with an annotated bibliography listing most of the Oracle's recent chroniclers, including the Englishman Oppé, the Irishman Dempsey, and the American Holland. With little restraint, it landed blows meant to banish all manner of preposterous theories from the halls of scholarship.

Amandry took on the trappings of geology to bolster his own authority, doing so to a much greater extent than Oppé had dared a half century earlier, seeking to raise his level of precision and persuasion. The move was clever but risky. Archaeologists of his generation tended to know little about the rocky earth and its study. Amandry could adopt the language of geology, but his knowledge of its methods, nuances, and accumulated facts was likely to be sketchy. At worst, he risked embarrassing himself with false claims, undermining the French position on the most contentious of Paris's many archaeological endeavors.

Despite the delicacy of the situation, Amandry came on strong. He dismissed the idea that ages of earthquakes, rockslides, and mudflows could have closed the crevice and stopped the fumes, as Dempsey had argued. The cleft was simply not there, past or present, and no amount of conjecture could make it so. The temple, he wrote, rested on clay and shale, both fine-grained sediments. Deeper still was limestone, a rock from ancient seas. None could support a fissure, he wrote. Yes, shifts of the limestone could change the flow of ground waters. But that motion was very unlikely to have closed or opened a crevice from which gases rose. Such phenomena, he stressed, were unknown in the Delphi region. The closure hypothesis, he concluded, was useless.

He also declared the area incapable of producing mind-altering vapors because of its lack of volcanic activity, echoing Oppé. The terrain at Delphi, Amandry insisted, could never have put the Oracle into a state of natural ecstasy.

He dismissed Holland's thesis about the mysterious block, claiming that the American was so desperate to intoxicate the Oracle that he replaced natural vapors with artificial ones. The image of the intoxicated Oracle that had come down from the ancients was the result of a disinformation campaign run by the early Christians, Amandry argued. The fathers of the church had taken scraps from the ancient Greeks and Romans and spun them into a fairy tale of frenzy that colored all subsequent interpretations. For the church founders, he wrote, the Oracle was a "symbol of paganism sinking into the convulsions of hysterical delirium."

Stripped of ecstatic inspiration, the Oracle of Amandry's book became a poor, pathetic creature who owed all her achievements to Delphi's clever priests. She was a front, a comely veneer on a corrupt bureaucracy. "It will be admitted with difficulty that an illiterate woman, lacking the gifts of a Cassandra, chosen only for her moral virtues, could give the response instantaneously, formulated in prose, let alone in hexameters," he wrote. "One can scarcely believe that, for a political affair such as a treaty of alliance, the response was not dictated to the Pythia."

It was as if a god had spoken. The scholarly debate ended, and the unruly Americans dropped their onslaught. Instead, quite remarkably given the long history of friction, a new mood of deference seized the world of classical scholarship. In the aftermath of Amandry's opus, the French findings were accorded almost universal acclaim and were repeatedly and reverentially cited during the second half of the twentieth century, a time, in any event, when science often came to dominate the academic agenda at the expense of other inquiries.

The doubters had won. Scholars no longer tried to reconcile the ancient record with modern findings, no longer tended to speculate on the psychoactive effect of springs or smoke or the possibility that the Oracle in her prophetic outpourings had in fact displayed any hint of real psychic powers. The dissenters—a few holdouts who believed in the existence of the Oracle's vapors, mainly a handful of Greek scholars who felt it reckless to dismiss ancient authorities such as Plutarch as cheats or simpletons—were ignored. Consensus, that rare thing in the normally fractious world of academic discourse, spread like a fog.

> 1963: "As for the famous 'vapours' to which the Pythia's inspiration was once confidently ascribed, they are a Hellenistic invention," wrote Eric R. Dodds. "The French excavations showed that there are to-day no vapours, and no 'chasm' from which vapors could once have come."

> 1978: "There was no vapor and no chasm," wrote Joseph Fontenrose. "The Pythia experienced no frenzy that caused her to shout wild and unintelligible words."

> 1989: "The excavators have found no cleft, either natural or artificial, for hallucinatory fumes," wrote Saul Levin. "Nor is there any pharmacological effect from the substances to which the Pythia was exposed."

And so it went in dozens of books and articles and encyclopedias published from Berkeley to Stuttgart. In 1956, Parke and Wormell, the Dublin scholars, set the tone for much that followed by giving what was considered one of the most authoritative summaries in English of the new consensus. They repeated the French geologic mantra, saying the terrain at Delphi could never have "emitted a gas with any intoxicating properties." No external force swept the Pythia off her feet. The action had more to do with manipulation and mind games. Echoing Amandry, they argued that, at best, the Oracle had been a pawn in the hands of savvy priests.

"Probably the majority of these women, particularly when they came of ordinary peasant stock, were simple tools," they wrote. "The priests may have chosen them for their suitability, which may have manifested itself most easily in an intense devotion to Apollo and his worship. The signs of emotional instability and a tendency to abnormal behavior may have been a recommendation. . . . If due allowance is made for the circumstances, modern psychology will find no special difficulty in accounting for the operations of the Pythia." The chief temptation and challenge for the priests was to take the "confused and disjointed remarks" of the women and somehow turn them into words befitting a god.

Nowhere in the new consensus was there room for the obvious intelligence of a Clea, for the possibility of intoxicating fumes, or for the prospect that the Oracles possessed the kinds of occult powers that had so fascinated Myers and the founders of the Society for Psychical Research. The excavations at Delphi and the vigorous French interpretation of the findings had all but ruled out such prospects. Doubters had undone them all. The woman who once electrified the ancient world was now generally seen as a dupe, if not a conscious fraud.

Remarkably, the men who made the skepticism so fashionable knew astonishingly little about the fundamental aspects of science that supposedly informed their hypotheses and conclusions—little of geology, faults, volcanoes, rocky strata, hydrology, and the evolution of the earth's crust over billions of years. They were archaeologists or classicists or men of letters who were out of their depth, dilettantes who professed to know more than they really did. The gods, if interested in such things, might have judged it a shocking display of hubris and decided that the situation called for the assessment of an earth scientist who actually knew what he was talking about.

THREE

Inquisitive Man

*J*ELLE ZEILINGA DE BOER grew up in Indonesia on the flank of a volcano. Occasionally, the ground would shake and one of the neighboring vents would wheeze and hiss and erupt, sending clouds of ash into the sky. It was the kind of activity that would capture the attention of anyone, especially a young boy.

One day when de Boer was six, his father and he were driving over the mountains in their new Chevy. Suddenly, his dad slammed on the brakes. A crack had opened in the road. Up shot a curtain of brownish water that rose higher than the hood of the car. Astonished, father and son watched the water play in the air for what seemed like forever before it came rushing down the road toward them and splashed off to the side. The shock waves from an earthquake—too small for them to feel—had compressed the land and forced out the groundwater. It was a revelation. Most people never see dramatic evidence of how water can saturate layers of rock. What de Boer had witnessed burned in his memory.

The de Boer family lived on Java, the most developed and populous of the seventeen thousand islands that make up Indonesia, and home to its capital, Batavia (now known as Jakarta). They were part of the legacy of colonialism in the Dutch East Indies that was rooted in the spice trade and nurtured in rich volcanic soils that proved ideal for tea and coffee plantations. Java has more than thirty volcanoes in what comprises the planet's most active volcanic region. West of the de Boer residence, in the strait between Java and Sumatra, smoke often rose from the ruins of Krakatoa, whose eruption in 1883 killed nearly forty thousand people. Java's volcanoes are mostly active but usually harmless. The small eruptions that regularly blow off ash and steam act as safety valves; it is the lack of venting that can prove deadly.

Their own volcano was a sulking giant known as Welirang. Its summit consisted of miles of cones and craters, sulfur deposits, and small vents emitting gas and steam. Past cycles of explosive fury and relative quiescence had given the surrounding region a surreal look. Huge boulders sat in languid rivers. Mounds of ancient mud and ash stood where torrential flows of wet volcanic debris had come to rest. In Holland, the land was flat and calm, mud and clay. The contrast made de Boer appreciate Java all the more. It possessed not only rich highlands but dense jungles and Hindu temples, fragrant spices and exotic flowers.

His own corner of this world was paradise. De Boer's father was an architect who had built his dream house on the side of the volcano, where the climate was cool and the views extraordinary. A stone bridge ran over a stream at the home's entrance. Nearby in the forested hills, waterfalls splashed on rocks and hot springs filled the air with mist.

The family had loyal servants and a good life that centered on their four children. Jelle (pronounced YELL-a) was the youngest. He rode to school on a pony, traveling under canopies of old trees and down narrow mud paths between rice fields. The de Boers sent their two older children to school in Holland, but their home retained a lively air because they had adopted several Indonesian children. A favorite sport was fighting kites, a Javanese tradition. After the monsoons, the winds would blow steady in the afternoons and the children would sail bamboo kites that swooped and dove and sometimes managed to cut the lines of rivals, setting them free.

War ended this idyll. Tokyo, eager for Indonesia's oil, rice, and rubber, invaded in March 1942 and tried but failed to force the colonial government into an alliance. Instead, the Japanese devised their own way to run the archipelago. Military authorities tore de Boer's family apart. They put his father to work on the Burma railroad as a slave laborer, threw his sister into a concentration camp, and held his mother and him captive in an old prison. The Japanese considered boys of ten to be men. In early 1944, when de Boer was nine and a half, they took him from his mother and put him into a concentration camp with hundreds of older Dutch boys and old men, many dying. The hardships were legion: beatings, filth, near starvation, dysentery, endless work, lice, bedbugs, clouds of mosquitoes. When the guards got drunk, the prisoners would sneak up to the barbed-wire fences and try to sell their clothes to local Indonesians for food. Boys who got caught were tortured.

Small and thin, de Boer was asked by some of the older men to try to get more food. To do so surreptitiously he had to crawl through a muddy ditch filled with human excrement. The third time, he got caught—with grim consequences. Afterward, the nuns in the small camp hospital treated his wounds as best they could.

Allied planes flew over the prison camp on August 23, 1945, parachuting in crates of peaches, butter, Spam, corned beef, and Vegemite, a paste loaded with vitamins. It was de Boer's eleventh birthday. Soon, the gates opened. But the situation was still dangerous. No Allied troops had arrived, and Indonesian snipers, eager for independence after centuries of servitude, fired on the Dutch as well as the Japanese.

De Boer fled the camp with a group of boys. Without shirt or shoes, dirty and brown from the sun, he might have passed for a local Indonesian except for his blue eyes. The boys took handouts or stole food during the furtive hunt for their families. Some were shot. De Boer suffered leg and head wounds. Eventually, after nearly a year, he found his mother and sister. His father was dead, killed in the war's last days. The remnants of the de Boer family reunited in Holland.

Jelle had trouble settling into a routine life and had difficulty in school. He often got into fights. In time, a friend of his father's from Indonesia came to live with the family and proved to be a stabilizing force. Jelle grew proud of his new last name, Zeilinga de Boer. He learned to study hard and excel at sports. He became an excellent fencer. In high school, he dreamed of becoming a navy pilot but was rejected because of eye trouble. Depressed, he wandered Utrecht, the great old university town of the Netherlands, seeing what, if anything, might interest him.

Beside a canal he bumped into a friend from the concentration camp, an older boy who had shown him much kindness, finding him extra food, probably saving his life. The friend said he was studying earth science and invited Jelle to come take a look. They went to a stately old building that turned out to hold many graduate students who had grown up in Indonesia. The land's natural liveliness had, as with Jelle, piqued their curiosity about the earth, and now they were preparing to make it a career.

De Boer felt as if he had found a new family. His chaotic past now seemed to point toward a meaningful future. He plunged into hard courses and exhilarating fieldwork that took him to the Alps and Pyrenees. He fell in love with a beautiful Dutch girl who had grown up in Indonesia and, like Jelle, survived the Japanese camps. They married and had a child. He was becoming educated and settled. He felt a growing sense of purpose.

HIS TIMING could hardly have been better. As de Boer began graduate school at Utrecht in the late 1950s, geology was starting to undergo a revolution that transformed it from a staid descriptive science into a prodigy that could explain the origin of the planet's main features and, with some precision, predict their future arrangements.

The old school of earth science had taught that the continents and oceans remained in fixed positions with respect to one another. For instance, it held that the Atlantic and Pacific oceans had forever bounded the Americas. The revolutionaries found that, to the contrary, the earth's face had undergone constant rearrangement. For instance, the Old and New Worlds had once been part of a primeval supercontinent, with evidence of their union in how the shoulder of Brazil could tuck neatly into the armpit of Africa. The earth's seemingly rigid surface turned out to be an ever-changing mosaic.

The main discoveries came in the early 1960s. Global inquiries showed that the tiny motions had accumulated over the ages to cause continents to merge and spread, mountains to rise and fall, oceans to open and close. It was a violent epic, albeit an extremely slow one, happening about as fast as fingernails grow. The new picture also explained why some volcanoes erupted and others went extinct, why some lands shook violently and others lay quiescent. The underlying theory was called plate tectonics (after the Greek word *tekton,* or builder). Its popular name was continental drift. The theory held that the earth's surface was made up of a dozen or so huge plates that floated like rafts on a hot sea and constantly slid around and collided, carrying about the continents and ocean basins.

At Utrecht, de Boer studied with eminent Dutch scientists who helped nudge this revolution along. A giant of the field, literally and figuratively, was Vening Meinesz, a large man who for many years crammed himself into small Dutch submarines to study the rocky abyss. He did so regularly off the southern coasts of Java and Sumatra, mapping a huge trench that plunged nearly five miles beneath the waves. The trench, it turned out, marked an intersection where one giant plate was colliding with another and getting pushed down into the hot earth. As the plate melted, parts of it rose in molten globs back to the surface to erupt as volcanoes, forming the elongate isles nearby.

So it was that de Boer learned how tectonics explained his own past. The new science showed that the astonishing shudders of his childhood were, very simply, repercussions of plate migration and melting. As a student, de Boer participated firsthand in this rush of discovery. The Utrecht scholars were leaders at tracking the long history of plate movements by hunting in the rocky crust for subtle patterns of old magnetism, what is known as paleomagnetism. They discovered ancient magnetic signatures in rocks all around the globe, including some made by the slow accumulation of sediments in ancient seas. These signatures arose when tiny magnetic mineral grains that floated in the water became aligned with the earth's magnetic field as they descended and slowly accumulated with other debris on the bottom. The rock that eventually formed preserved the magnetic orientation of the grains as if they were swarms of tiny compasses. The same thing happened in volcanic rock. When cooling, it allowed tiny magnetic grains to align themselves with the earth's magnetic field and freeze in position. Geologists learned to read the old alignments as a way to track how far the sampled regions had moved with respect to the planet's current magnetic field. The art was difficult, but the results were so powerful that its practitioners were sometimes referred to as paleomagicians.

De Boer emerged from Utrecht as an expert in this new science, using it to illuminate the origins of lands extending from northeastern Spain to southern France to northeastern Italy. While doing so, he paid close attention to an additional factor that might seem alien to a newly minted geophysicist: ancient life. He was not, after all, a biologist or paleontologist. But an important aspect of his work was to look for signs of fossil creatures in the rocks he studied and to weigh their significance. For instance, de Boer's Alps bristled with ancient coral reefs. In his analyses, he would cite the presence of identical fossils in widely separated mountain ranges as evidence that, long ago, the animals had dwelled in similar regions or environmental conditions, citing such parallels as a way to bolster his paleomagnetic findings.

A related aspect of his education involved terrains of limestone, the sedimentary rock formed in old oceans and often riddled with fossils of ancient sea creatures. Every summer, de Boer would go on field trips, often to south central France. He found its limestone areas fascinating, their texture and ambience different from anything he had known before. Compared to granite or volcanic basalt, limestone is quite soft. Over the ages, rain and groundwater can reshape the pliant rock, especially along preexisting cracks and fissures. In southern France, the erosion had formed thousands of caves, sinkholes, and subterranean rivers. Such a landscape can seem thirsty and dry. But it can surprise, too. The networks of subterranean waterways, when near the surface, tend to spill out into the open as springs and crystalline pools, which gain more attention than they might otherwise.

De Boer came to feel great affection for the limestone region—the stony hillsides and aromatic plants, the thyme and sage, the sudden expanses of clear, cold water where you could drink and swim, the caves where prehistoric humans had painted murals. It was so different from Java. Eventually, his family, his wife's family, and he and his wife bought homes there; his own cottage was in Ségur-le-Château, a small medieval village. He went there as often as he could.

By THE EARLY 1960s, de Boer and his peers had discovered that the Mediterranean was, in geologic terms, a fairly recent creation that had formed as a much larger and older body of water had shrunk dramatically in size. It was a relic. That meant the Mediterranean's basins and flanks and coastal regions had gone through age after age of geologic upheaval, and that its rocky strata were not fresh expanses devoid of fossils (as would be the case, say, for a new volcanic isle) but virtual museums of past life. It explained why fossil coral reefs dotted parts of the Alps.

The ancestral body of water, they found, had dominated a large swath of the earth during the age of dinosaurs, especially during the Cretaceous period, from roughly 65 million to 145 million years ago. Straddling the equator, soaking up sunlight, the predecessor ocean had seethed with warmth and energy, storms and waves. To the north lay the huge, isolated supercontinent of Eurasia, to the south the similarly disconnected landmass of Africa and its adjoining Arabian lands. Geologists call this bygone ocean the Tethys, after a sea goddess of Greek mythology.

The climate of the earth during this period was warm, easing the burdens of survival. Life flourished. The Tethys in particular teemed not only because of its equatorial location but because of its proximity to giant continents whose rivers and runoff fed it a constant supply of nutrients. Its waters swarmed with fish and reefs, plesiosaurs and mosasaurs, alligator-like predators up to sixty feet long that undulated their bodies like snakes. Primitive sharks knifed about, their teeth extraordinarily large.

In the parade of life, some of the smallest members, but perhaps the most important because of their sheer numbers, were the clouds of floating plants and animals—the plankton. There were algae and diatoms, foraminifera and radiolarians, their tiny shells as varied as snowflakes.

As life came and went, the spent bodies and shells rained down through the waters of the Tethys and piled up on the bottom along with silt, sand, and clay, forming layers of sediments. Over time, the beds turned to rock, including ones rich in organic matter. This ooze was vast in quantity and similar in composition because most living things are made of the same building blocks—long chains of hydrogen and carbon atoms known as hydrocarbons.

The shells of bygone animals, rich in calcium, fused to form limestones and marbles, which are simply limestones that get compressed into dense arrays of crystals. They also formed beds of chalk that in time produced such formations on land as the White Cliffs of Dover. (Indeed, the Cretaceous period was named after the Latin word for chalk, *creta*.) Some Tethys limestones took shape without the aid of old life when waters supersaturated with calcium precipitated the rock directly, as occurs today in some shallows of the Bahamas. However, many strata were rich in biologic remains, the oily matter turning them brown and blackish. The rocks could also hold sulfur, a common element of seawater and life, where it helps form amino acids and proteins.

As these rocky beds grew thicker, the weight of the accumulated sediments pushed them deeper into the earth and closer to its hot interior. The rising heats and pressures cooked ("cracked" in the argot of oil geologists) their layers of organic sludge, breaking the long molecules into simpler hydrocarbons of oil, tar, bitumen, and such gases as methane, propane, and ethylene. The latter gas is unusual because of its sweet bouquet. Depending on the composition of the raw materials, the products could also be smelly with sulfur—in oil-patch jargon, sour rather than sweet. In short, ages of sedimentation led to the formation of petroleum (Latin for rock oil).

Over time, the lighter of these hydrocarbon deposits, far less dense than their rocky surroundings, tended to rise upward toward the surface. To the naked eye, the average stone looks too dense to allow such movement. But most rocks in the upper few miles of the earth's surface are in fact riddled with tiny pores, cracks, and fissures through which water and other fluids and gases can pass quite easily if they have sufficient time. By volume, up to 40 percent of most rocks—even ones that look solid—are open space. If the rising hydrocarbons reach a layer of dense, impermeable rock, they tend to pool, often in large reservoirs.

The oil of the Tethys moved around a lot, and not just because of upward migration. Another factor worked violently to reposition the oily rock. For eons, the African plate had slowly inched northward across the earth's face toward Eurasia. Then, the two supercontinents began to collide. The initial contact came toward the west, where Africa slowly pushed into the area that would become Spain. At this time, the Tethys still stretched endlessly to the east. But during the collision, Africa started to rotate counterclockwise, its movement compressing the beds and islands and shallow banks of the eastern Tethys, squeezing the rocky masses

PANGAEA'S BREAKUP

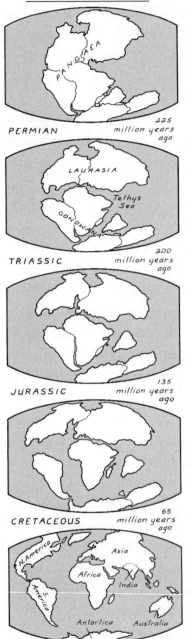

PERMIAN   225 million years ago

TRIASSIC   200 million years ago

JURASSIC   135 million years ago

CRETACEOUS   65 million years ago

PRESENT DAY

together into a smaller and smaller area and prompting many of the beds to fold, buckle, and rise. The climax came at the end of the Cretaceous, about sixty-five million years ago, when the ascending right side of Africa slammed into the belly of Eurasia, closing off the eastern Tethys to form an inland sea, the Mediterranean.

So it was that Tethys deposits containing oily limestone came to lie scattered around the Mediterranean and far beyond to the Middle East and India. The tectonic vise continued to tighten as the African plate kept inching northward and pushing below the Tethys remains. In response, mountains rose across a vast belt that would one day include Spain and Italy, Armenia and Turkey, Azerbaijan and Georgia, Iraq and Iran.

The once vast Tethys bequeathed to the earth many new bodies of wa-

Starting some 200 million years ago, the breakup of the supercontinent Pangaea formed the present day continents and a large body of water known as the Tethys. It shrank over the ages to form the Mediterranean and, as its shallows rose and contracted, the Greek mainland.

ter in addition to the Mediterranean—the Persian Gulf, the Gulf of Oman, the Black Sea, the Caspian. These waters and adjacent lands hid bonanzas of hydrocarbons thanks to the bygone life that enriched the sedimentary rocks. Today, people get most of their energy from these stores of fossil fuels.

In the Mediterranean, the crumpling of the Tethys beds also produced a rocky promontory that came to be known as Greece. It resulted from a rare interplay of forces—not just the tectonic vise of Eurasia and Africa but lateral squeezes as Asia Minor pushed westward and Italy pushed eastward. Greece was caught in a three-way squeeze. It was like being in a serious traffic accident involving multiple cars, the one in the middle crushed beyond recognition.

The Greek peninsula bristled with young mountains, as did many of the nearby islands, which were simply rocky projections of the crumpled seabed. As the African plate continued to push against and beneath Eurasia, grinding in fits and starts, the mountains and islands of Greece rose ever higher and shook with frequent earthquakes, making the young land among the most violent places on earth. It is difficult for those unfamiliar with the immensity of geologic time (roughly 4.5 billion years) to grasp the extreme youthfulness of Greece. An analogy may help. If the history of the earth were condensed into a single year, the oldest rocks that survived the planet's birth would date to February. The cores of continents would have formed anywhere from March to May. Simple life, mainly plants and animals made of tiny cells, would have emerged from May to October. Rocks holding evidence of more complex life—everything from trilobites to primitive ferns—would date from November and December. The land that became Greece would have arisen in the calendar's final days, making its debut around Christmas and jelling into its current form on New Year's Eve. By the time Greece formed, the dinosaurs that had once roamed the continents were long gone. So its terrains hid none of their bones, unlike Asia, Europe, the Americas, and many other regions.

Reflecting its watery origins, the Greek peninsula bristled with vast limestone ranges as well as pockets of fossil seashells miles inland and hundreds of feet above sea level. Near the southeastern coast, a solid block of limestone rose at a place that would be known as Athens, the mound destined to be called the Acropolis. In all, mainland Greece is composed of about 65 percent limestone, most of Cretaceous age.

The western regions of the Tethys turned out to have been unfavorable for preserving the organic remains of past life, and thus for producing much oil and gas. Geologists traced this relative poverty to the high oxygen content of its shallow, often turbulent waters—a comfortable home for bacteria that dined on life remains in the process of organic decay. By contrast, the deep easterly waters of the Tethys had little oxygen, reducing bacterial decomposition and letting most remnants of past life turn slowly into petroleum.

Greece arose between these extremes. As a result, its rocky limestones tended to hold only limited concentrations of tar, oil, and gas, the amounts in most cases too small for commercial exploitation. Even so, in places, the land harbored pockets of petrochemicals that were concentrated enough to seep to the surface.

BY THE TIME he graduated from Utrecht in 1963, with a doctorate in geophysics, de Boer knew much Tethys history, especially on the origins of the northern Mediterranean. His thesis was on the birth of a complex segment of the Italian Alps. He considered working for Shell, the Dutch oil giant. Instead, he decided to apply to universities in America.

An attractive candidate because of his paleomagnetic skills, de Boer got several offers. Wesleyan looked interesting. It was a prestigious liberal arts college, one of the little Ivies. Located halfway between Boston and New York in the rolling hills of Connecticut, it seemed like it might have the same kind of pastoral ambience he had come to love in provincial

France. It had also just hired a prominent expert in rock magnetism with whom he was eager to work.

De Boer arrived at Wesleyan in late 1963 and threw himself into teaching and research, at first extending his European studies and then focusing on areas closer to his new home. He probed the Appalachians and the Connecticut Valley. He explored the Atlantic and Pacific as an adjunct professor of oceanography at the University of Rhode Island Graduate School. (One of his students was Robert D. Ballard, who eventually won fame for helping discover the *Titanic* at the bottom of the North Atlantic.)

At Wesleyan, de Boer worked hard to improve his research skills. He learned how to read subtle patterns of contemporary magnetic fields in addition to old ones, and became practiced in the field of aeromagnetism, so named because a plane would fly low over a target region to detect the invisible magnetic signatures. De Boer would gather the data and plot it back at the laboratory. The readings looked like contours on a topographic map and with proper analysis could be quite revealing. For example, abrupt changes could indicate hidden faults, and they, in turn, could reveal earthquake dangers for man-made structures.

Prompted by a love of adventure as well as the financial responsibilities of a growing family, de Boer consulted for industries and governments around the globe, often using his aeromagnetic skills to look for mineral and energy resources or to judge the likelihood of earthquakes. The advising took him to Benin and Nicaragua, the Philippines and Pakistan. There he saw old Tethys limestones black with tar and bitumen, deepening his appreciation of the ubiquity of life residues. When possible, he took his family. One semester he went on sabbatical leave for a United Nations project in Costa Rica, bringing along his wife and three children. They lived in the mountains and bounced around in an old jeep.

The wide travel and ensuing scientific papers developed his eye, his intuition, and his credentials. By 1974—a decade after leaving Europe—de Boer had been made a full professor at Wesleyan, and by 1977 he held an endowed chair. Academically, he had arrived.

.   .   .

*I*N 1979, a friend of de Boer's invited him to join a team of scientists that was going to Greece to assess the suitability of the nation's diverse terrains for the construction of nuclear power plants. The survey came in response to serious problems. Greece was suffering major energy shortages. Moreover, its massive burning of coal produced air pollution and acid rain that ate into old stone monuments and temples, destroying many treasures of classical antiquity. The coal was a brownish variety known as lignite, and its combustion released much sulfur into the air and produced acid rain that dissolved stone. The Greek government, with United Nations backing, was initiating an effort to investigate clean alternatives.

De Boer had no need of new challenges. But the idea of learning more about Greece—the cradle of Western civilization, a fresh example of tectonic forces at work, a logical extension of the investigations he had conducted in Spain, Portugal, France, and Italy—appealed to the old Tethys hand. Moreover, its limestone terrains were even more extensive than those of his favorite haunts in southern France. Intellectually and emotionally, it beckoned like few other places. He decided to go, taking a year's sabbatical leave. Quietly, from his days of government consulting, de Boer made inquiries and obtained a tool to aid the team—American reconnaissance photos. The images showed Greece's rocky terrain in detail, giving overviews more accurate than any map could disclose and revealing such subtle geologic features as long depressions that had resulted from faults and other breaks in the underlying rocks.

When de Boer arrived in the summer of 1980, it was a bit of a disappointment. The team got jeeps and aeromagnetic data and was promised much equipment, such as drill rigs to extract rock samples from deep underground. But things moved slowly, when at all. The geologists (all from the United States) ended up spending much of their time in hotel rooms waiting for government permissions and promised equipment.

The idle time nevertheless turned out to be productive. For reading, de Boer had brought along a collection of ancient and modern books that he hoped would reveal something of the nation's seismic history. The ancient Greeks, keen observers of nature, had often referred to these violent upsets, which early writers such as Homer and Hesiod attributed to the gods. Later, more than a dozen philosophers, including Plato and Aristotle, developed naturalistic theories to explain the causes of earthquakes and even tried to predict when their devastation might strike.

Among other authors, de Boer read Plutarch, the high priest of Delphi and friend of Clea. Slowly, he learned of the sanctuary's long history and the central role of the Oracle, absorbing it directly from the ancient Greeks rather than from textbooks and secondary sources.

Plutarch had considered whether earthquakes and other natural cycles had produced fluctuations in the strength of the pneuma, the wispy substance said to inspire the Oracle's divine madness. In so doing, he referred to the great earthquake at Delphi that "overthrew the city" and destroyed the temple in 373 BCE.

The two men, separated in time by nearly two millennia, bonded over science. De Boer judged Plutarch to be an intelligent man making plausible observations about nature, not a mystic lost in the clouds. The unusual phenomenon of the sanctuary's vapors and the crippling of the nearby city attracted the geologist, and he kept it in the back of his mind. Clearly, Delphi would be an interesting place to visit.

When de Boer and the team finally attempted to do the work they had come for, they often found their path blocked. On Evia, a mountainous isle off Greece's east coast near Athens, locals viewed the team with suspicion. A Communist newspaper threw fuel on the fire, claiming that the foreigners were part of a government conspiracy to promote nuclear power. Someone fired a gun at a graduate student. Thugs repeatedly harassed a woman academic on the team who studied population densities and social conditions. She suffered a nervous breakdown. Frustrated, the team carried on as best it could, fanning out in different directions, trying to keep a low profile.

De Boer headed for the Peloponnese, Greece's southern heartland, and inspected a proposed reactor site near ancient Olympia, home of the Olympic Games. As usual, he probed a zone that extended for some forty kilometers, or twenty-five miles, around the proposed site, looking for young faults that were active. The ring marked the risk area. Earthquakes inside it could in theory endanger a nuclear complex, rupturing buildings and destroying gear. Afterward, he headed north, taking a ferry across the Gulf of Corinth to its northern shoreline and driving eastward. Rugged mountains framed both sides of the narrow gulf, letting the geologist drink in a procession of inspiring views.

At Itea—a market town, whitewashed and Mediterranean in ambience, with palm trees lining the waterfront—he turned away from the gulf and again headed north. That road led to Delphi. He passed the side road that led to Kira, the ancient port of Delphi on the nearby coast, and entered a sea of olive trees, retracing the path that pilgrims took over the centuries, driving through the fertile plain toward the rocky, commanding heights where the sanctuary clung to the flanks of Mount Parnassus. The mountain's sides, visible up ahead, lay less than ten kilometers away. De Boer planned to linger at Delphi only briefly on his way to a proposed reactor site up north. As fate would have it, his short stay turned into repeated visits over the decades.

ASTRONOMERS LOOK at stars, biologists at life, meteorologists at clouds. Geologists who study the planet's exterior look at exposed rocks and surface features. Others delve deeper. Those who want to understand the underworld, the maze of differing blocks and amalgamations and fractures and pools and conductive zones that make up the subterranean realms, can have a hard time accessing and evaluating their subject matter. Every so often a volcano will spew molten rock from down below, producing a window into the earth, but otherwise the world of their interest is mostly hidden from view. They must struggle for bits of evidence.

Students of the terrestrial depths understand that much of what they do is based on educated guesswork. They have developed an arsenal of brutish and sensitive tools (drill rigs, rotary bits, seismometers, radars, explosive charges, gas analyzers, gravitometers, magnetometers, and so on) to glean clues about this invisible world and make deductions about its composition and fate. Geology may be founded on physics and chemistry and their elegant simplicities, but its subject matter is far more complex and uncertain and its variables far greater in number. As a result, its practitioners often have to strike tricky compromises between evidence and conjecture. The element of imprecision can make it harder in geology than in physics to reach a consensus and can stir fierce debates, rivalries, and skepticism. Continental drift remained a much-disputed theory for more than a half century, until, in the 1960s, the evidence became overwhelming and most geologists accepted the idea, some grudgingly.

De Boer was the kind of geologist who had spent much of his life visualizing the earth's invisible depths, in particular the slow turmoil of plate tectonics. The abstractness of it all was one reason he had thrown himself back into fieldwork, eager to strike a more satisfying balance between theory and investigation. So what de Boer saw outside Delphi came as a happy surprise. After ascending the steep wall of the valley, navigating the many switchbacks on the southwestern flanks of Mount Parnassus, and driving onto the somewhat level stretch of land before Delphi, he laid eyes on a geological feature that caused his heart to stir.

There at the bottom of the hillside, off to the left, a half mile or so away, he spied the beautiful face of an exposed fault. It rose perhaps thirty feet high in spots and seemed to run far along the hillside toward Delphi. In overall appearance, it seemed not unlike a wall or the kind of long cuts that construction crews make all the time through rocky knolls when building modern highways—except that in this case the cut was smooth and polished and entirely natural. In geology, such a feature is known as a fault scarp. To de Boer, it was an ultimate scarp, an example striking enough to grace any textbook.

He knew that, by definition, the exposed face marked the junction between two massive blocks of rock. Such faults lie hidden all over the planet, often extending down miles into the depths. They originate when monumental stresses build up to the point that something has to give. The resulting split manifests as an earthquake, during which the blocks slide past each other. The abrasive motion can leave their surfaces highly polished, like semiprecious stones.

De Boer got out of his car and walked up the terraced fields, dodging rocks and thorny bushes on the way. He was in his element—a stony hillside rich in thyme, sage, and wildflowers, a place reminiscent of his second home in southern France.

He read the rocky face like an open book. It was smooth, marbleized limestone, a bit of the Tethys frozen in time. Different bands of weathering that stretched horizontally spoke to a long history of jostling and displacement as the face lengthened during earthquakes. Each slip would expose an additional three or four feet. The history of slippage meant the top band had braved the elements for much longer and its soft limestone had become very weathered and pitted. At the very top, the pitting was so extensive that large cracks and holes had formed that acted like flowerpots to hold dirt and growing plants. Of the horizontal bands, the lowest one, at the bottom next to the stony field, was the smoothest, having been exposed most recently to the elements and sunlight.

De Boer judged that the fault was quite active, as suggested by the freshness of the lower face. Geologically, it was alive rather than the dead remnant of ancient jostling. The blocks had clearly slipped past one another repeatedly in the past few thousand years.

Which zone of weathering, he wondered, was associated with the earthquake that Plutarch had described, the one that "overthrew the city." De Boer stepped back and looked along the length of the rocky face to the east, toward Delphi. With few exceptions that he could see, the face stretched in a clear line, more or less straight, his eye also detecting subtle undulations along its length.

He set off on foot. De Boer slowly traced the face, climbing over piles of crumbled limestone and around occasional tangles of thorny bushes and pine trees. Every once in a while, he pulled out a special tool with a built-in compass—known as an inclinometer—to measure the face's angle and jotted down the figures in a notebook. Yes, it was running true. It was a major exposed fault if ever he had seen one.

Eventually, after hiking roughly two miles along the rocky face, taking measurements all the way, he came to a rise that overlooked the town of Delphi and the sanctuary. The view was magnificent. Mountains loomed all about, gray and diminishing in the distance. Far to the right lay the sea of olive trees and, partly obscured by a mountain range, the edge of the Gulf of Corinth and whitewashed Itea. To the other side, he could see the valley of the Pleistos River in front of the sanctuary and, higher up, the cleft in the side of Parnassus that sheltered the temple, the jagged cliffs forming a kind of natural amphitheater.

De Boer looked back from where he had come and forward to the sanctuary. He looked again. The fault disappeared from view. The exposed face was unmistakable on the hillside leading up to Delphi but seemed to vanish upon entering the sanctuary itself, apparently buried under the ruins and rubble. Back at his car, de Boer got out a reconnaissance photo of the region and inked in a thin line.

H̲E HAD LUNCH in Delphi. The ramshackle village of nearly a hundred years earlier had survived its transplant and transformed itself into a decent tourist town with a number of good restaurants. There was no time to linger, however. De Boer loved the exposed fault and the thrill of being able to see what was normally hidden from view. But in truth, the fracture was, at best, a sideshow for the nuclear survey. It was too far from the potential reactor site to be much of a risk. Even a major earthquake at Delphi would unlikely menace any power facility that was built in the northern valley. Tracing the fault was more of a personal impulse than a professional necessity. It had just been too lovely to pass up.

De Boer continued his northward drive. Near an open-pit mine for extracting bauxite, an aluminum ore, he marveled at an underlying strata of gray limestone dark with tar and bitumen—the same kind of oily residues he had come across in Pakistan. It was more evidence of Greece's formation under the sea, and of the ubiquity of past life in the rocky foundations of the region.

Eventually, he rejoined his colleagues and compared notes. They found that the overall feasibility of the government's reactor plan seemed to diminish with most every new fact and insight the team gathered. Most of the proposed sites were too unstable, too prone to seismic upsets, or too close to population centers. The few that did appear suitable always seemed to have some other drawback or deficiency. One site turned out to be rich in old artifacts and historic remains, a sure way in Greece to kill any kind of development.

Suddenly, out of nowhere, the gods—more specifically Poseidon, the earth shaker—delivered bad news to the Greek government in the most direct way possible. Strong earthquakes hit Athens and parts of central Greece on the evening of Tuesday, February 24, 1981, as well as into the next morning, killing at least fifteen people and seriously injuring fifty-three others. Hundreds of buildings collapsed. At museums in Athens and Corinth, the jolts threw antiquities to the floor, smashing them to pieces. At the Parthenon, cracks appeared in some of its marble columns. The police and military distributed food, blankets, and tents to crowds of people afraid to return to their homes and apartments.

At Corinth, close to the quake's epicenter in the Gulf of Corinth, the quakes leveled four hotels. Fearing new tremors, thousands of people fled Athens, Corinth, and Thebes for open spaces, with tens of thousands of people camping outdoors. In an attempt to dampen fears, the authorities broadcast announcements saying that rumors of an impending new earthquake were unfounded.

Poseidon struck again a few days later, the strong earthquake and its many aftershocks taking at least one more life and injuring thirty people. Residents of Athens rushed into squares, while people in rural areas saw many previously weakened houses collapse. Old adobe structures simply fell apart.

While a nightmare for most people who survived them, the earthquakes left the American geologists fascinated. One aftershock struck while some team members, at an outdoor restaurant, watched in amazement as their lunches began to jump and spill. Though suffering no injuries, the team understood the human tragedy all too well. This was their calling, what they were paid to predict, to visualize the hidden workings of the earth and how they might end in sudden violence that tore apart cities and the fragile intricacies of civilization. Their work in Greece, protracted as it was, had already put them on edge about the potential for new earthquakes, and now their edginess had been borne out in disaster.

The jolts captivated de Boer no less than the others. To him, the destruction not only drove home the riskiness of the reactor project but opened a new window on the hidden processes that were still shaping Greece. He decided to quit the team and study what the quakes revealed about the land. The unexpected revelation of the exposed fault at Delphi helped inspire him.

In his travels, de Boer had never seen a place quite like Greece. Elsewhere on the planet—in France and Italy, Connecticut and Massachusetts, the Philippines and Pakistan, Panama and Costa Rica—faults at the earth's surface usually lay hidden in valleys or were hard to discern under layers of soil, vegetation, and eroded rock that had accumulated over the ages. Greece was different. It was young and rising rapidly out of the surrounding seas. Its arid Mediterranean climate and light rainfall had kept the accumulations of soil and sediments to a minimum. Moreover, the wide deforestation from ancient times had quickened erosion, often washing away what little soil did develop. Most important, the youthful vigor of its mountain building often made its faults quite prominent, almost naked, giving much of the landscape a chiseled hardness. This rawness had increased over the ages when, in waves of earthquakes, blocks slipped and the faces of exposed faults grew in length.

Now, de Boer judged, the faces near the epicenters of the recent earthquakes would be fresher, longer, and easier to read. And the rocky exposure at Delphi—close to the epicenters in the Gulf of Corinth, as well as being a fault of similar type and origin—would provide a good site for comparative study. For him, the aftermath of the quakes seemed a rare opportunity to better understand the ties between clues at the surface and what took place down below.

STARTING IN 1983, he began returning to Greece in the summers, usually with students from Wesleyan and other schools in tow. He immediately focused on Delphi. This time, instead of driving up from the west and the Gulf of Corinth, he took the meandering easterly route over the mountains from Athens. As he approached the sacred area, de Boer once again saw something remarkable—a beautiful exposed fault, this time to the east of the sanctuary but similar to the one he had already examined to the west.

It had once been less conspicuous, covered by dirt and limestone debris that had fallen into the valley. But a Greek highway crew, while widening the road outside Delphi to make room for tour buses to pull off or around, had carefully removed part of the veil and exposed the face, making it more prominent. Parts of the exposure seemed to run fifty feet high.

Excited, de Boer and his students went to work analyzing the eastern fault face, seeing its unveiling as a wonderful stroke of luck. Intuition told him that it was closely related to the western original. But only analysis would tell. During his previous visit, he had made forty or fifty measurements of the western fault face. Now, he and his students swarmed over both, taking a hundred or so readings along the rocky exposures.

Their efforts revealed that the two had many features in common. Both, of course, were made of polished limestone and both seemed to be of the same general age. Both had the same general alignments, east-west. Moreover, both faces possessed the same kind of subtle undulations across their lengths, running concave, convex, concave, and so on. Finally, both had grooves slightly inclined from the vertical that cut across the faces at exactly the same angle, showing that the direction of the periodic slips of the blocks during earthquakes ran ever so slightly sideways.

The evidence was overwhelming, de Boer concluded. The two faults were one and the same. What appeared to be distinct east and west exposures looked very much to be different expressions of the same fracture. And it ran under the sanctuary.

THE HISTORY of science is filled with dramatic episodes of discovery in which the protagonists suddenly realize that they have changed our understanding of nature for all time. The early star of such a drama was Archimedes, who supposedly exclaimed "Eureka" ("I have found it!") upon discovering how to measure the volume of an irregular solid and thereby deduce the purity of a gold object.

De Boer's experience at Delphi was nothing like that. He knew from his studies and explorations that dozens of major east-west faults ran through central Greece and assumed that his visualization of one beneath the temple was no great revelation. He imagined that experts more knowledgeable than he—Greek geologists who had searched the region for valuable ores, or perhaps even the original French excavators of the sanctuary of Apollo—had already made the connection between the fracture and the vaporous emissions. Certainly, the crack was obvious once you did the fieldwork. The potential tie between the fault and the oracle's long history, he reasoned, had probably been investigated decades ago and, with additional fieldwork, had been proved right or wrong, likely or unlikely.

Wide reader though he was, de Boer knew nothing of the debate over the crevice and vapors that had echoed through the halls of archaeology during the twentieth century, nor about the rough consensus that had dismissed both features of the oracle's world as fictions. He knew only about the clues he had seen with his own eyes as well as the Delphic lore he had learned from Plutarch and the other ancient writers.

If the gods had any interest in illuminating the history of ancient Greece, in helping a new age rediscover the Oracle, they might have concluded that what de Boer needed at this juncture was a knowledgeable partner, perhaps an archaeologist who could understand the audacity of what the geologist had concluded.

Sleuths

OHN R. HALE COULD hardly have been more different from Jelle de Boer in terms of his life history. He grew up in a large, musically gifted family
spread across the rolling hills of southern Indiana.
The music would sometimes go till dawn as friends
and relatives joined in on cellos, violins, and pianos.
His grandmother gave him books about ancient
Greece and Rome. By third grade, he knew what he
wanted to be.

Hale loved to explore the woods around his
home, uncovering old jars, tools, stone walls, and
bits of houses that had vanished long ago. His
grandfather once found an Indian ax that came to
symbolize the treasures just waiting to be unearthed. Try as he might, Hale and his friends never
found any Indian artifacts, even as caches of them
seemed to appear every time someone dug a foundation for a new house.

He followed the family tradition of going to
Yale. There Hale met Donald Kagan, a prominent
classicist working on his four-volume *History of the*

Peloponnesian War (and father of historian Robert Kagan). Students loved his lectures. Kagan would have them overlap their notebooks to mimic how Greek soldiers locked their shields together in defensive barriers. Early on, Hale bumped into Kagan one day on campus. The professor surprised the new student by asking many questions. Hale told of being a rower on the sculling team and Kagan suggested he might turn his avocation into scholarly insights about ancient sea battles. They talked for an hour.

Hale took every course from Kagan that he could, as well as studying ancient Greek and archaeology. For graduate study, he went overseas to Cambridge University, doing his doctoral dissertation on the Bronze Age boats of Scandinavia, the forerunners of the Viking longships. But the magnet of home and family eventually drew him back to southern Indiana and a job teaching archaeology at the University of Louisville.

He moved into his great-grandfather's house, built in the 1870s on a bluff overlooking the Ohio River, and filled it with thousands of books, curios, antiques, and a harmonium, which he played with brio. The house was an ideal retreat for the bachelor scholar—more library and museum than residence. Music was still a large part of his life. He listened to classical recordings at home, and came to direct concert planning for the Louisville Bach Society.

Starting in 1984, the lanky archaeologist, full of spunk and ambition, traveled repeatedly to Portugal. His new passion was Torre de Palma. The large Roman villa, set in the gentle hills of southeastern Portugal, had flourished in the heart of Iberia from the first through the early fifth centuries. After the Visigoths swept in, it slowly fell into ruin.

For many summers, Hale directed a large team of researchers, faculty members, and student volunteers who excavated the site. It was easy to get people to come because of Portugal's allure and the area's rustic charm. Even so, it could get warm, and work typically started very early in the day so a fair amount of progress could be made before the afternoon heat set in. The team uncovered a complex of houses, baths, barns, stables, granaries, dormitories, gardens, slave quarters, laundries, cemeteries, workshops, a blacksmithy, and olive and wine presses.

No strangers to horse racing, coming as they did from Louisville and the Kentucky Derby, Hale and other members of the team developed a theory about the villa's name, Tower of the Palm. In Roman Iberia and other parts of the ancient Mediterranean world, palms were worn as laurels were in ancient Greece, as garlands of victory in athletic games. The villa clearly traded in horses, undoubtedly for riding as well as for chariots, to judge from the bridles and other paraphernalia found all over, as well as a horse mosaic discovered near the master's office. Clearly, the estate had been very large and successful. Hale and his colleagues decided that Tower of the Palm was the self-congratulatory name of the region's largest stud farm.

By the summer of 1995, his twelfth season, Hale knew every inch of the excavations and much about Portugal, rural and urban. He had worked on the artifacts not only at the villa but at a museum in Lisbon. At the Roman estate, he oversaw some of the dig's most daunting aspects, including the dating of structures, the assigning of likely functions to rooms, and the preservation and interpretation of human remains, including many bones.

A mystery that long puzzled him was what had shaken up a section of the villa where its walls had shifted off their foundations and where stonework had collapsed or been destroyed. The damage seemed quite possibly the result of an earthquake. But Hale and his colleagues could not rule out fire or some other natural disaster. Whatever it was, it had been a turning point in the villa's life, preceding a bout of rebuilding on an even grander scale that included many rich mosaics. From coins in destroyed rooms, the archaeologists dated the mayhem to the third century. Hale spoke of the puzzle with many colleagues. One said she knew an experienced geologist with an interest in history who might be able to lend interpretative aid. His name was Jelle de Boer. And that summer he happened to be in Portugal researching a book.

．　　．　　．

DE BOER ARRIVED at the villa in June 1995, just as the season was getting under way. The rains were over, the wildflowers in bloom, the isolated stands of trees clothed in new foliage. Hale, a generation younger than the geologist, found him impressive right from the start. Everything about de Boer seemed to crackle with confidence: his brisk manner, his trim mustache, his shock of white hair, his European charm. De Boer always rose to meet a lady. Here was a star of hard science, a man of discernment who had carved out a distinguished place for himself in academia. He looked the part, too. Central casting could have done no better. Even his Dutch accent seemed to reinforce his civilized air. In truth, Hale felt slightly awed.

De Boer toured the site. An earthquake had obviously done the damage, he said. He pointed over the grassy hills toward the coast and the distant Atlantic, indicating the origin of the waves of destruction.

Late in the day, toward sunset, the two men walked up a nearby hill that overlooked the site and opened a bottle of Portuguese red known as Dão. The mood became increasingly mellow. As they talked, the two men discovered a mutual love of Greece. De Boer told of the reactor project and how it had evolved into a wide study of the effects of earthquakes not just on Greece but on human civilization. He was gathering material for a book. The idea was to make geology come alive for students by demonstrating the cultural impact of natural disasters. For instance, the earthquake that leveled Lisbon in 1755 produced not only great suffering but such triumphs as *Candide,* which satirized the optimistic philosophy of the day. De Boer made no apologies for his fascination with epics of destruction. The disasters echoed his war experiences and seemed like good lessons in the ephemerality of man.

Hale—still a bit dazzled by the geologist, and feeling like a student after their tour of the archaeological site, a place he thought he knew well but now saw through the somewhat intimidating lens of geology—tried to highlight some of his own accomplishments.

The enthusiastic rower told of researching a book on the Athenian navy and its surprising victory over the Persian Empire with oared galleys. One of his ideas, Hale said, was that the simple Greek rowing cushion—a modest technical advance—had acted like the cavalry stirrup or the medieval longbow to decide the fate of nations. It was probably lubricated with olive oil, he said, letting Greek rowers take long sliding strokes that increased the trireme's overall speed and maneuverability. He was writing up his findings for *Scientific American,* where they were to appear next year.

De Boer asked many questions, clearly interested. The men found that they shared a common enthusiasm not only for Greece but for the region around the Gulf of Corinth, the narrow body that separates northern Greece from the Peloponnese. Hale told of traveling there two years earlier to learn about Phormio, one of the legendary admirals of ancient Athens. His brilliant naval campaigns in the gulf had twice defeated superior forces. The archaeologist recounted his frustration in tracking one of Phormio's most important naval battles. An island where the admiral had sheltered his fleet had vanished, inexplicably. In Athens he had found a map of the gulf from the eighteenth century in which the isle was plainly visible and identified by name, Isle de Chalcis. But it was no longer there, on charts or in the gulf.

De Boer grew excited. This was exactly his kind of thing, studying the repercussions of earthquakes along the Corinth rift. He had already learned how a massive quake in 373 BCE (apparently the same one that struck Delphi and destroyed its temple) had caused two cities on the south shore of the Gulf of Corinth to sink below the sea. Now, what Hale told him appeared to allude to a kindred drop on the north shore.

What was the likely date of the disappearance? the geologist asked. Was there other evidence? Had anyone linked the isle's vanishing to an earthquake? Hale said no one seemed to know much about the episode, or Phormio, for that matter. He was devoting much time to chronicling the life of the forgotten sea hero. The archaeologist noted how, during his trip to Greece, he had traveled to Delphi to look at a monument in front of the temple where some of Phormio's trophies had been put on display. The Athenians, he said, had praised the admiral in an inscription.

For the first time, Delphi was in the air.

De Boer chimed in, adding recollections about his own travel to the ancient sanctuary. He told of how, a decade earlier, he had found a fault there that ran under the temple of Apollo. He said he was beginning to think that maybe fumes did rise at Delphi to intoxicate the Oracle, as the ancient writers had reported.

Hale stiffened, the mood suddenly cool. That was highly unlikely, he thought. He had seen nothing like a fault during his own visit, even while driving the same roads. Still somewhat on the defensive and looking to assert himself, he plunged into a rebuttal.

That's impossible, Hale said flatly. There is no such fault. The French dug at Delphi and proved there was nothing there. Not one textbook says otherwise. The claims about the vaporous cleft, like so much the ancient Greeks and Romans wrote about, turned out to be wrong. The ancients have been debunked. It was all a delusion if not a lie. Hale drove his point home, confident he had the upper hand. No, he told the geologist. You couldn't have seen a fault. That's quite impossible.

A silence ensued. The sky was on fire.

Would you know a fault if you saw one? de Boer asked abruptly. Have you read Plutarch? Strabo? Do you know what they said? Both told of fumes that inspired the Oracle to divine madness, with Plutarch noting that the vapors had a sweet smell. The authorities are clear about what happened, de Boer said, as is the physical evidence for a fault if you have an opportunity to examine it.

Hale blanched, caught off guard. In truth, he knew only the secondary literature that he had read in school, only the rough consensus of archaeology, only what his teachers had taught him. In contrast, here was a man of some authority who obviously knew the primary literature as well as the site, a man who had pondered the evidence and, based on expert knowledge, come to his own conclusion.

Hale protested as best he could, putting on a brave face.

Oh, you can't take the ancient literature so seriously, so literally, he insisted. After all, the French found nothing. It was an example of how modern scholarship could correct the mistaken notions of the past.

Have you read the French reports?

No, Hale replied, feeling more foolish by the minute. He admitted that his knowledge was secondhand. Shaken, Hale began to reevaluate his position and ask his own questions. How can you be so sure? What's the evidence?

De Boer said it was one of the most conspicuous faults he had ever seen, describing how it ran east and west of Delphi. It was a beautiful thing to behold, a rupture unusual in prominence that appeared to extend under the sanctuary and the temple.

Can faults emit gas? Hale asked.

Yes, de Boer replied. Such releases happen all the time but people are usually unaware of them. Along the San Andreas fault in California, geologists have installed sensors that sniff the air to detect escaping gases. Such projects seek warning signs of earthquakes.

Well, Hale said, if what you say about Delphi is true, you have made an important discovery.

Now it was de Boer's turn to scoff.

How could it be important? he asked. Anybody who has taken Geology 101 can see the fault. All you have to do is open your eyes. It can't be significant when the fissure is so obvious.

Hale assured him that it would be extraordinary if what he said turned out to be true, and grew more interested even as de Boer grew increasingly matter-of-fact. Maybe it was real, he thought. Maybe de Boer had stumbled onto something. Maybe in looking at Delphi with different eyes he had seen things that other people had missed out of bias or ignorance. And maybe an archaeologist could aid the reevaluation.

It was getting late. The sun was down and the night sounds were starting up. Like a ghost, Delphi hung in the air. As they made small talk, the geologist found himself liking the archaeologist, despite his rather bold contentiousness. Hale was hard-nosed, if not argumentative. But he also seemed to have an open mind. He seemed like the kind of person you could convince with evidence. And that, after all, was the essence of how science worked, organized skepticism that in the end after all the bickering and argumentation respected the facts. De Boer also liked Hale's ambition and professionalism. Finally, he had to admit that they were both enthusiasts for Greece and the Gulf of Corinth, where they had gone down parallel paths. They already had much in common. Now, their paths were converging.

Come with me to Greece, de Boer said. I'll show you what I'm talking about.

Okay, said Hale. It's a deal. And while we're there we can investigate what happened to the island.

In studying the sanctuary of Apollo, the two men agreed that Hale would concentrate on the archaeological evidence, and de Boer on the geology. They would do it in their spare time, such as it was. No big commitment—just a cooperative study of a tantalizing possibility. Their skills were obviously complementary, and perhaps their styles too.

They shook on it.

CHANCE ENCOUNTERS among scholars often result in plans for joint projects. Most, however, despite the best intentions and even the investment of considerable time and energy, go nowhere. Not so with Hale, not this time. He quickly talked himself into a genuine fascination with the Delphi question and made plans to move ahead smartly, despite what promised to be a busy semester. By this point, Hale not only taught archaeology but directed his school's liberal studies program. It let students create multidisciplinary programs or independent majors, echoing Hale's own diverse interests.

The archaeologist sent de Boer a postcard from Portugal and, in the fall of 1995, upon returning to Louisville, set himself to roaming libraries and assembling literature. Soon, his file included the writings of Plutarch, Strabo, Pausanias, Diodorus, Pindar, and many others. His modern list featured Holland, Amandry, and Parke. While reading the moderns, he enumerated all the doubts and negative findings: the myth of the fissure, the inability of the bedrock at Delphi to produce gases, the lack of volcanism suitable for gas generation, the possibility that even genuine intoxication had nothing to do with the Oracle's trance and influence.

In October 1995, he flew to Connecticut to visit de Boer at Wesleyan and plot strategy. Upon arrival, he got a reminder of how little he knew about geology. Hanging in the hallway outside the geologist's office was a large multicolored map of the earth by the United States Geological Survey, "This Dynamic Planet," with thousands of dots indicating recent earthquakes. The Pacific rim had thick bands of them. But Greece stood out, dark with dots from one end to the other, almost obliterated.

The tumult fascinated the archaeologist, who had falsely assumed he had a fair understanding of Greece's physical environment from his decades of study and travel. Now, geologically, it turned out to be one of the most active places on earth. The two settled into the geologist's office, a comfortable, cluttered place of plants, rocks, fossils, large seashells, and mounds of paper. On the floor was a weathered old gravestone that de Boer had found in the Connecticut woods.

Drawing on a lifetime of study, the geologist gave Hale a quick overview of the tectonics of Greece, explaining how the African plate slid beneath Europe to cause earthquakes on land and volcanoes in the blue Aegean. Tiny Greece, de Boer said, shook with some 15 percent of the world's seismic energy, much of it released around the Gulf of Corinth. Given the country's network of fissures and all the jostling going on in its depths, it would be quite unusual if no gas ever rose to the surface. Waters rising along faults were under great pressure, he explained. When they emerged at the surface, any gases would quickly bubble out, like the fizz in a fresh bottle of seltzer.

After de Boer finished his geological overview, Hale got out the results of his Delphi literature search and went through the main points, especially on how skepticism over the intoxicating fumes had arisen during the twentieth century. De Boer was amazed at what Hale had been able to dig up in such a short time.

The two made plans to visit Greece during the winter break in February 1996—no students, just them. They would do a field survey at Delphi and look for traces of the lost isle. Hale took out his eighteenth-century map, showing de Boer where the island once lay, not far from Delphi.

BACK IN LOUISVILLE, Hale pressed ahead. One weekend he drove up the river to the University of Cincinnati, a major center for the study of archaeology and classical antiquity, its Burnam Library one of the world's most comprehensive for advanced research in the classics. The university was a little more than an hour away, and Burnam's stacks held nearly two hundred thousand bits of treasure. Hale knew it well. More important, he had discovered that it held a rare book he needed.

At the library, he tracked down the progenitor of all serious archaeological literature on the subject: *Fouilles de Delphes (Excavations of Delphi)*, the official French record. Only a few copies existed in the United States, and Hale handled the tomes with a mixture of awe and apprehension. After all, he had now tentatively embraced de Boer's thesis, yet the official French records promised to be the most thorough refutation of the idea that the foundations of the temple of Apollo hid anything resembling a vaporous fissure.

Sitting in a stately reading room, delighted to be surrounded by so many rare books, Hale paged carefully through Courby's contribution to the encyclopedic effort, tome 2, dated 1927. Hale grew increasingly excited with descriptions of how the archaeologists had worked their way through the rubble, eventually finding the holy of holies. The report had become a thriller. The secondary literature had never given this kind of detail, had never reported the drama.

Below the *adyton,* Courby wrote, the team had tried to dig deep but the hole kept filling with water. Finally, the dig's leaders had brought in pumps and sucked the hole dry. Then they peered at the ancient bedrock, the deep foundations of the temple of Apollo laid bare, perhaps for the first time in ages, perhaps ever.

What Hale read next leapt off the page.

Le roc fissuré par l'action des eaux.

The rock fissured by the action of the waters.

Hale couldn't believe his eyes. He reread the passage. Maybe he had erred in translation. After all, his French was acceptable but not perfect. No, his translation was correct. His heart pounded.

There, in black and white, Courby contradicted the secondary literature and everything Hale had ever learned in school about Delphi. Quite suddenly, the most important things he thought he knew about the French excavations appeared to be wrong.

The French team, Courby wrote, having dug into the western foundations of the temple to a depth of six meters, or nearly twenty feet, discovered that flowing waters had fissured the bedrock—fissured, as in fractured, split into cracks, broken into lines interspersed with tiny gaps.

Hale's mind reeled. It was just what the experts had all agreed the French had never discovered. Instead, this crucial document, contrary to the conventional wisdom, reported that the French themselves found that bedrock was rent by openings, all potential conduits into the deep earth.

Why had no one ever said so? How could scholarship on the subject be so wrong?

Then, in reading the next two sentences, Hale had his answer. Courby went on to contradict himself and say the French team had never discovered the kind of fissure he had just described. Moreover, the key phrase had been italicized for emphasis, as if to drive home the disavowal.

Ainsi, au niveau où les fondations Ouest ont été établies, le sol est vierge, sans débris de poteries, sans trace de bouleversement. *Il n'y a jamais eu de fissure en cette partie,* encore moins d'excavation artificielle ou naturelle.

Thus, on the level where the Western foundations were established, the ground is virgin, without the remains of pottery, without a trace of upheaval. *There never was a crack in this part,* much less an artificial or natural excavation.

Hale concluded that a possible explanation for the contradiction was that the French had never discovered a major fissure, a prodigious crack in the earth's crust that led into the abyss. After all, their expectations had probably been quite high. Even if discounting reports of a cave, they probably hoped to find the "chasm of Parnassus," the kind of large crevice that Lucan and other authors had described.

But as Hale reflected on the startling passages, he concluded that the simple, unadorned truth was that the French archaeologists had burdened one of the most important areas of the official report on the excavation at Delphi with a fundamental contradiction—a fissure but no fissure, a crack but no crack. It was a major inconsistency. On further reflection, Hale came to suspect that a senior French archaeologist in charge of editing Courby had forced the younger man to hew to the party line, italicizing it for emphasis. Seniority often worked that way in science. It was part of the culture.

Whatever the origin of the contradiction, Hale realized that, at a minimum, what he had been taught was wrong. The French had not ruled out a fissure. Perhaps they had eliminated the possibility of a major chasm, but not of conduits into the deep. In essence, the French archaeologists had left the question open.

Hale walked out of the reading room in a state of quiet excitement, his head spinning. De Boer, it seemed, was onto something.

WHILE ON CAMPUS, Hale visited the geology library, eager to discover more about de Boer's specialty. There he learned that its administrators were getting rid of materials that were either surplus or out-of-date.

Once again, for the second time that day, Hale found himself surprised and delighted. In the giveaway pile, he came upon an official Greek geological map of the Delphi region. It was large and quite detailed—layered with topographic lines and brightly colored to delineate the differences among the area's rocky strata and mineral deposits, all described by extensive captions in both Greek and English. Tiny picks indicated active mines.

At Wesleyan, de Boer had never shown Hale such a map or mentioned its existence, and the archaeologist doubted that the geologist knew about it. The discovery seemed like a wonderful stroke of luck.

The map's top caption identified its maker as the Institute for Geology and Subsurface Research—in Greece a main government agency in charge of studying the earth. A note at the bottom said the institute had done the fieldwork in 1958, 1959, and 1960, and published the map in 1964. So it was more than three decades old. Remarkably, Hale reflected, it had appeared just as the archaeological consensus over Delphi had formed, with the ranks of scholars undoubtedly ignorant of the basic facts about the region's physical makeup.

Hale saw to his amazement that de Boer had been right—professionals, if not Geology 101 students, could easily track the Delphi fault. The map showed it extending east and west from Delphi, a major crack running

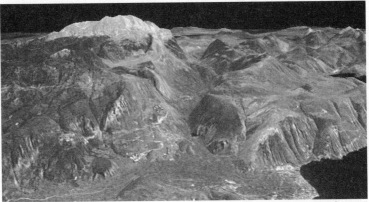

Mount Parnassus in central Greece rises just north of the Gulf of Corinth,
as seen in this view from a modern satellite. North is to the left and east
straight ahead. The valley running down the middle of the picture from
west to east holds, on its upper left side, the ruins of ancient Delphi.
The sanctuary is invisible from this distance but lies just before the
Castalian gorge, seen here as a dark streak rising from the valley
floor up the southwestern flank of Parnassus.

through the middle of Greece. There was even a broken line through the
sanctuary that connected the fault's two sides. The map's legend called it
a probable fault, just as de Boer had concluded.

The archaeologist was further astonished to see that the Delphi fault
extended for a distance of at least twelve miles, or twenty kilometers, and
perhaps much longer since it simply ran off the page. Its great length
seemed further evidence that it extended under the sanctuary as well. After all, Delphi was the one small place on the map where the long fault
was dotted. Why should it be the exception to the rule? Wouldn't a crack
in the earth's crust over such a long distance be continuous, as the map
generally depicted? Yes, maybe the fault was hard to see in the sanctuary,
where people had been cutting stone and building terraces and rearrang-
ing things for thousands of years. But the map offered fresh evidence—
even if it wasn't proof—that a fissure did in fact run under the temple.

Hale found the considerable length of the fault to be a happy revelation. In general, it seemed to bolster the case, showing that de Boer was not out on a limb in this theorizing and that the fault was probably substantial enough to extend beneath the sanctuary.

But something about it also troubled him. Like a minor ache that swims in and out of consciousness, the disquieting thought kept recurring as Hale drove back to Louisville through the rolling hills of the Ohio River valley.

The question had to do with distinctiveness. If the fault was so long, what made the section that ran through Delphi special enough to act as a conduit for underground gases? Or, flipping the question on its head, why didn't the whole fault emit some kind of vapor? That had obviously never happened. So, if the de Boer thesis was correct, the team had to find some other factor that made the geology of Delphi special and perhaps unique. What was it? What in addition to the fault could have let gases from deep within the earth rise to the surface? What could have made the stimulation unique to the site of the Oracle and not somewhere down the road?

Hale was slightly uneasy as he drove home. It had been a very good trip, an excellent trip, really, because of the two major surprises. A veteran of such endeavors, he knew all too well the empty feeling that came when research produced little or nothing of value.

But it was equally true that success could produce new puzzles. Among his findings, he now realized, he had stumbled upon a question that, unless answered clearly and with authority, had the potential to throw the project into limbo.

$\mathcal{D}$E BOER STARED at the old photograph, delighted, taking pleasure in its details the way a connoisseur would savor a fine wine. It was a page from the Courby tome that Hale had located and copied. The geologist saw the

An old French photo of the temple's interior showed not only a springlike pool but fissures (hard to see here without magnification) in the bedrock, suggesting a specific pathway by which intoxicating gases could have risen into the Oracle's sanctum.

scene as a confirmation of his physical intuitions. He felt a quiet sense of vindication.

The vivid black-and-white photograph—obviously taken by an old box camera, its giant negative capturing impressive detail—sprawled over a full page of the large book. It showed an interior view of the temple's southwestern corner where the French had excavated down to the bedrock. Top to bottom, it revealed a layer cake of limestone blocks that made up the temple's outer wall and, in the rocky clutter below, rather prominently, a pit filled with water.

What delighted de Boer was not so much the verification of a spring-like pool at the heart of the temple as the revelation of the bedrock's composition. Where a layman might see a confused jumble, he saw the physical truth behind the French report's contradictory words. There, right above the water line, the photograph clearly showed vertical fissures running up through the bedrock. No denials could hide that fact, no scholarly disclaimer could obscure the reality of what lay before his eyes. The fissures were as real as he was, a network of spidery cracks in solid rock.

Moreover, the fissures rose through a chaotic region where it was obvious that the cracks had repeatedly been filled with mineral deposits and broken apart again and filled again—what geologists call a cemented limestone breccia, where sharp bits of rock have been glued into a fine matrix. It was more evidence of tectonic jolts and protracted flows of mineralized water. Finally, de Boer saw that some of the limestone blocks atop the wall slumped down slightly over the region of the fissures, yet another sign of upheaval down below, of an active geological site, of shifting and rearrangement.

He judged that the evidence strongly confirmed the presence of an underlying fault. In particular, it strengthened his inference about a large fissure running under the temple of Apollo. But this time the clues came not from his investigation of hillsides outside the city, not from exposed fault faces. They came from the depths of the sanctum itself.

. . .

$\mathcal{D}$E BOER AND Hale flew together from New York City to Athens, arriving during the winter break. The Mediterranean sun shone bright and hints of spring wafted through the air, with some low areas already showing evidence of the season's first wildflowers. They drove over the mountains in a rental car to Delphi, closing in on what was once the holiest place in all of Greece. It got colder. The sky clouded up.

Snaking along the southwestern knee of Parnassus, glancing down at the Pleistos River far below, they passed cedar and almond trees and a run of flags from different nations flapping in the breeze. The flags honored the site's past centrality. "Delphi, Navel of the Earth," read a sign. "The World Heritage. Every intellectual human being of free will deserves to be regarded as 'citizen' of the town of Delphi."

The town had the air of a quaint mountain village despite the numerous souvenir shops. Its sidewalks were made of cut stone, its Greek Orthodox church proud, its views astonishing. It offered everything from deluxe accommodations with spas and swimming pools to youth hostels and campgrounds. The Greek government rates hotels by class. The top is AA, the bottom E. In Delphi, most hotels were at the middle or top of the list, and most boasted views of the surrounding mountains or the Gulf of Corinth, a splash of blue beyond the olive orchards. The grandeur could make even a humble place seem magnificent.

The modest choice of the scholars was a category C hotel de Boer had frequented during his stays, the Kouros, Greek for "youth" and, appropriately enough, a symbol of Apollo in ancient statuary. Run by the same family for many years, the Kouros had no pool or other amenities but did offer small clean rooms with their own bathrooms. The hotel, like the others, lay on the town's defining slope. With the Kouros as their base camp, the two men set out on a whirlwind tour of the region. They had only a few days. The light overcast had given way to darker clouds and a cold rain, the day pensive. First, they went to the nearby sanctuary, sheltered from the main road by dense foliage. On its edge sat the Delphi museum. There they met Rozina Kolonia, an official who had the authority to grant them access to areas of the ancient sanctuary normally off limits to tourists, including the temple's interior, access roads, and the museum's archives and storerooms. She expressed strong interest in the project and the possibility that the ancient Greek authors may have known what they were talking about.

Both men had been to Delphi before, but never with the door open so wide. They walked up the multicolored slabs of marble and limestone that formed the Sacred Way, heading toward the temple, passing countless relics of past splendor and glory. A high retaining wall of massive polygonal blocks formed the temple's ramparts, producing a long terrace meant to level the ground and strengthen the temple's foundations against the jolts of earthquakes. They marveled at the wall's seamless beauty and its countless inscriptions relating to the freeing of slaves. Hale said the wall, pieced together some twenty-five centuries ago, had been one of the few things found largely intact under the former town.

Rising higher, they came to the remnants of Apollo's home. It consisted of massive foundation blocks, a handful of tall stone columns, and a chiseled entrance ramp. In all, the pieces added up to perhaps half of the original structure, perhaps less. The temple, though a ghost of its former self, nonetheless possessed an aura of majesty. Just the girth of its surviving limestone columns, five or six feet wide, hinted at the building's original massiveness. Most important, the temple dominated the sanctuary. Its high terrace gave a panoramic view of everything downslope, not just the treasuries and memorials but stunning vistas of the Pleistos gorge and the surrounding mountains. It fostered the illusion that you could see forever.

The two men walked carefully across the limestone blocks that made up the temple's periphery, focusing inward, glancing down to keep from tripping on a gap or uneven edge. Most of the original floor of the temple had vanished, so its center was a sunken area of packed earth. Toward the temple's rear, on its southwestern side, they came to the area the French had identified as the *adyton*. It was a major letdown.

Hale had told de Boer all about the discoveries in Cincinnati and both men had read Courby's excavation report. But one glance told the rest of the story—the French had filled in the hole, probably long ago. The two men could see none of the lower reaches of the *adyton* that the photograph had revealed. Instead, it had been filled with a couple meters of dirt, so they could see only the upper temple foundation, just the top four or five feet. Moreover, the packed earth showed no sign of a spring or water other than superficial dampness of the rain.

Without discussing it in detail, the two men understood the unpleasant significance of this development: they had no access to the central mystery of the place. Worse yet, it promised to stay that way. Their permit allowed them to wander the sanctuary at will but prohibited any digging, sampling, moving, or removing of antiquities. That would be virtually impossible to do, they realized. First of all, Delphi was still one of the most venerated sites in Greece, and the authorities were unlikely to consider a request for a new dig at the heart of the most sacred area. Moreover, the French still held much influence over what archaeological work was done at Delphi, perhaps with veto power. It seemed unlikely that they would approve a major endeavor whose thesis contradicted one of their most celebrated findings.

Despite the disappointment, de Boer's eye caught sight of potential evidence. He noted many breaks among nearby foundation blocks. The pattern bespoke damage from an earthquake, much like that in Portugal. From the alignments, he could tell that the wave of destruction came from the far western end of the Gulf of Corinth. He guessed that it not only shattered foundation blocks but possibly closed off cracks in the earth that fed the spring, silencing the Oracles.

Possibly more important for solving the riddle of Delphi, de Boer noted the presence of water—lots of it, though in the sanctuary's distant past. The evidence, most everywhere, was travertine, a form of the mineral calcite. The soft, light-colored crusts, much like sponge cake in color and porousness, often formed around springs, like those of Yellowstone in the United States, and in caves, like those de Boer knew so well in southern France. Travertine was the stuff of stalactites and stalagmites. It formed as water ran underground through limestone formations and picked up the calcium left over from ancient seashells and oceans. When such waters emerged into the air, they reacted with oxygen and carbon dioxide to form travertine, which precipitated in layers, often where a spring splashed to the surface. In a dry area, it was hard evidence of past wetness.

De Boer saw travertine all around—chunks of it scattered in the temple's foundations, veins of it in nearby rocks, a flood of it on a large retaining wall just behind the temple. The latter deposit probably arose from the Kassotis, which Pausanias, the travel writer, identified as flowing into a basin above the god's shrine and also welling up inside the temple. The flow of travertine on the wall was thick and wavy, like a frozen waterfall. In places, it formed stalactites, where the drip, drip, drip of water had made icicles of rock. Perhaps its flow, de Boer speculated, increased after the earthquake shut down the temple spring.

Whatever its source, the travertine bespoke centuries of water rich in minerals running around and under the temple, probably through the fissured bedrock that the French had discovered. It was a kind of subtle evidence that was invisible to nongeologists. But to de Boer, it spoke of a time when the *adyton* held more than dry dirt.

They climbed down from the temple. Behind it, de Boer spied a large block of limestone placed for prominent display by a footpath. It was the alleged epicenter of the *adyton*—the base for the Oracle's tripod, according to Miller and Holland. He inspected it closely. Though it too once held a heavy coating of travertine, that was now gone. The French archaeologists had carefully removed the layers of soft rock, leaving the stone bare of watery evidence.

They walked around the temple to the southern area just outside the *adyton* and there found more strong evidence of past water—a system of ducts that led from the temple's lower foundations into its massive polygonal retaining wall. The stone ducts appeared to be an elaborate drainage system into which overflows from the interior could spill. It too was now dry.

After lunch, the men walked up the steep path behind the temple and through the switchbacks, rising higher on the slope. Near the top, at the base of a rocky limestone face, they came to the Kerna spring, once alive but now vanished since Greek engineers had rerouted its waters to supply the town of Delphi. An ancient springhouse, the size of a small swimming pool, stood empty by the side of the path, the cracks in its stone floor starting to show the season's first grasses and weeds.

The Kerna, a modern name, interested the men greatly because in times past it had probably flowed down the slope and fed branches lower down near the temple, including the ancient Kassotis. If so, it was probably the mother of much of the travertine.

They stepped off the path and picked their way through the boulders and brambles higher up the rocky slope. At the very back of the sanctuary, they surveyed the rocks leading to the precipitous limestone cliffs, an area de Boer had previously given little attention. They could find no large exposed fault faces. The implication was that the fault—the hypothetical fault that seemed to grow more real with each new piece of evidence—lay farther down the slope beneath the temple.

THE NEXT DAY, they drove out of town. On foot, de Boer led Hale on a methodical survey of the east and west fault faces, with the geologist taking the measurements and the archaeologist writing them down. De Boer was basically redoing his old studies, but he wanted Hale to understand the logic and the process that had led him to conclude that the two exposures were different aspects of the same fault. For Hale, it was his Geology 101 inaugural field trip. The climbing tired him but the intellectual stimulation and sheer beauty of the views—attractively moody on a cloudy day—more than made up for it, leaving him feeling exhilarated. He felt he was doing the right thing, even if it was professionally risky, even if the depths of the *adyton* now lay beyond their examination.

After dinner, the two men returned to their rooms at the Kouros to talk over their findings, the next day's agenda, and the outstanding issues. Near the top of the list was the origin of the gas, if that was what had in fact sent the Oracle soaring aloft.

De Boer kept recalling the gulls he had seen a couple of decades earlier while looking for a rock collection that a school had discarded at a dump site in Hartford down by the Connecticut River. The gulls had evidently come under the influence of some kind of gas from fermenting trash, probably methane. There was a sweet smell in the air, the kind you get in an old barn filled with hay and cows. Some of the gulls behaved oddly— wobbling and teetering and trying to fly by flapping just one wing, as if they were drunk. The ones farther away had no problem. It was just the birds rooting around in one area of the dump, the ones that had probably inhaled some kind of gas.

Maybe the Oracles were like the gulls, de Boer theorized. Maybe the principle was the same. After all, pockets of oil, gas, and tar lay through- out the bedrock of the Mediterranean and Middle East. In theory, the Or- acles could have come under their influence. But in truth, beyond that, the questions were almost too numerous to tally: How did the gas get into the temple fault? What was its composition? How did it rise into the *adyton* and accumulate there and act on the Oracle to promote her trance?

His intuition told him that the network of faults beneath the Gulf of Corinth probably acted as a pipe. The run would be perhaps fifteen or twenty miles and the faults would pass through pockets of hydrocarbons and transport them in some kind of gaseous form to the surface, to the tem- ple, to the Pythia. The periodic quakes that shook the region would keep the plumbing open and the gases flowing. It was not implausible. On the other hand, there was no hard evidence to back it up. It was just a hunch.

As the two men talked, de Boer looked distractedly at the Greek geological map that Hale had discovered in Cincinnati. The archaeologist had been right in thinking it was unfamiliar to the geologist. De Boer had found it interesting but, on the whole, not that informative. In particular, he questioned the dotted line that the Greek experts had drawn in the sanctuary between the east and west exposures. The geologists had made incorrect assumptions about the attitude of the fault plane and where it intersected the slope, de Boer argued. But he felt no smugness about it. He had an advantage, he realized, because he had studied the Delphi region for so long and had zeroed in on a tiny part of the big picture. By contrast, the Greeks had been interested in the faults of the region mainly as boundaries between different kinds of mineral deposits and had focused on finding valuable ores, especially bauxites rich in aluminum, one of the country's top exports. As field geologists working for a relatively poor country, they were pursuing vital issues of economics and prosperity, not the nuances of curvilinear faulting that only academics might find interesting.

De Boer spread out the map. With it wide open for the first time, he examined not just the central depictions but the legend. It explained what the map's various colored areas stood for, what kinds of deposits and formations the Greek geologists had identified.

Yes, there were the bauxite deposits, which he already knew about in general from his travels around Greece. The legend showed them as small orange, black, and blue pockets sandwiched between immense layers of limestone of many different ages and compositions. The map identified the various limestones with a variety of different colors, dark green, green, teal, and light teal.

His eyes widened.

He reread the entry on the dark green limestone and glanced back at the sanctuary.

Yes! The colors matched!

His face lit up.

John, de Boer said, you're not going to believe this. It's here. The petro-chemical source is right here.

He threw the map at Hale and gave a whoop.

It's here, below the sanctuary, de Boer said. It's been here the whole time.

Confused, Hale asked what he was talking about.

The limestone, de Boer answered, talking fast. The limestone beneath the sanctuary is bituminous. It's riddled with hydrocarbons. It's full of pitch, maybe not enough to burn if you struck it with a match but cer-tainly enough to produce gas.

De Boer laughed and showed Hale what he was talking about. The leg-end ran down both sides of the map, laying out explanatory paragraphs for more than a dozen colors and markings. On the left, it labeled the dark green limestone as Turonian-Senonian, a term in European geology for the late Cretaceous, the twilight of the dinosaurs. It said the local limestone of that age was bituminous, black or gray in color, and charac-terized by fragments of rudist fossils. The rudists were ancient bivalves re-lated to oysters. During the age of dinosaurs, they dominated the earth's shallow tropical seas, especially the Tethys, where they built massive reefs that could dwarf those of corals.

Moreover, the rocky beds were not minor features that might get lost in the geological chaos of the region but sumptuous. The entry said the bituminous layers of rudist fossils tended to have a thickness of up to 100 meters, or 350 feet. That was longer than a football field. The beds were relatively big, built up over millions of years as untold generations of rud-ists and other animals came and went on the shores of the primeval Tethys.

Examining the map, the two saw a belt of the bituminous limestone, dark green in color, around and below the sanctuary. Its extended length ran for kilometers. Clearly, the rocky depths beneath the temple of Apollo held no small amount of the dark, sticky material.

The men couldn't believe their luck. De Boer, deeply moved, thanked

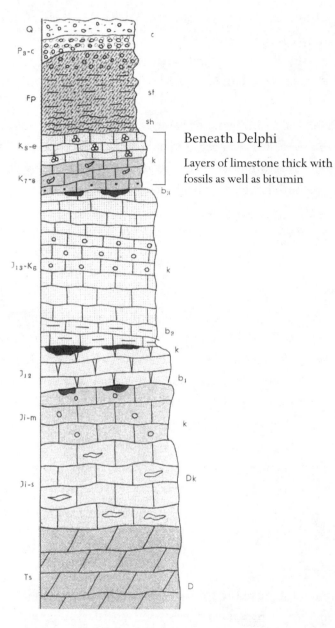

Beneath Delphi

Layers of limestone thick with fossils as well as bitumin

A eureka moment came when de Boer, the lead American investigator, laid eyes on a 1964 Greek geologic map. It showed that rocky layers like those under the sanctuary of Apollo included bituminous limestone riddled with hydrocarbons, a common source of intoxicating gases. This cutaway view comes from the map's legend.

Hale profusely for finding the map. As the implications of the discovery sank in, they marveled at the strange juxtaposition: a riot of old hydrocarbons lay behind the Pythia and her centuries of prophecies and visions and convulsions. It was almost too good to be true, better than fiction. It was the eureka moment they had never dared to hope for.

In a flash, de Boer gave up his theory about the gases originating under the Gulf of Corinth. It had been a false hunch he no longer needed. The likely factors that enlivened the Oracle turned out to be much closer and more compelling than he ever imagined.

De Boer recalled some of the bitumen he had seen in his travels—in Pakistan, in northern Greece, even in Connecticut near Wesleyan. He would take students on field trips up Highway 9, to East Berlin. There, by the side of the road, they would examine the bituminous rocks and crack them open with a hammer and smell the pungent odor. In places the bitumen was so thick you could see it running in rivulets through the cracks, like asphalt. Bituminous limestone under the temple could produce gaseous emissions that rose to the surface. One possibility was that violent shifts along an active fault—probably the fault he and Hale had mapped that very day—produced friction that heated and vaporized the bitumen and drove off its lighter fractions. The same kind of thing happened when refineries cracked crude oil into its component parts.

Yes, he told Hale, earthquakes and violent shifts along active faults could produce that kind of heat. In some cases, they could boost gas emissions for years, decades, even centuries. Equally important, they reopened fractures, providing new pathways for the gases. Deep under the sanctuary, he suggested, the episodes of heating and venting might have alternated with periods of stagnation, accounting for the kind of erratic performance of the Oracles that Plutarch mentioned.

The two men knew that, all things said, the link between the Oracle and the bitumen was still just a hunch. But the guess was grounded in a set of impressive facts about the makeup of the land beneath the sanctuary. It was much more than speculation. The pieces of the puzzle were falling into place. The two had discovered not only a fault but a way it could have conveyed gases to the Oracle.

*H*ALE ONCE suffered a major professional embarrassment while leading an archaeological dig. It occurred at the start of his career and he took it as a lesson never to be repeated. Just out of graduate school, he was directing the field assessment of a site proposed for industrial development in Jefferson County, Kentucky, the area around Louisville. His responsibility was to see if it would disturb any ancient artifacts. He had been given little time but the job nonetheless required great care. The survey site was in the Ohio floodplain, an area known to be rich in Indian tools and cultural items dating back thousands of years when dense settlements of Native Americans dotted the river's banks.

Hale crackled with zeal. Sure he was about to make a great discovery, he bent over backward to do everything by the book. His team came to a creek after cutting its way through dense brambles. There, just ahead, lay a large mound. Louisville once bristled with Indian mounds that had been lost or destroyed before the days of careful archaeological analysis. Now, an untouched one seemed to loom. This was his big chance. Hale told his team to spare no effort. For days under the hot sun, they cleared away shrubs, put down a grid, and began the painstaking process of uncovering the mound, cutting into its rich black dirt millimeter by millimeter. This, Hale knew, was his Troy. He could already hear the speeches and the applause.

Up came a piece of glass. Hale, unshaken, said a rodent or tree root could have pushed it under. Minutes later, a chunk of brick emerged, then a long iron chain. Hale told his four teammates to take a break. He left the site and located the nearest farmhouse. After introducing himself to the woman at the door, he asked if she knew anything about a nearby Indian mound. No, she answered. Then he described the site with greater precision, saying it lay in a U-shaped bend of the creek. Oh, she said, that's where my husband dumped all that stuff years ago.

Afterward, Hale formulated a simple rule for himself, one he had never learned in school: People living close to an archaeological site probably know more about it than an initial survey by trained professionals could ever reveal, so the first step is always to talk to the locals.

He now applied it to Delphi.

A gregarious man by nature, Hale swept the city, going from store to store, asking if anyone knew of nearby springs or crevices that emitted unusual odors, any places where gases came out of the ground. His aim was to see if Delphi's earthquakes had rearranged the bedrock and possibly diverted the Oracle's vent to a new location, as Plutarch had suggested.

Late in the day, he hit paydirt. The site of his inquiry was a kind of eclectic antiquities shop filled with goat bells, religious icons, leather goods, old stirrups, an olive press, rugs, horseshoes, coins, watches, wooden rakes and shovels, and, inexplicably, delicate molds for making fancy communion wafers. Two men sat at its rear. There's a place just beyond the edge of town, far from the temple, a crack in a rocky face, they said. It's called the wind hole, *anemo trypa.* We used to play there when we were kids.

Thrilled, Hale worked his way down the town's main street, asking in bars if anybody knew about the wind hole.

Yes, one man said. I remember when I was a kid you could smell sulfur coming out of it sometimes and you could see vapor hanging above it in the winter.

Hale was speechless, his mind filled with visions of intoxicating vapors. He knew that many hydrocarbons such as coal and oil contain sulfur, and supposed that bitumen could, too, giving it a familiar odor.

Look for a gate, someone said. A metal gate now covers the hole.

Why? Hale asked.

So nobody will fall in.

Hale had always dismissed reports of the Oracle's tripod straddling the temple's fissure as a safety feature. Now he wondered if that was true.

It was late. The night was cold and no stars were visible. But Hale, warmed by wine and growing excitement about the wind hole, hit another bar, the only establishment still open. He talked to a young couple. Neither knew of the wind hole, but as the archaeologist described the project, both grew eager to find it. The man and his wife mounted their motorcycle and Hale ran after them on foot. The site was easy to find. It lay just outside town along the road down to the Gulf of Corinth, presenting itself as a craggy wall of limestone. The woman turned the motorcycle's light on the gate so Hale and her husband could inspect what lay beyond. It was a miniature cave, a narrow crack perhaps a meter long from top to bottom that widened a bit before disappearing into the depths. There was no odor, no wind. There was also no chance that anyone other than a very small child could have fallen into the opening. They could see some small stalactites and that layers of limestone had coated its inner surfaces. It was a small doorway to the inner earth.

Hale went home happy. The find was no big discovery but it did evoke possibilities about the bituminous roots of the area, and possibly how the temple's vent had shifted location over the centuries. For now, there was no obvious leakage of hydrocarbons. But maybe there had been in the past. At a minimum, it was another clue.

THE SKY looked threatening and the air had turned icy. A woman at the Kouros said snow was on its way, maybe a lot. Despite the forecast, the two decided to drive over Parnassus to the coastal plain that held Thermopylae, where the Greeks had held off the Persian army and where de Boer had often watched the nearby springs bubbling away. He wanted to show them to Hale, sure that such an experience could drive home, as no textbook could, the everyday reality of gas bubbling up from deep inside the earth.

The springs of Thermopylae, literally "the hot gates," lay along a very active line of faults. De Boer had visited the steaming pools previously while mapping fractures for the reactor project on Evia, the mountainous isle off Greece's east coast. Around one spring lay an abandoned spa where laborers and their families had once gone for relaxation, letting the heat ease their muscles. De Boer himself planned to plunge into the large pool that lay where the hot water welled up, even if it was snowing. From past experience, he knew that the bubbles rising from the bottom of the pool were not intoxicating but instead contained gases of carbonate, like bubbles in soda or seltzer water. There was no evidence of bitumen or exotic hydrocarbons. Still, as the eagle flies, Thermopylae lay just twenty miles north of Delphi, and the site made an arresting parallel to what might have percolated up at the sanctuary of Apollo.

The snow began to fall as the two men set out and it came down harder as they drove up the switchbacks of Parnassus. Soon, it was a gale, the snow horizontal and visibility all but gone. They turned back after passing a snowplow stuck along the side of the road and decided to call it quits in a tiny upland town. Further progress was dangerous, and in any event, the rumor was that the passes up ahead were closed.

The isolated town had few hotels, none open. After a search, they found an inn where the proprietor agreed to open up and make a fire. The men warmed themselves and began talking again, eventually in a more personal way. It somehow seemed appropriate. Hale told of descending from a line of doctors and teachers, preachers and small businessmen. Little by little, de Boer told of his childhood in Java, his internment in the concentration camp, and his lucky initiation into the field of geology. At one point, he pulled back his hair to show the scar on his forehead from a bullet wound he got while fleeing the Japanese camp, the scar red in the firelight.

Hale had had no idea. He felt new respect for de Boer and fresh commitment to the project.

· · ·

*D*E BOER was indisputably the project's senior member by virtue of age, experience, academic stature, and primacy in making the first critical observations about the unusual geology under the temple of Apollo. Likewise, there was no question that Hale was the junior partner.

But after the first round of investigations in Greece, a subtle shift took place in which Hale played a leading role in shaping the agenda. Part of it was raw determination. Hale knew a good thing when he saw one, and the de Boer thesis now appeared to have gone from implausible to likely. After all, they now possessed—in addition to the testimony of the ancient writers—a large body of circumstantial evidence supporting the idea of oracular intoxication. In no particular order, it included the gull metaphor, the French report on the *adyton*'s fissured rock, their own observations of the fault passing through Delphi, the Greek map's confirmation of the fault, the discovery of bitumen in the bedrock below the temple, the observation of travertine in and around Apollo's shrine, and the evocations of the wind hole. On balance, it seemed increasingly probable that a spring or fissure had let some kind of gas rise up to the temple and, over the ages, inspired a succession of Oracles.

Hale, as junior partner, stood to gain more career advancement from a solid discovery at Delphi, and that perhaps made him more deeply vested in the project. By contrast, de Boer had already arrived academically and even a major success at Delphi would be unlikely to raise his standing markedly. After all, he was already the Harold T. Stearns Professor of Earth Science at Wesleyan, with his endowment paying for most of the project's costs. His native curiosity made him deeply interested in solving the mystery of Delphi, but in terms of his career, he was probably less driven to achieve a major advance. In a way, de Boer had reached that station in academic life where he had the freedom to relax or do something daring and run the risk of striking out. Either outcome was acceptable. Hale, on the other hand, had no endowed chair and, while directing

Louisville's liberal studies program, could easily aspire to becoming a dean or provost or president if he followed the administrative route. In whatever direction he went, Hale had ample opportunity for promotion, and a solid discovery would do that prospect no harm. Their ages suggested the divide. De Boer was sixty-one, Hale forty-four.

Probably more important than any personal differences between the two men were professional factors that gave Hale an incentive to press ahead forcefully. Most important, the two were questioning a conventional wisdom that in character was archaeologic, not geologic. There was nearly a century of archaeological writing and discovery, observation and debate about Delphi that had ended up dismissing the idea of a fissure and intoxicating fumes. The geological world had no such tradition. It would be a novelty for de Boer to talk about Delphi in a geological journal, perhaps a first in some cases. But Hale, in writing for an archaeological audience, would come up against a long line of predecessors who, for the most part, preached skepticism on the ancient sources. He would face a potentially hostile group of reviewers and readers who, if open-minded at all, would likely be persuaded only by a wealth of compelling evidence. The alternative was unthinkable. Hale had no intention of becoming the laughingstock of archaeology.

So too, the men faced wide differences in how their respective fields viewed the subject matter. To archaeologists, Delphi was a holy grail, one of the most famous sites of classical antiquity, on a par with the Parthenon in Athens and the Colosseum in Rome. By contrast, Delphi was all but unknown to most geologists. At best, it was a sideshow compared to mobile plates, tectonic boundaries, and rising mountains ranges.

Finally, their respective fields had very different standards of evidence and proof, and in Hale's case those differences contributed to his incentive to press ahead boldly. Though geology is considered a hard science, much of it, especially aspects that seek to understand the depths of the earth, deals in a range of intangibles—implied boundaries, invisible convective currents, inexact zones of melting and solidification. By contrast, much in archaeology can be seen, picked up, and subjected to testing and analysis. It is tactile and sensory, even when missing parts of a particular puzzle force an investigator to rely on inference. To a degree, Hale sought to impose his own discipline's methods on those of geology.

Perhaps personal psychology also came into play. De Boer was a hardened survivor, at times headstrong, whereas Hale could be quite sensitive to the approbation of his peers.

Such factors combined to make the archaeologist eager to gather the most convincing possible evidence. He wanted to be very sure of himself. It was a situation ripe with the potential for friction and resentment, especially if de Boer felt Hale was challenging his authority. On the other hand, it was the kind of creative tension that often marked collaborations. In theory, the benefits outweighed the risks.

The issue on which the men's differing perspectives now came to bear was the question of publication, of setting their discoveries before a wide audience and making a public case for oracular intoxication. At this point, in early 1996, de Boer, who had the benefit of fifteen long years to meditate on Delphi's unusual geology and its implications for antiquity, felt they probably had enough evidence to go into print. It would be no big deal, he argued. The two of them could pitch an article to one of the geological journals. Hale disagreed. They needed more evidence, better ways to back up their claims, to go from "it could" to "it did." De Boer had no problem with pushing harder. It could do no harm and might help. Years later, in recalling the period, he praised Hale as a perfectionist, illustrating his compliment with differing notions of what constituted acceptable knowledge in their respective fields. Geologists, he said, were often satisfied if their findings were, say, 75 percent certain. But Hale wanted to be 90 or 95 percent sure that their conclusions were correct.

As the two men drove to Athens and flew back to New York, they talked over how to move the project forward. A key part of the hypothesis for which they had no hard evidence was the flow of bituminous vapors up through the rocky earth. How, Hale asked, could they prove that?

Was there any method that could throw light on what petrochemicals had reached the temple, especially in the distant past? Was there any way to reach back, to discover what gases were bubbling up around the temple thousands of years ago?

De Boer thought about it for a long time, weighing the possibilities. Finally, he spoke.

The travertine, he said. It offered only a small chance of success but was perhaps worth trying. The idea had a lot of ifs, he said. If the flow of gas up to the temple had been abundant back then, if the rock had formed quickly, if the gas had proved stable over long periods of time, if most of the gas hadn't leaked through the porous rock, then perhaps some of the gas might have became trapped in the rocky pores as the travertine formed during the age of Oracles and stayed imprisoned there for thousands of years. De Boer was not optimistic, however. He knew of no such discovery of ancient gases. If it worked, it would be new science.

And of course, de Boer added, almost as an afterthought, it seemed likely that the authorities at Delphi would disapprove. Getting permission to chip away at the site's travertine would probably be viewed as a violation of the holy sanctuary. It just wasn't done.

*H*ALE SETTLED back on the plane for the long flight home. It had been a good trip, despite the disappointment of finding the *adyton* filled with dirt. He was confident they had already gathered important evidence and had also come up with a plan for realizing a new level of precision, for testing the hypothesis, for collecting data that could prove them right or wrong. That, after all, was how science worked. You proposed a bold idea and then subjected it to experimental verification. Hale was sure they had made a good start.

What continued to nag him, though, was the problem of the length of the fault and the question of what had made Delphi—of all locations, if the thesis was correct—such a hot spot of intoxication. After all, the fault ran for at least twenty kilometers along the flank of Parnassus. The riddle of Delphi's uniqueness, revealed by the Greek map, had gotten lost in the blur of subsequent travel and inquiries and discoveries. But now that things had settled down, it came back with renewed force.

FIVE

X Marks the Spot

*T*HEIR ATTEMPT TO WIN approval for rock sampling began a few months later, in May 1996. Though doubtful of success, de Boer wrote Rozina Kolonia, the Delphi official who had given them permission to roam the sanctuary. He explained how travertine scattered around the temple of Apollo might hold a memory of past gases, and requested that they be allowed to test the idea by removing four fist-sized chunks of rock.

That the wheels of government turn slowly is a universal fact of life that appears to hold especially true in Greece. Moreover, the socialists then in power seemed to take special joy in thoroughness. On proposals that threatened to affect some kind of change to the country's prized classical antiquities, a foundation of Greek national pride, officials in Athens could show a meticulousness that bordered on fanaticism.

Kolonia was courteous. She said she appreciated the interesting science involved. But only an archaeologist could formally apply for such permission. That was the rule. And it was Athens that would decide.

In September 1996, Hale submitted an application for a permit to take travertine samples at Delphi, doing so through a distinguished intermediary, the American School of Classical Studies at Athens. Only it had the credentials, the scholars learned belatedly, to make a request that the Greek Ministry of Culture and the Central Archaeological Council would find acceptable. Boldly, Hale raised the proposed number of samples from four to ten and asked for larger chunks. The rocky specimens, he said, might range in diameter up to fifteen centimeters, or six inches—about two fists wide. Though Hale prepared the proposal and took the initiative in dealing with the American School, the document listed de Boer as a main investigator, putting him forward as the team member bearing the best credentials.

Privately, the school warned the scholars that the Greeks—if they went along with the plan at all—would be reluctant to approve letting the scholars take the rocky samples outside the country for testing, as the plan envisioned. The authorities liked to keep such work at home. The two men nonetheless decided to press ahead, convinced that American laboratories were best suited for the analysis.

As weeks turned into months, as the winter holidays came and went, and as 1997 got under way, de Boer shifted his focus from helping with the application to pondering Hale's last question—what added factor along the length of the Delphi fault might have given the temple region a monopoly on intoxicating gas. Unlike Hale, de Boer knew a lot about the natural variability of faults, about their undulations and irregularities, their quirks and surprises. Fickle portals to the depths, they could often be bone dry where a specialist might expect them to gush with cool water. He knew such frustrations personally. So the question of what made the long fault of Delphi leak gas at some places rather than others struck him as intrinsically less interesting than it did Hale, who knew only that the long black line portrayed on the Greek map failed to explain why Delphi was different.

Still, de Boer felt Hale's question was fresh and worth exploring. Who knew what they'd find? Maybe a novel mechanism would come to light. He sensed that an answer might lay in the undiscovered presence of other cracks in the earth's surface that crossed the Delphi fault at something close to a right angle, forming an X. That would enlarge the path from the bituminous limestone to the surface, increase the amount of friction on the two fractures during earthquakes, and generally ease the rise of gases. In terms of geometry, it would transform a vertical plane into an intersection of two vertical planes, their juncture forming a pipeline to the surface. Of course, if the idea had merit, the X would have to cross right beneath the temple of Apollo.

Behind de Boer's hunch lay a deep knowledge of crisscrossing faults he had acquired over decades of study. He knew them not only from books and college courses but from fieldwork he had conducted around the globe from Pakistan to Connecticut. Such intersections are not rarities of nature but—across the vastness of the planet's face—fairly common features. Their ubiquity is suggested by the large size of the crisscross family: its members include tear faults, strike-slip faults, conjugate faults, gash fractures, feather fractures, transfer faults, transform faults, transcurrent faults, and more.

In Greece, de Boer knew the world of intersecting faults quite intimately because of his long explorations of the Corinth and neighboring rift zones. A 1985 report on his research in Greece to the National Science Foundation bore several maps that depicted crisscrossing faults, most especially in the areas north of the Corinth rift, including Delphi. The maps showed that the area's main faults—including the ones responsible for the 1981 earthquakes—generally ran east-west, while the crosscutting ones ran north-south.

De Boer dug into his field notes and journals to look for evidence of local crosscutting faults at Delphi. He found plenty. During his early surveys of the sanctuary, it turned out, he had plotted swarms of baby cross fractures in the hillside above the temple near the high cliffs. The small fractures, roughly two dozen in number, strongly implied the presence of a mother fault. They were the rocky equivalent of echoes.

But where was the big one? And just as important for the public aspects of the scientific process, in which an investigator must not only prove the validity of ideas but persuade skeptics of their importance, how

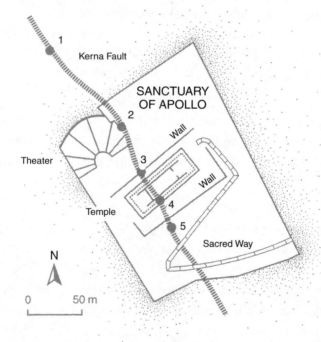

De Boer found a clue to the existence of a second rocky fault at Delphi in how five old and current springs lined up, suggesting a common geologic origin. Only the first—the Kerna—is active today.

could he demonstrate its existence? De Boer explored the scientific literature on Delphi as well as nearby libraries, driving, for instance, to New
Haven to visit Yale. He mulled ideas at work and home. His house, nestled
in wooded hills near the Connecticut River, was ideal for reflection. It had
a large meadow out back as well as a stream and a pond where his children
once hunted frogs and snappers.

As he read and meditated, de Boer hit upon a potentially strong piece
of evidence: the old springs, today mainly represented by the accumulations of travertine. On the Delphi hillside, they lay in a straight line that
ended just below the temple, implying, de Boer reasoned, that the waters
arose along a common fault that passed beneath Apollo's shrine. Moreover, it turned out that their lineup paralleled the baby swarms he had
mapped so carefully.

He judged that the sanctuary region at one time or another had bubbled with at least five springs that ran in a straight line down the hillside,
all now virtually dry or rerouted. From the top, they started with the
Kerna near the rocky cliffs, emerged next at a springhouse adjacent to a
large theater above the temple, then splashed over the retaining wall
where so much travertine had accumulated, then welled up in the *adyton*
(as suggested by the system of ducts leading from the temple's lower
foundations), and finally spilled out below the temple at a place known
alternately as the spring of the muses or Gaia, the site's original goddess.
Their lineup was almost perfectly linear.

Finally, de Boer pulled out his old reconnaissance photos of the region
and examined them carefully, searching for evidence in the most expansive of all possible views. There it was, hints of a crosscutting fault dis-
cernible in the shadows of hills running north and south of Delphi. The
bits of circumstantial evidence added up to strong but not conclusive
proof of an intersecting fault. What would cinch it was an exposed fault
face, like those east and west of Delphi. He promised himself that, during
his next visit, he would look for one.

. . .

DE BOER ALSO investigated the nature of the gases that would most likely have welled up from the X to intoxicate the Oracle. He talked at length with friends at Texas A&M University, who studied the nearby Gulf of Mexico and had learned a good deal about its gases, oil deposits, and hydrocarbon leaks in a region underlain by a massive limestone complex. The gulf seemed like a good analogue. De Boer became fascinated by a Texas project that investigated an area of major hydrocarbon leakage some 200 kilometers (or 125 miles) off Louisiana, where a large mound on the seabed released streams of bubbles. The gases, arising along a pair of faults, were found to include methane, ethane, propane, and butane. Methane and ethane are the main components of natural gas.

A significant piece of the Delphi puzzle seemed to fall into place when de Boer learned that the gases bubbling up from the mound flowed intermittently—only when the gulf warmed up. No bubbles could be detected when the water was cooler. To the geologist, that potentially answered the question of why the Oracles had spoken on behalf of Apollo only during the nine warmer months of the year. Perhaps the temple's spring bubbled little during the winter months, releasing insufficient amounts of the stimulating vapor needed for prophetic sessions.

Curious about how such gases would affect people, de Boer consulted with Wesleyan colleagues in the chemistry department and started his own literature search. Methane, ethane, and butane, if inhaled in sufficient quantities, turned out to produce mild intoxification. The problem was that they were odorless.

Inspired by Plutarch's description of the pneuma, de Boer looked for something with a sweet odor, like the fragrance of an exotic perfume. He found it in ethylene. Surgeons around the turn of the century had used the powerful, aromatic gas for anesthesia. Even in extremely light doses, it produced feelings of aloof euphoria, a kind of pleasant, disembodied high. The gas samples from the Gulf of Mexico, de Boer learned, might have seethed with ethylene, but its presence would have gone undetected because its identification was difficult and the gas had little economic value, making it irrelevant to the Texas specialists. A cocktail of ethylene and a few of the other gases appeared to possess all the needed attributes, with ethylene the strongest in terms of human intoxication. And its effects wore off quite quickly. Once inhalation stopped, a person would come down from the high in just a few minutes. The modern facts seemed to fit the ancient evidence.

As de Boer sought to understand the underlying science, he talked and corresponded with Hale. The archaeologist reported that he had still heard nothing from the Greek authorities about the sampling request but had made a breakthrough that helped put the Oracle into historical perspective. It turned out that the ancient Greeks had built not just Delphi but several major temples over springs and gaseous vents. All were located in Asia Minor, home of many imposing Greek ruins, and all seemed to have been modeled loosely on Delphi, which predated them.

A temple of Apollo had stood inland at the bustling city of Hierapolis on a rise overlooking brilliant white pools of travertine, Hale reported. A spring known as the Plutonium, dedicated to Pluto, god of the underworld, had bubbled nearby, the effects of its gas not heady but deadly. Priests would demonstrate their powers by throwing in small animals and birds and watching them die.

On the west coast at Claros, in a more rural setting, another temple of Apollo had operated as an important center of prophecy. Deep in the interior of its ruined temple, archaeologists found an *adyton* where a spring welled up. According to ancient accounts, the priests had sipped the sacred water to achieve inspiration.

Finally, Hale told of a site known as Didyma, lower down the west coast, hidden among rolling hills. Its temple of Apollo could swallow the Parthenon. Like Claros, its *adyton* held a holy spring from which priests would drink as part of the prophetic ritual.

.   .   .

*B*Y EARLY 1997, de Boer felt they had gathered enough evidence to go public and raised the possibility of giving a talk on their findings. Hale, despite his initial reservations about publication, went along with the idea. After all, it was only a talk, a standard way to report scientific work in progress and tentative ideas rather than a formal publication of findings that were set in concrete. Moreover, de Boer was to present it to geologists, his peers—not to archaeologists, arguably a tougher audience. Finally, the geologist was indisputably the project's leader, so he had every right to make a presentation if he wanted to. And perhaps, Hale reasoned, the talk would produce some feedback that might aid the project.

He warned de Boer that many people would be interested in a revisionist history of the Oracle of Delphi and to expect some attention. In late April 1997, de Boer flew to London and presented his paper at a conference entitled "Volcanoes, Earthquakes and Archaeology" that was sponsored by the Geological Society of London. It was held in Piccadilly at the group's headquarters in Burlington House, an elegant old building that housed learned societies. Founded in 1807, the Geological Society was the oldest such body in the world, its library bursting with journals and a bust of Charles Lyell, an Englishman who helped found geology. Importantly for de Boer, it was a European venue. He considered it an appropriate place to disclose news about an ancient aspect of European civilization.

He laid out the thesis and the evidence, telling his audience of the possible existence of bitumen and faults beneath the temple. Over the centuries, he said, earthquakes may have vaporized the bitumen and shaken the fissures, moderating the flow of gases. Venturing further, de Boer suggested that sweet ethylene may have been one of the intoxicants.

The unveiling demonstrated de Boer's faith in his own intuition, despite the lack of hard evidence that the layers of bitumen had actually produced a flow of intoxicating fumes. Only time would tell if his presentation was mistakenly premature or presciently bold.

Among dozens of talks from around the world, his made the big splash. Delphi, after all, was Delphi, a place of solemn importance in the history of human civilization. More subtly, de Boer's paper went against the meeting's grain in an intriguing way. Most of the talks looked at volcanoes and earthquakes as agents of destruction. De Boer's postulated a benefit. For the ancient Greeks, the rumblings of the earth had helped inspire their religious life. The news media loved it. The *London Times,* the BBC, the *Daily Telegraph,* and *New Scientist,* a British magazine, peppered de Boer with questions and ran stories.

The French geologists at the meeting, sitting at the back of the presentation room, showed no reaction whatsoever, their arms crossed, their faces hung with great stony expressions as De Boer became the center of attention. It was unclear if they understood that the American geologist had just assailed a monument of French learning.

*M*ost people who go to Zakynthos have no knowledge of, or interest in, its ancient tar pit. The island lies off the west coast of Greece in the Ionian Sea. Flights from northern Europe are quite short, so tourists flock there, especially young people. They seek its beaches and smart hotels, bars and pounding nightlife. Rows of rental umbrellas and sunbeds dot the sands, as do sleek, tanned bodies.

Beyond the tourist bustle lies an attractive green isle. With little development and lots of charm, it features old farming villages, fertile plains, rugged mountains, dense forests, and blue caves that the sea carves in limestone cliffs. The farms grow citrus fruits and grapes for raisins. The island takes its name from a legendary companion of Hercules who was supposedly laid to rest amid the rural beauty.

De Boer and his Wesleyan students came to Zakynthos for its geologic riches. Unbeknownst to tourists, a major fault bisects the island. It runs roughly north to south for more than twenty miles, a mighty gash through the limestone bedrock that goes from one coast to the other. To the fissure's east lie flat lands and sandy coasts, and to the west, mountains with dramatic cliffs and secluded beaches. The geologist wanted to explore the fault and the land's other features not only for the Delphi project with Hale but for his own work and interest as well, perhaps for his earthquake book. In 1953, a major jolt shook the isle, leveling most buildings and setting many fires. The Venetians, who ruled Zakynthos from 1484 to 1797, had filled its capital with many beautiful icons, churches, and buildings. The quake destroyed most of them.

De Boer had never before visited Zakynthos and happily led his students—three young women and a young man—on a tour. From the maps he brought along and from his review of the scientific literature, he saw the island as a rather extreme version of Delphi, its foundations rich in bituminous limestone and split by a long fault that bubbled with springs and hydrocarbon seeps.

He had first learned of the tar pit from Hale, who knew it from Herodotus. The father of history had described a site on Zakynthos from which people extracted pitch and put it into jars, apparently for export as well as local use. Among other applications, the ancient Greeks smeared the sticky material on wooden ships to seal joints.

De Boer wanted to explore Zakynthos as a possible test of the Delphi hypothesis. Perhaps its tar pit exuded fumes similar to those that intoxicated the Oracle; if so, sampling them and documenting their composition promised to strengthen their case. It was June of 1997—just after school let out, two months since the London meeting, and more than a year since Hale and he had first gone to Delphi. They had yet to receive permission to sample the travertine around the temple of Apollo. Eager to keep their options open, de Boer saw Zakynthos as an analogue to Delphi and a possible backup for sampling.

The group bypassed the tourist areas and headed straight to the island's southeastern coast, home of the famous (at least to a few scholars) tar pit. The area was known as Keri beach. It was a natural magnet for de Boer, since the pit seemed to arise atop the main fault, which soon thereafter plunged into the sea.

A dozen signs for boat shops and sea cave adventures marked the Keri turnoff. A winding drive led to a little town and a stony beach dotted with shade trees. Motorbikes buzzed along the shore road. No European tourists were visible, but a few Greek families relaxed in the shade as children played in the sandy, shallow water.

The tar pit lay in a swamp just behind the beach, surrounded by green hills. Pockets of gooey blackness oozed up among tall reeds and grasses and pools of water that stretched over a flat region about the size of a football field. The students scrambled around the black puddles, poking in sticks and rocks and stones. The pungent odor was familiar—like a road project that had just laid down fresh coat of asphalt.

The marsh was no tourist mecca. A row of trash receptacles ran along one side. Near its center lay a rusted blue pickup truck, its engine gone. In the tar pools, a few pipes and metal gadgets stuck out where moderns, like the ancient Greeks, had once gathered up the sticky substance. Nearby in the town of Keri, a sign announced a concession to tourism where part of the gooey expanse had been packaged for public display. "Herodotos Spring, 50 meters," said the sign in Greek and English, with an arrow pointing down a roadway. Out behind a building stood a white stone gazebo with a red tiled roof. Inside lay a well six or seven feet across, its depths oozing with black tar. The students again poked at it with long sticks, pushing them down quite deep, impressed by the sheer massiveness of the goo. It was much thicker than among the marsh pools.

Back in Connecticut, the team had assembled a large kit of sampling paraphernalia—bags, bottles, jars, pens, labels. Now, under the geologist's supervision, the students unpacked a jar and filled it with tar. The black material was like Super Glue, getting stuck on their fingers and shoes and not easily coming off. But they had their specimen. De Boer considered it a possible backup. If the need arose, he would have a skilled chemist redo the sampling and probe the results for clues. It would have to be done carefully to avoid contamination and rule out false positives. The geophysicist, a global authority on the risks of paleomagnetic misinterpretation, knew that the chemical world held similar pitfalls and that navigating them lay beyond his experience.

Across from the tar pit, back on the road, the Super Market Herodotos beckoned with signs for ice-cream bars and cones. After a snack, de Boer and the students went back to the beach, plunging into the cool waters, frolicking and chatting. Nearby lay a small harbor and jetty. De Boer walked out, admiring the colorful boats and the view.

He got a whiff of something. There it was again, that rotten-egg odor that high school chemistry students know so well, a sign of hydrogen sulfide, of sulfur. He looked around. Sure enough, he could see a few lines of bubbles rising from the seafloor to the surface—not nearly as many as at Thermopylae but with about the same steadiness. The bubbles were probably some mix of sulfur and petrochemical gases released from the underlying bitumen. It was just the kind of thing he hoped they might find, more evidence of the vanished Tethys and its bygone life.

Like most scientists, de Boer knew that sulfur had a strange history and contradictory reputation. Once known as brimstone, associated with hellfire and heavenly wrath, the flammable element over the ages had been made into matches and gunpowder. In addition, sulfur eventually won a reputation for healing. Modern tonics featured nutritional sulfur, proclaiming it as a key to healthy skin, hair, and nails, where it aided the formation of proteins.

The students got out the sampling kit. They lowered bottles into the seawater, then inverted them over the bubbles to capture the gas. On nearby seaweed, they also found some paraffinlike residues and collected samples of the oily substances. Asking around, de Boer was told that, in the evening, when the winds died, the smell could become quite unpleasant.

Along the beach, the team found an outcrop of thinly layered sandstone cut by small fractures. The rock was dark brown in places and smelled of bitumen, with asphalt filling some of its fractures. The alignment of the baby faults suggested a parallel mother fault below the swamp and that its direction was more or less at right angles to the major fault that cut Zakynthos in two. Possibly—just possibly—the mother represented one arm of an X that was leaking tons of hydrocarbon goo.

After dinner, the exhausted team went back to their hotel, which was perched on a bluff overlooking Keri Bay. De Boer had a bad feeling about the place. The walls were marked with dull red patches where mosquitoes full of human blood had been squashed. Ever since his long nightmare of the Japanese concentration camp, de Boer had hated mosquitoes. The nearby marsh seemed to be an ideal breeding ground. No one had noticed that during the day as fresh breezes kept blowing. But now the winds had died, making it easier for the mosquitoes to fly around and hunt down humans. De Boer plugged all the holes he could find in the screens of his room and went to sleep. The buzzing came in waves. Soon, he was standing on his bed, flailing his arms, waking the dazed male student he shared the room with. After two or three hours, de Boer gave up, retreated to the car, and shut its windows tight.

The next day, groggy but glad for the bright sun, the geologist led his students on a survey of the peninsula on which their hotel sat, walking higher and higher up the dead-end road. It was all an expression of the rocky fault that split the island in two. They found outcrops riddled with hundreds of small fractures, many impregnated with oil. They took out their hammers and chisels and broke off samples. The also climbed down the embankment to Keri Bay, again getting whiffs of sulfur in places but this time seeing no bubbles. They scraped oily deposits off some of the nearby rocks and put them in sample bags.

After lunch, the team drove into the hinterlands of Zakynthos, ready to track the twenty-mile fault. It was fairly easy to see at a distance, since the island's middle roads paralleled it. On a smaller scale, the setting was similar to the American plains where the Rocky Mountains suddenly loom up, sheer and commanding. But getting close was difficult. Few of the island's roads cut into the mountains. Where they did, the group explored the exposed fault faces and environs quite closely, looking for signs of oil and gas, carefully sniffing the air. They found none, despite a long day of searching. It seemed like it took more than a simple gash in the earth to free what lay below.

Toward the end of their stay, they drove along the fault all the way up to the island's northern coast. According to a paper by Greek geologists that de Boer had located, a beach there fairly seethed with hydrocarbon springs and clumps of solids that looked much like fat or paraffin. Indeed, the site was known as *Xygia*, Greek for "fat." The isle's tourist literature called the beach picturesque but delicately noted that it bore a strong odor of sulfur. Despite its unappealing aspects, the local Greeks were said to covet its sulfur-rich waters, believing them restorative. They used them in face creams and lotions and as cures for rheumatism.

The team's drive was inspiring but treacherous, the final push over a precarious track. Xygia turned out to be isolated and quite deserted, with none of the families or bustle of Keri. It was just a small, stony beach located between rocky promontories, like a pirate's cove. So far, de Boer smelled no sulfur, just a fresh ocean breeze and the wonderful salt air.

He eyed the rocky site. The promontory to the right—where part of the long fault face plunged into the sea—towered over them, rising maybe twenty meters, the top a sheer cliff fringed with trees and dark vegetation. He drank in the sight, exhilarated.

No exhibitionist faults had been visible near the tar pit. There, the cracking of bedrock that allowed the upward migration and pooling of hydrocarbons had been hidden beneath the wide marsh, out of sight. Here, the window into the depths was on public display, magnificently so. For a geologist who had spent decades contemplating the invisible workings of the inner earth, it was a joy. The massive vertical wall of rock, its face level and smoothly polished, loomed over de Boer and his students, a showpiece like that of the Delphi fault, another example of nature's glory.

As he looked around, de Boer saw that the site was even more significant than he had thought at first glance. Unexpectedly, it put on clear display not just a single, magnificent fault but an intersection of two of them, the junction plainly visible. The converging fault lay at the back of the beach, a beautiful rocky outcrop parallel to the waterline and almost at right angles to the exposed fault of the giant promontory.

The two formed an unambiguous X—an X at Xygia.

De Boer and his students crawled up and around the cross fault, which was much smaller and apparently older than the main one. Working their way along the beach in the smaller fault's direction, they clambered into a rough area of broken rocks and cavities and small caves. Some of the gnarled limestone was marked with patches of pale yellow discoloration, a sign of sulfur. They headed back to the stony beach and decided to swim to the sea caves where most of the hydrocarbons were said to bubble up. The waves were small and the caves only about one hundred meters away, around the larger of the two promontories. Tourist brochures called them the White Cave and the Devil's Throat, the latter undoubtedly because of the sulfur smell.

De Boer and the students were a bit apprehensive about the swim but dove in, their sampling gear tucked in their suits. The water was chilly. It was June, many weeks from the warmth of late summer. The five of them swam out and around the point, navigating a cluster of jagged rocks that seemed to guard the sheer face of the promontory. A cave came into view. It did in fact gape like an open mouth, the water lapping at its rocky sides and gurgling softly within. The geologist noted that the water had turned quite milky, with a faint odor of sulfur. The whitest water was closest to the throat.

He treaded water at the entrance as the students swam in. They reported that the limestone overhead was lightly colored, very beautiful, sculpted over the centuries by the action of the waves. They could smell the sulfur strongly now, the students reported. It got stronger the deeper they went in. They could see a waxy deposit on the walls. The cave ran perhaps thirty feet deep.

Get the paraffin! de Boer yelled. He was turning blue as he churned the cold water.

Two students began scraping deposits off the walls just above the waterline while the others helped with the sample bags. The material was a light yellowish paste. They pushed it into the plastic bags and sealed them as best they could with slippery fingers.

Back on the beach, they congratulated themselves on the success of their mission, marveling at the gooey substance, admiring their handiwork. It looked like old grease—but with a faint sulfurous odor.

Later, they celebrated at a restaurant up the road, drinking in the coastal views. After a tough day, de Boer relaxed, warm and content. On Zakynthos, he had not only been able to provide his students with memorable fieldwork but had learned much that could illuminate Delphi. The hot depths of Zakynthos obviously acted like a petrochemical refinery, transforming the bitumen into a mix of products. The student team had collected tar, oil, gas, and paraffin. The broad range of substances implied high temperatures down below, which made sense. After all, in the wide context of the Mediterranean, Zakynthos sat close to the juncture where the African plate pushed down below the Greek mainland, churning and heating and shaking most everything nearby.

As any petroleum engineer knew, or any geologist who had once considered a career in the oil industry, it took very little heat to release simple gases from crude oil, less than a hundred degrees Fahrenheit, or forty degrees Celsius. After all, the gases were made up of chains of carbon atoms that were quite short, just one to five atoms, and the molecules were thus quite volatile. It took increasingly high temperatures to separate out the more complex hydrocarbons—gasoline (five to ten carbon atoms), kerosene (ten to twelve carbon atoms), fuel oil (fifteen to eighteen carbon atoms), grease (sixteen to eighteen carbon atoms), paraffin wax (twenty to thirty carbon atoms), and tar and asphalt (thirty to fifty carbon atoms).

Their inquiries on Zakynthos had demonstrated that it was no dream to think that Greece, a land poor in exploitable resources of petrochemicals, nonetheless possessed many derivatives of crude oil that could rise to the surface. In fact, they did so with more vigor and variety than de Boer had anticipated. The isle, unbeknownst to the sun worshippers and disco fans, harbored a wide variety of petroleum byproducts. The strong implication, de Boer concluded, was that the earth's depths at Zakynthos seethed with inner heats to a greater degree than at Delphi.

Not that Delphi's underworld had to boil. De Boer knew that it would take very little heat to do what was required to the bituminous limestone below the temple of Apollo, to liberate the kinds of gases he assumed the Oracles had inhaled.

Now the question was whether he and Hale could find convincing evidence of ancient gases at Delphi, just one hundred miles away from Zakynthos across the Ionian Sea and the Gulf of Corinth. The signs were favorable. The two sites were not only in the same neighborhood but appeared to have features in common.

As de Boer meditated on the findings and what lay ahead at Delphi, he took special pleasure in recalling the beauty of the intersecting faults at Xygia beach. It was rare to see such phenomena so elegantly and clearly laid out, so accessible to investigation. The rocky juncture was as vivid a scene as any he had recently come across as a geologist. On Zakynthos, he and his students had found no oil, gas, or bitumen along the midsections of the fault that bisected the island. But at Xygia, the petrochemicals arose where two faults intersected. Perhaps the same held true at Keri beach as well, though they had no way of knowing for sure because of their inability to see the rocky fractures below the swamp.

In any case, their discoveries on Zakynthos added up to fresh support for the idea that crisscrossing faults at Delphi lay beneath the temple of Apollo. Increasingly, it seemed, de Boer had an answer to Hale's question.

.   .   .

$\mathcal{H}$ALF A WORLD away in Louisville, Hale fairly writhed in nervous anticipation. A packet had arrived from the Greek Archaeological Service of the Greek Ministry of Culture, postmarked Athens. This was it, the reply they had long awaited. A year had passed since they had made their first sampling request. It was now 1997. The archaeologist, like de Boer, had personally decided that his American School colleagues were probably right and that the Greeks were never going to grant permission.

The letter was in Greek. His knowledge of the language centered on the ancient tongue and he knew too little of the modern idiom to make sense of the letter and its enclosures, all of which looked very official, heavy with stamps and seals. The sheer size of the packet lifted his spirits. It seemed unlikely that a "no" would be so lengthy. He dared to hope that Athens had granted their request.

Searching through his liberal studies program, Hale found a student who belonged to a Greek Orthodox church in Louisville.

No, she said, she did not speak the language but had friends who did.

A little past noon, Hale walked into the City Cafe, a downtown eatery known for its good lunches. The student's friend, a young man, was already there. After introductions and chatting, Hale pulled out the Greek documents. The young man fell silent as he read. In a second, his face lit up.

Yes, yes, he said, your hopes were right. You got permission.

At first, Hale was too excited to speak. The impossible had come to pass. The man gave a rough translation. Officials at the archaeological museum at Delphi, the letter said, would have the final say on the sampling process and procedures but the authorities in Athens had given their overall approval. The two proceeded to eat an enjoyable meal, with Hale glad to pick up the bill.

Still doubting his good fortune, he went to the main library at the University of Louisville. A large Greek dictionary helped him render a careful word-for-word translation. He wanted to miss no nuance or caveat. It was true, as advertised. They had received permission. It got better. Exactly as requested, the team would be allowed to take ten samples of Delphi travertine and transport the precious rocks outside of Greece for analysis.

$\mathcal{T}$RACKING DOWN university professors in the summertime can be difficult because many fly away like leaves in the wind. They travel. They rove. They flutter here and there. In June, Hale had been in Portugal. It was now late summer 1997, and the archaeologist, though a close collaborator of de Boer's, had difficulty locating him. It turned out that the geologist was in France, vacationing at his cottage. In August, Hale was able to get a number and place a call.

We got it, Hale bubbled. We got permission to sample the travertine.

De Boer became quite excited, uncharacteristically so given his normally taciturn manner. At last, after blizzards and downpours, it seemed like sunny Apollo was smiling on them. The two men talked of when to go back. The earliest possible date was next year's spring break, in March 1998. It would be around the second anniversary of their first visit.

Hale also told de Boer of his plans to give a talk on their project. Little by little, the archaeologist was overcoming his worries about the adequacy of their evidence. His new confidence even extended to his Louisville office, where he had hung a life-size, nearly floor-to-ceiling color reproduction of Collier's painting of the Oracle. Its depictions of vapors swirled over his desk.

After the fall semester passed uneventfully, Hale in late December flew to Chicago to present his paper at the annual meeting of the American Philological Association. It was the main learned society in the United States for the study of ancient Greek and Roman languages, literatures, and civilizations. The title of his talk reflected his new sense of self-assurance. There was nothing in it about evidence or speculation, nothing that suggested hedging or equivocation. Instead, it flatly contradicted half a century of teachings about the Oracle. "Chasm and Vapor at Delphi," it read.

.　　.　　.

Weeks later, Hale's morale rose further still. While browsing a book-shop during a visit to Stanford University, carefully inspecting shelves he had once ignored, he stumbled on a title that riveted his attention: *A Geological Companion to Greece and the Aegean,* written for the Cornell University Press by a father-and-son team. Their complementary strengths paralleled those of Hale and de Boer. Reynold Higgins had worked on Greek antiquities at the British Museum for three decades, and his son Michael Denis Higgins taught geology at the University of Quebec. It was a rare thing—a geologist exploring ancient Greece with an antiquities expert and writing the results up for publication.

Hale flipped to the section on Delphi and saw to his astonishment that the pair had independently come close to one of de Boer's recent insights.

The sanctuary at Delphi, they wrote, had a series of ancient springs that ran down the hillside and under the temple of Apollo in what appeared to be a straight line, suggesting that the waters arose along a fault. Hale felt a sense of relief. It was more evidence that he and de Boer were on the right track, that the geologist was correct in his geological intuitions and interpretations. And though Hale could be intensely competitive, he felt the book posed no threat to their priority in discovery. Higgins and Higgins, while finding evidence of a north-south fault, had completely missed the one that ran east-west under the temple. They failed to see the X.

They did, however, reject the received archaeological wisdom and speculate on a physical mechanism that may have put the Oracles into a trance. But here again, their picture was incomplete, leading to a shaky conclusion. The pair made no mention of the layers of bitumen under Delphi, which they apparently knew nothing about. Instead, they suggested that the Oracles may have breathed in carbon dioxide gas—the kind of bubbles that came up at Thermopylae and many other limestone springs around the world. However, Hale knew that carbon dioxide had no known psychoactive effects and in sufficient concentrations could be lethal if it displaced oxygen in the air. That was what he had discovered to be the case at Hierapolis in Turkey, where the priests had sacrificed small animals to the god of the underworld.

Overall, Hale was quite happy. Even if Higgins and Higgins were wrong on some of the particulars, they were kindred spirits trying to make sense out of what the ancients had claimed about Delphi. They made him feel less vulnerable, especially about the geology. Most important, they had gone out of their way to challenge many decades of conventional wisdom, to question the idea that the Oracle's euphoria had no physical basis. Instead, they lent a modern voice to the proposition that the earth itself played a role in her ecstatic union with Apollo.

*I*N MARCH 1998, de Boer arrived at Delphi a few days ahead of Hale and a Dutch film crew that had asked permission to make a documentary about the investigation. Both the geologist and archaeologist had readily agreed, increasingly sure of the rightness of their discoveries, increasingly happy to share the news. The weather cooperated this time. There was no rain, no snow, no dark sky—just sunshine and the almost narcotic warmth of early spring, the wildflowers up, the air clear and sweet. Goats ate the new greens voraciously.

After checking into the Kouros, de Boer headed for the hills, eager to see if he could find an exposed face that would help nail down the existence of a major fault running north-south beneath the temple. De Boer felt it was a prerequisite if they were to make a convincing public case for the presence of the X. As an experienced geologist, he himself judged that they had already gathered conclusive evidence and felt that the vast majority of his peers would agree. Higgins and Higgins offered evidence of that. But it was his responsibility to make sure the case was strong enough to sway doubters and skeptics, archaeologists and historians, classicists and other nonscientists who would know little or nothing about the nuances of geology and would want to see the issue in high relief.

The twin limestone cliffs known as the Phaedriades, "the Bright Ones" or "the Shining Rocks," rose up behind the temple to a height of perhaps a thousand feet. It was their intersection that formed a deep recess in the southwestern flank of Mount Parnassus, creating the lofty backdrop that had helped make Delphi a religious stage of the ancient world. On this spring day, the cliffs, living up to their name, seemed to glow as the sun bathed them and the whole Pleistos River gorge in an ethereal light.

De Boer turned to the rugged highlands north of the cliffs in his search for the fault face. He knew it was there, somewhere. The baby swarms and the line of springs and the satellite photos all said so emphatically. Now it was just a matter of discovering it, of confirming the reality of a feature that he had already described nearly a year earlier to an international group of prominent geologists. He smiled to himself at his own cocksureness and how it often left Hale slightly unnerved.

De Boer headed into the hills on foot, climbing up the ancient trail of carved limestone that zigged and zagged its way up the side of the cliffs and then cut behind them. The views were superb and kept getting better the higher he climbed, the sanctuary laid out below in miniature. Like much at Delphi, the trail too was a relic, preserved from the days when young Greek women would sing and dance their way up the slopes to honor Dionysus, seeking mystic union with the god, climbing high to worship him in the flickering depths of the Korykian cave.

The terrain behind the cliffs leveled off and narrowed into a valley lined with rocks, grass, and dark bushes. It ran northward, at a right angle to the sanctuary's east-west fault. As he moved deeper into the ravine, stands of pine trees began to dot its sides, evidence of the higher altitude and more water. To de Boer, the very presence of this long gouge in the earth seemed to suggest still more evidence of the hidden fault. He could feel it, almost taste it. He was sure the grove marked the interface of two massive blocks of limestone. It was probably one of the shadows he had seen in the satellite photos.

His prey materialized out of nowhere, up on the right, alongside the ravine—the beautiful exposed face of a limestone fault. The smooth wall emerged from a gnarled slope. Its face was perhaps sixty feet long and in places up to twenty feet high. It was not nearly as grandiose as the fault exposures east and west of Delphi. But it was nonetheless solid proof of a major crosscutting fault. They had it in their hands at last.

De Boer unpacked his instruments and proceeded to take a dozen measurements. Having done that, he looked in his notebook and compared the readings to those for the swarms of baby cross fractures on the hillside

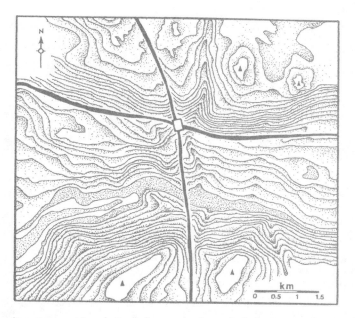

The American team envisioned two faults crossing beneath the sanctuary of Apollo to form an X—their intersection a pipeline for the rise of intoxicating gases. The topographic map shows the Pleistos River valley. Each line marks a change in altitude of fifty meters and the triangles mark high points. The Pleistos River flows at the foot of the southern cliffs, and, to the right of the sanctuary, the Castalian gorge cuts into the northern cliffs.

above the temple. The alignments were indeed the same. They were different expressions of the same underlying crack in the earth's surface.

He felt no thrill of victory. The face, after all, was what he had expected. De Boer had been studying the region for more than a decade and a half. It was simply a matter of digging a little deeper and finding the connective tissue. The emotion he experienced was a sense of professional pride, a calm sureness about his understanding of the world that made the day all the more agreeable.

Hale grew quite excited when shown the face. Little by little, the subterranean X was coming to light. This most recent of findings gave their argument new weight and increased his confidence in the whole thesis and project. More and more, it looked as if the intersection of the two faults was real.

In life and art, bestowing a name helps personalize the world and make it a bit more manageable. Now, like proud parents, the two men agreed to name the newly discovered fault the Kerna, after the main spring atop the sanctuary.

BACK AT APOLLO's home, the two prepared to sample the travertine. Rozina Kolonia had now become director of the museum and proved quite accommodating. She authorized them to chip away where they liked as long is it was done carefully and with an eye to making as few scars as possible. De Boer got out his chisel and hammer. He started near the back of the sanctuary, removing pieces of travertine from where the Kerna spring had once bubbled up. Lower down the slope, close to the temple, he chipped away at the retaining wall where so many layers of travertine had accumulated. After a few blows, a large chunk fell away, its insides revealing a labyrinth of holes and pores. It looked a little like whole-grain bread, with scores of tiny hollows. Their hopes lay on such minuscule voids. Perhaps in ancient times the holes had formed fast enough to trap a little bit of gas. Or perhaps not. They would find out. As de Boer hammered away, Hale put the chunks of rock into white cloth sample bags equipped with sturdy tie strings. He carefully wrote up labels that noted where and when they had taken the samples.

Finally, the men did the easiest collecting of all, crawling through the bowels of the temple. The archaeologist got down on hands and knees in an open space below the foundations, finding several chunks of travertine just lying there, waiting to be picked up. The temple sampling, if hard on hands and knees, was quite pleasant visually. The periphery of the foundation acted like a greenhouse to block the winds and concentrate the sun, making the dirt inside explode with a profusion of spring plants and wildflowers.

For the testing, de Boer had canvassed his peers and settled on a laboratory at Florida State University in Tallahassee. A geochemist there, Jeffrey P. Chanton, had earned a wide reputation for accuracy in the delicate art of measuring the concentration of hydrocarbon gases. Using a technique known as gas chromatography, he analyzed samples taken both on land and at sea. De Boer carefully wrapped the rocks to avoid new breakage and got them ready for shipment to Florida.

At the end of their stay, the two men headed for Thermopylae, de Boer still eager to show Hale the extravagance of the bubbling spring. This time, the weather cooperated. No snowdrifts blocked their passage over Mount Parnassus. Bulbous deposits of travertine lined the banks of the stream that splashed away from the spring. The bubbling water was hot, sending clouds of vapor into the cool air. The men donned bathing suits and slipped into the pool's steaming water.

They relaxed and talked and relaxed. It was paradise, the nearby mountains topped with snow, the heat slowly unknotting their muscles. They had found the X and done the sampling they had thought they would never do. Their faces became slack with contentment.

Hale studied the bubbles. They came up in little lines, one after the other, like beads on a necklace, rising from the bottom of the rocky pool. It was amazing. Who would have thought?

·   ·   ·

*T*HEY RETURNED to the United States eager for news about the sampling results but heard nothing for a long time and made no real progress on other fronts. Slowly, the sense of euphoria faded. De Boer began to assume the worst. The silence meant that the results would be negative, that they would show no sign whatsoever that the rocky pores of the travertine had managed to trap any kind of ancient gases.

The spring semester ended. Still there was no news. Hale, as usual, went to Portugal, which distracted him for several weeks. By midsummer the two men grew despondent. In the August heat of 1998, de Boer called Hale to discuss some old articles about Delphi he had found. Hale talked of going ahead with the evidence they had gathered to date and writing up their findings for the *American Journal of Archaeology,* one of the most prestigious forums of his profession. But he decided against it. Publishing without the travertine results would be like writing a play without the final act. They needed the sampling data.

The fall semester was almost over—the winter holidays just two weeks away—when Chanton finally called de Boer. It had been nine months since the Delphi visit.

You were right, Chanton said calmly, those travertine samples turned out to hold some gases. We found ethane and methane. Not that much but enough to show that the gases were definitely present in Delphi's spring waters. The highest concentrations came from the area of the temple. Despite his excitement, de Boer managed to match Chanton's relaxed tone, as if they were discussing the weather.

Really? That's great. What about ethylene? Did you find any?

Ethylene was the old anesthetic with the sweet aroma that produced feelings of aloof euphoria. More than ethane and methane, which could act as mild intoxicants, it seemed like it should be the main ingredient of a Delphi cocktail. It was also the gas that, the previous year, de Boer had brought to the attention of the Geological Society of London as the most likely agent for the Oracle's high. It was a theory for which he had gone especially far out on a limb.

Sorry, Chanton replied, we found no ethylene—just ethane and methane.

Chanton e-mailed de Boer the detailed findings, which showed the measurements in parts per million. The geochemist's work was a triumph of precision. One part per million equals one drop in ten gallons—by any measure an infinitesimal quantity. The data revealed a gradient in which the gas concentrations tended to increase the closer the sampling got to the temple, reinforcing the idea that crisscrossing faults there had expedited the rise of the gases.

De Boer was delighted with the results and not at all put off by the small amounts. The findings revealed that the principle was correct but said nothing about the original quantities of gas that had bubbled up long ago at Delphi. The concentrations in parts per million referred not to the gaseous intensity back then but rather to what had survived ages of diffusion through the travertine's rocky pores as well as the artificial conditions that Chanton had been required to create to do the measurements. The most important finding was the mere presence of the hydrocarbon gases, and secondarily that they emerged in a gradient suggesting that de Boer had indeed uncovered the site's geological secret. The very old rocks had been persuaded to talk.

De Boer called and faxed the results to Hale, who reacted with delight. The archaeologist told a friend that it seemed like the clinching piece of evidence. Their collaboration of more than three years had ended in success. Hale added that he was now determined to send off a paper to *Nature,* a leading science journal with a global audience. It was where Watson and Crick had announced their discovery of DNA's structure.

De Boer, while elated, wanted more. Since returning from Zakynthos and Delphi, finding the intersecting X and the north-south exposure, and learning about Higgins and Higgins, he had switched places with Hale in terms of initiative. Now it was the geologist's turn to insist on the need for more evidence. They were very close, he argued. Now was not the time to slack off. By pushing just a bit harder they could turn a convincing case into one that was rock solid. His ardor had something to do with momentum and something to do with credibility. In London, he had gone public with detailed speculations about Delphi that had yet to prove totally accurate. His strong personality and professional status tended to make him fairly relaxed about weathering the opinions of his peers. But being right—and being perceived as being right—had its attractions, even for de Boer.

In particular, he found himself baffled and fascinated by the elusive ethylene, which he still felt must be the main intoxicant. At Wesleyan, he now redoubled his study of the gas and discovered some potential reasons why Chanton had found none. Ethylene turned out to be extremely volatile and fleeting. Lighter than air, it had perhaps long ago escaped the rock, leaving the heavier gases behind.

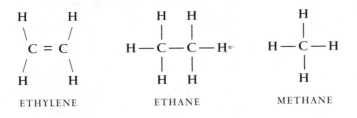

More important, he found that ethylene's chemical makeup is quite different from that of methane and ethane. They are what chemists call saturated hydrocarbons, holding as many hydrogen atoms as is physically possible—four in the case of methane, six for ethane. But ethylene, despite having two carbon atoms (like ethane), carries just four hydrogen atoms. That makes it more reactive, more dynamic. The chemical term for its state is *unsaturated*. In its volatility, it resembles the unsaturated fats, which also have fewer hydrogen atoms compared to saturated fats and are better to eat because their reactivity makes them more digestible and less likely to clog arteries. Ethylene is filled with a kind of chemical yearning to interact and merge with its surroundings, to form relationships, to change its form. In short, its character is fundamentally different from that of ethane and methane. At Delphi, since emerging from the ground, it could have morphed into another gas or wafted into the sky.

Soon, de Boer came up with a plan not only to renew the hunt for ethylene but to do much wider sampling at Delphi that in theory could strengthen their case, perhaps greatly. He proposed to test the water. They had considered that initially but had put it aside in favor of focusing on the travertine. After all, water samples would give no hint of what had been happening thousands of years ago. But now, having found strong evidence of past gas flows, they could examine the springs to see if the underlying bitumen was still enriching the waters—an open question, since the flows had presumably diminished a lot since ancient times. On the plus side, the simple act of collecting water would likely require no permit. And, best of all, they might finally discover signs of ethylene, however faint.

De Boer's overall idea was to test the two springs that were still active at Delphi and see if the comparative results supported the thesis. In theory, the Kerna spring, bubbling up along the north-south fault at the back of the sanctuary (and still accessible for testing though siphoned away by the city of Delphi), should have relatively high concentrations of hydrocarbon gases. But high compared to what? As a baseline, they could sample the Castalia, the sacred spring a half mile east of the temple's grounds. If their hypothesis was correct, gas readings from the Castalia should be lower or absent altogether. To widen the comparison, they could also sample the waters at Zakynthos, the Delphi analogue. In theory, it should give the best readings of all because of the extremely high levels of hydrocarbon leakage.

In late 1998, de Boer discussed the plan with Hale. Of course, the archaeologist said, let's do it. He called Chanton, and the Florida geochemist agreed to go to Greece after classes let out next spring, in May 1999. De Boer knew they faced another long wait to complete this new round of testing—half a year until Chanton went to Greece, and a few more months after that to get the results. All told, it would probably end up being three years since they had first asked the Greeks for permission to sample the travertine at Delphi and more than two decades since he had first agreed to go to Greece to study its rocky foundations. But he felt the potential outcome was worth it.

*E*VERY ART has its tools. For water sampling, the prerequisite is glass bottles. They are carefully engineered to make them not only impermeable to any gas but hard to break and easy to fill. Moreover, their sides are gently rounded so that stray bubbles quickly exit the top rather than getting trapped inside. And instead of screw tops or plastic lids, which might hold subtle contaminants, the glass bottles are closed by means of tapered glass stoppers. Overall, they look like old-fashioned apothecary bottles, though usually smaller.

In May 1999, after school let out, Chanton and his eleven-year-old son flew to Greece, taking along a plastic cooler full of sample bottles. The pair turned the field trip into an adventure. Driving a rental car, camping across Greece, sleeping in a small tent, they headed first to Zakynthos. On the sunny isle they picked up a bag of ice and packed it into the cooler. Then they drove to Keri beach. At the stone gazebo, they reached down into the pit. Water flowed over the tar, cool to the touch and obviously welling up from deep within the earth. It was the perfect place to start. Chanton knew he had to avoid splashing water into the bottle, since that would mix in atmospheric gases. Instead, he pulled out a large medical syringe. Attaching a section of plastic hose, he placed the tip into the cool water and pulled back on the syringe. He then gently transferred that water to a bottle, letting it overflow and quickly plugging in a stopper.

After drying off the bottle, he wrapped its seam with black electrician's tape to make sure the top stayed on. He carefully labeled the bottle and put it in the cooler. Like a refrigerator, the ice would slow the multiplication of any bacteria that happened to be inside. Some could feed on hydrocarbons, making the chemicals disappear. So countering any bacterial action was an important step. Then he redid the procedure, filling a second bottle as a backup.

The next day, the pair climbed into their car and drove north toward Xygia beach. They could smell sulfur as they traveled down the shore road but missed the turnoff to the cove and ended up higher along the northern coast. At a restaurant, they found boats available for hire, rented one, and motored back down the shoreline, admiring the sculpted bays and rugged beaches.

At Xygia, the cave area stood out because of the cloudy water. It smelled. They pulled close. The rocky face looked menacing, full of sharp angles, the limestone gnarled. Chanton would have worried about smashing the boat except that the waves were modest. Donning life vests, plunging into the cold water, they swam into the cave's open mouth. They carefully submerged a sample bottle and filled it with cloudy water. They filled two more as backups.

Later in their visit, they rode the ferry back to the mainland and headed to mountainous Delphi. Their campsite west of town was set on a high flank with remarkable views. In the distance they could see green olive orchards, the turquoise gulf, and, farther off, gray mountains, some capped in white.

After settling in, they performed the same procedures as on Zakynthos. At the edge of the sanctuary, they filled bottles at the Castalia spring. Chanton's son explored grottoes cut into the canyon's limestone walls. They waited until late in the visit to take the most important sample of all, that from the Kerna spring above the temple of Apollo.

$\mathcal{T}$HE YEAR 1999 had its distractions. In Washington, the Monica Lewinsky scandal hit the Clinton presidency hard, resulting in his impeachment and acquittal. Texas governor George W. Bush announced his candidacy for president, and Hillary Rodham Clinton announced a run for the Senate. All the while, a speculative frenzy over new technologies sent stock markets soaring to record heights.

De Boer and Hale passed the time as patiently as they could. And, as before, the wait was painfully long. Once again the holidays were approaching. It was December—a year since they had received the travertine results—when Chanton finally called de Boer to report the water findings.

Yes, he said. There are hydrocarbons all over the place. And yes, we found ethylene.

Chanton reported that, at Delphi, the Castalia spring off to the sanctuary's eastern side produced the lowest hydrocarbon readings of all, as expected. That supported the thesis. The unremarkable geology of the Castalia area presumably gave little access to the layers of bitumen far below. The water that Chanton sampled there turned out to hold 4.9 parts per million of methane and no signs whatsoever of ethane or ethylene. By contrast, Chanton found all the gases to be more abundant at the Kerna spring on the hillside above the temple of Apollo, where the team judged that the water bubbled up along one of the area's two main faults. In parts per million, the Kerna yielded 15.3 methane, 0.2 ethane, and 0.3 ethylene.

De Boer smiled to himself. Ethylene at the temple—ethylene at last. His muse had been right. The results weren't bad considering that the ground at Delphi had reportedly stopped venting its mysterious pneuma some eighteen hundred years ago.

Also, as expected, Chanton's overall findings were even better for Zakynthos. Its depths had clearly stirred the subterranean crude into a froth. At Keri beach, the samples from the tar pit turned out to contain an impressive 109.4 parts per million of methane. Strangely, the water samples held just 0.1 parts per million of ethylene—two-thirds less than the Kerna spring had produced. It seemed to de Boer that much of that light gas had probably evaporated from the tar pool prior to its sampling.

The best news came from Xygia beach, on the isle's north coast, where paraffin rather than gooey tar emerged from the earth. Chanton found the methane to be almost off the charts at 169.8 parts per million. So too, the ethane reading was relatively high at 1.6 parts per million.

De Boer savored the next measurement. At Xygia, the concentration of ethylene turned out to be the highest of all the readings from Delphi and Zakynthos—but only by a hair. The 0.4 parts per million found at the sulfurous cave slightly outdid the 0.3 reading from the Kerna spring near the temple of Apollo. Statistically, the two were in a dead heat. That made sense. The team was finding that the greatest concentrations of ethylene arose from places that showed the strongest evidence of intersecting faults. Elsewhere, little or none of the potent gas emerged. To de Boer, that finding reinforced the reality of the physical scenario he had come to visualize over the years. Of the gases, ethylene was not only the most powerful in terms of human intoxication but, once set free, the mostly likely to evade human capture. Its presence was detected only where it gushed from the depths, only where a rocky pipeline carried it swiftly upward, only where it had little time at the surface to escape or change form. In short, the geologist saw the nearly equivalent ethylene readings as yet more evidence that the team had truly come to understand the geology beneath the temple, that the rocky paths from the depths really did crisscross in the sanctuary and, in the past, had encouraged the flow of gases that promoted the Oracle's union with Apollo.

In another way, the reading from the Kerna spring spoke to the richness of the god's sanctuary. After all, if the bituminous depths of Delphi ran cooler than Zakynthos, yet produced roughly equivalent amounts of ethylene along the intersecting faults, it seemed to suggest that the temple region had a predisposition for making the gas. The geologist saw more evidence of that in the percentages. At Xygia, ethylene made up 0.2 percent of the sampled gases. At Kerna, the percentage was roughly 2 percent—ten times higher. And that tendency, he reflected, was probably even more pronounced thousands of years ago during the sanctuary's early days.

De Boer, while relishing the implications of Chanton's water analysis for their overall thesis and the understanding of Delphi's ancient rites, still found the ethylene reading from Zakynthos to be especially pleasing. It resonated with his worldview as a born-again field geologist, as a man hungry for physical evidence. With its rocky promontories, the cove at Xygia set the intersecting faults on bold display, in marked contrast to Delphi, where he had to infer their existence beneath the temple. De Boer valued Xygia as a signal piece of evidence. It was the only place in all their studies where they knew for sure—he had seen it with his own eyes, had contemplated its beauty, had spoken of its significance with his students—that two faults crossed to form an X.

SIX

Rapture

*I*N MAY 2000, Hale sailed the Aegean on a cruise sponsored by the Yale Alumni Association. He and his mentor, Donald Kagan, the classics scholar, had teamed up to lecture on great battles of antiquity. The ship made stops at Troy, Salamis, and other historic sites. But at the time, Hale was understandably focused on Delphi, not epic wars. In the ship's salon one day, he pulled down the shades, turned on a slide projector, and proceeded to give passengers and crew members an overview of the team's findings.

Newly excited by the water-sampling results, Hale went on at some length about how the sisterhood of Oracles had most likely come under the influence of intoxicating ethylene. At the end of the lecture, one of the alumni, a medical doctor from Woods Hole, Massachusetts, stood up. He volunteered that he used to study why ethylene had such a strong effect on people even in light doses. The gas, he said, turned out to be unusually potent.

Hale almost hugged the man. It was a key issue

the team had yet to explore and understand, how a mere whiff of the gas could induce euphoria. And here—in the middle of the Aegean, not that far from Delphi, in fact—a knowledgeable expert had materialized to make a number of intriguing comments and suggestions. The gods had smiled again.

The two men exchanged contact information and pledged to stay in touch, speaking repeatedly during the remainder of the voyage. Hale felt he had just discovered a critical fourth member of the team, a kind of instant soul mate. After arriving back in the United States, he eagerly told de Boer about the unexpected encounter.

Hale wrote the physician. Weeks and months went by. He wrote again. Nothing. Eventually, Hale gave up. The physician was probably too busy or away on travel. Whatever the reason, the new teammate was not to be, leaving a gap. Moreover, the desire to add a specialist experienced in medicine, physiology, and neuropharmacology—someone who could explain the role of the Delphic gases in promoting euphoria—kept growing. A book by the Geological Society of London containing their first paper on Delphi was due out in September 2000, finally, after an editor's death had delayed its publication. That paper was heavily geological, as was a manuscript that de Boer, Hale, and Chanton were preparing for *Geology,* a publication of the Geological Society of America, the oldest and most prominent such group.

If they wanted to satisfy their own curiosity about the Oracle and reach a wider audience with their findings, they needed to achieve a more complete understanding of what had actually occurred at Delphi, the men agreed. The disciplines of geology, archaeology, and chemistry were a good start but not enough to illuminate the complex whole. They needed someone who understood the nuances of the body and how different gases could affect human consciousness.

The lucky break came in the summer of 2000. In the months after the voyage, Hale had worked on a number of civic projects in Louisville that touched on South America. One was a show of folk art. Another was arranging for a South American politician to come to the University of Louisville as a visiting professor. In so doing, Hale spoke repeatedly to Henry A. Spiller, known as Rick, a local health professional who knew much about Central and South America, having grown up in Paraguay. Spiller was director of the Kentucky Regional Poison Center, an arm of Kosair Children's Hospital. Hale knew Spiller in general terms as a civic activist.

At the time, Hale, in addition to his usual blur of academic and community projects, was undergoing medical tests to see if he had lung cancer—which fortunately turned out to be a false alarm. One day in August, he went downtown to visit a doctor at Medical Towers South, a large complex. There, Hale noticed that the Kentucky Regional Poison Center resided in the same building and decided to stop in and say hello to Spiller, whom he had never met face-to-face. The director greeted him. Lean and athletic, a decade or so younger than Hale, father to a brood of young children, Spiller turned out to be quite gregarious and talkative—much like Hale. The two hit it off. As they chatted, Spiller expressed interest in archaeology. Hale told of studying the Roman villa, the Athenian navy, and the Delphic Oracle.

Spiller in turn described how the poison center handled thousands of calls every year concerning street drugs, pharmaceuticals, overdoses, household toxins, and so on. Many callers faced real emergencies, some life-and-death.

It began to dawn on Hale that Spiller might know quite a bit about the science of intoxication. The archaeologist mentioned how the team had found evidence of hydrocarbon gases at Delphi and had lots of questions about their inhalation.

What a coincidence, Spiller said. I'm studying the same thing.

A toxicologist, Spiller explained that he was investigating a hidden epidemic of huffers, kids who have too little money to buy street drugs and instead get high on such cheap, legal products as glue, gas, solvents, lighter fluid, and so on—all different kinds of hydrocarbons. The effects could include sensory distortions and damage to various organs. Huffers inhaled the substances through their mouths, or sniffed. At the time, inhalant abuse had exploded into a minor epidemic, especially among grade-school kids. Federal statistics showed that the previous year, 1999, the United States had produced more than a million new inhalant abusers.

I'm basically trying to understand the effects of light hydrocarbon gases on human subjects, Spiller said. Right now I'm writing a paper on inhalant abuse. For Hale, the moment was similar to meeting de Boer in Portugal. Suddenly, a new world beckoned.

Can the vapors be fatal? Hale asked.

Not usually, Spiller answered. But asphyxiation had been known to kill some children. And sometimes—especially if the inhaler got spooked or surprised—he could suffer heart failure.

Hale struggled to contain himself. Here they were already discussing specifics, already drawing likely parallels between huffers and the Pythias, discussing the one who died when forced to prophesize under adverse signs. Spiller would make an excellent addition to the team, Hale quickly concluded. He had the credentials, the clinical experience, the research abilities, and the street smarts. It even seemed possible that his knowledge of contemporary drug culture might shed light on the Oracle.

Hale mentioned the team's findings about ethylene and how they had come to see it as a main stimulus behind the Oracle's intoxication. Adding detail, he noted de Boer's discovery of how physicians had used it as an anesthetic around the turn of the century.

Fascinating, Spiller said. I know nothing about it. But I'd love to learn.

THE RELATIONSHIP grew fast, nurtured by interest and proximity. Like Hale, Spiller lived in the suburbs of Louisville just north of the Ohio River. The two men talked regularly and the toxicologist threw himself into the research. A quick survey of the literature showed that ethylene, ethane, and methane all had the ability to create states of mental elation, but their potency varied with the gas. Ethylene was stronger than ethane, and ethane stronger than methane. Even so, ethane had nearly the same strength as ethylene, so the two could reinforce one another. When inhaled, they moved quickly into the lungs and bloodstream, around the body, and into the brain.

Spiller found that the two gases could ease pain and induce euphoria and dreamlike states, usually with a sense of physical detachment and a loss of inhibitions. He also discovered that they differed quite a bit from narcotics, which tended to slow the brain, causing drowsiness. Moreover, narcotics were usually addictive. By contrast, the Delphic gases in light doses worked like analgesics, relieving pain without dulling consciousness. Quite rapidly, the gases could change moods and the interpretation of pain, rather than obliterating it. A person under their influence might feel something unusual but not particularly care.

Spiller explored the origins of ethylene and found that it arises not only from oil deposits and commercially from oil refineries but also—to his surprise—from fruits and flowers, which make the sweet gas in minute quantities. It acts as a hormone, helping guide the ripening of fruit, the shedding of leaves, and the opening of flowers. Though he could find no study that addressed the point, Spiller found it conceivable that the feeling of relaxed contentment that comes from sniffing a particularly rich floral bouquet might arise, at least in part, from a few ethylene molecules stimulating the brain's pleasure centers.

His main investigation centered on how people came to breathe the gas, and that research quickly led to his reviewing the birth of anesthesia back in the late eighteenth and early nineteenth centuries. Its early days fascinated him because serious thinkers penned graphic descriptions of their altered states of consciousness, even though their experimentation with the first gas—nitrous oxide—long predated the advent of ethylene. The testimonials nonetheless evoked Delphi. The descriptions, completely subjective and uncolored by modern preconceptions, seemed to hint at what the Oracles might have experienced thousands of years ago.

Humphry Davy, a young British chemist, began the explorations. He first inhaled nitrous oxide in 1798 and found to his surprise that it produced a soaring euphoria and fits of laughter and sobbing. He dubbed it laughing gas, even while reporting unpredictable effects. One inhalation produced "a thrilling, extending from the chest to the extremities," he wrote.

> I felt a sense of tangible extension highly pleasurable in every limb; my visible impressions were dazzling, and apparently magnified, I heard distinctly every sound in the room, and was perfectly aware of my situation. By degrees, as the pleasurable sensations increased, I lost all connection with external things; trains of vivid visible images rapidly passed through my mind, and were connected with words in such a manner, as to produce perceptions perfectly novel. I existed in a world of newly connected and newly modified ideas. I theorized—I imagined that I made discoveries.

Elated by his findings, he got friends and acquaintances to try the gas and record their impressions. The poet Samuel Taylor Coleridge reported "great extacy." The air of excitement eventually led to nitrous oxide parties and Davy's book, published in 1800, *Researches, Chemical and Philosophical, Chiefly concerning Nitrous Oxide, or Dephlogisticated Nitrous Air, and Its Respiration.* There he made an astute suggestion. Since the gas "appears capable of destroying physical pain," he wrote, "it may probably be used with advantage during surgical operations."

His suggestion went nowhere, and all the first experiments with the new gas focused not on medical insensibility but how it produced dramatically altered states of consciousness and feelings so extraordinary that poets likened them to paradise. Only decades later did physicians and dentists, especially in Boston, begin to pioneer the use of ether and nitrous oxide for surgery and tooth extraction. As had been the case with Davy and friends, but even more forcefully as anesthetics became widely available, a number of investigators looked into their potential for throwing open the doors of perception.

It began in earnest with Benjamin Paul Blood, a farmer and philosopher living in Amsterdam, a small town in upstate New York. In 1860, Blood went to the dentist, inhaled nitrous oxide, and found himself transported into what he later described as a transcendental realm. He repeated the experience and after some fourteen years of investigation, in 1874, published a pamphlet, *The Anaesthetic Revelation and the Gist of Philosophy.* He argued that all the great philosophers from Plato to Hegel had experienced something akin to what he felt while inhaling the gas. The revelation, he argued, was primordial, inherently incommunicable, and available to anyone. It was drug mysticism—something shamans and religious figures had enjoyed for ages—but in a powerful new form.

Blood sent his pamphlet to leading American thinkers of the day and helped inspire a small group of philosophers to try nitrous oxide. Rather than dismissing his claims as mindless drivel, they tended to affirm and even enlarge upon his conclusions, agreeing that the anesthetic produced some sort of mystic revelation.

Among the group's most celebrated members was William James, the Harvard professor and philosophic visionary who eventually served as president of the Society for Psychical Research. In an 1882 essay, he described a life-changing ecstasy that he urged on others. "With me, as with every other person of whom I have heard," he wrote,

> the keynote of the experience is the tremendously exciting sense of an intense metaphysical illumination. Truth lies open to the view in depth beneath depth of almost blinding evidence. The mind sees all logical relations of being with an apparent subtlety and instantaneity to which its normal consciousness offers no parallel; only as sobriety returns, the feeling of insight fades, and one is left staring vacantly at a

few disjointed words and phrases, as one stares at a cadaverous-looking snow peak from which sunset glow has just fled, or at a black cinder left by an extinguished brand.

James noted with some disappointment that the scribblings he made during the intoxication verged on incomprehensibility. An example: "By George, nothing but othing! That sounds like nonsense, but it's pure on-sense!" He judged that his most coherent sentence ran thus: "There are no differences but differences of degree between different degrees of differ-ence and no difference."

Two decades later, in 1902, James fondly recalled his nitrous oxide days in his signature work, *The Varieties of Religious Experience,* saying the gas re-vealed life's hidden dimensions. "One conclusion was forced upon my mind," he wrote. "It is that our normal waking consciousness, rational consciousness as we call it, is but one special type of consciousness, whilst all about it, parted from it by the filmiest of screens, there lie potential forms of consciousness entirely different."

SPILLER FOUND the descriptions by Davy and James to be much more de-tailed, personal, and expressive than those by the men who discovered the medical uses of ethylene, which debuted long after the era of laughing gas parties and anesthetic mysticism. Like many discoveries in science, their insights grew out of an accidental observation, this one in the early years of the twentieth century.

Gentlemen in those days often wore a carnation through the button-hole of a jacket as a boutonniere. Charlie Chaplin's last silent film, *City Lights,* featured him falling in love with a blind girl who pinned a carnation on his tattered jacket. An extensive business lay behind the scenes. In Chicago during the winter of 1908, carnations in a bank of greenhouses warmed by gaslight suddenly began to mature too quickly. Investigators traced the problem to gas leaks and, eventually, to ethylene, which they found to make up about 4 percent of the illuminating gas. Its dramatic effect on the plants led experimenters to investigate its effect on frogs, white rats, and a dog. The tentative results suggested that ethylene had anesthetic properties.

Fairly quickly, physicians began to study ethylene for human anesthesia and tried the gas on themselves, first tentatively, then boldly. Their reports were clinical and dry. They had no time for foolishness. These were serious men and women of science, not farmers or philosophers. Working at eminent institutions, they embodied the spirit of a new century that was moving as fast as possible to advance science and disregard the numinous. They wanted facts, not metaphysics.

Even so, their writings hinted at how the gas could cast an other-worldly spell. In 1923, the *Journal of the American Medical Association* published a long article by Arno B. Luckhardt and Jay B. Carter, investigators at the University of Chicago who did their initial work on mice, rabbits, and cats before lying down on a couch to inhale the potent gas. Under a light dose, Carter experienced what he recalled as "a sense of well-being and exhilaration." The effect was even more pronounced for Luckhardt, a physician and the senior of the two men. He expressed contentment enough to want "to lie there under the influence of the gas for all time." Throughout the experience, he felt he never lost consciousness.

The investigators found that once a person stopped breathing ethylene, the effects wore off quickly, seemingly even faster than with nitrous oxide. The two men upped the dosage on volunteers. To test the depth of anesthesia, they would pull up a pinch of forearm skin and push through a blunt-nosed safety pin. Archer C. Sudan laughed a great deal before complete anesthesia took hold. On recovery, he talked excitedly and incoherently about his experience, his speech returning to normal after several minutes. He recalled no safety pin.

As with nitrous oxide, the effects could be unpredictable. Carter, one time while coming out of deep anesthesia, became so excited that ob-

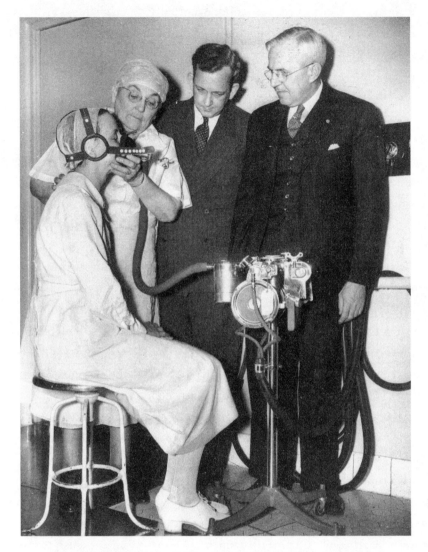

An important clue emerged when the team discovered that surgeons in
the early twentieth century had used ethylene for anesthesia. Medical
experimenters, shown here in Chicago around 1923, found that the potent
gas could produce feelings of aloof euphoria—a kind of pleasant,
disembodied high conducive to trancelike states.

servers found it necessary to hold him down. After testing a dozen subjects, the two men concluded that ethylene had many advantages over nitrous oxide. In high doses it produced not only complete insensibility to pain but total muscular relaxation and no detrimental side effects other than the possibility of slight nausea and loss of appetite, both quite temporary. Moreover, regulating the dose proved to be quite easy because the gas took effect and let go quickly. If a patient started to revive too soon, a small increase in the flow of ethylene would rapidly put her back under. And conversely, if a patient went too deep, cutting back on the flow would quickly bring her out.

Unconsciously describing what might have happened at Delphi, they found that low concentrations of the gas induced a trance that was often quite benign. The patient would remain conscious, sit up and respond to questions, feel euphoric, experience out-of-body sensations, and remember little afterward. But occasionally things got violent. Some patients uttered wild, incoherent cries and thrashed about.

Spiller's investigations of the literature showed that, from the 1920s to the 1970s, ethylene became one of the world's major anesthetic gases. As its popularity grew, scientists did numerous studies to explore its nature. One described how the gas worked extraordinarily fast, reaching concentrations in the brain sufficient for full anesthesia in less than two minutes. A 1964 report showed that, compared to nitrous oxide or ether, ethylene was nearly three times as potent.

Spiller also found that the gas's popularity eventually wore thin. By the 1970s, a half century after its introduction, ethylene had lost its following because of a constant, serious drawback: the reactive nature of the gas molecule meant that ethylene had a tendency to explode, especially when mixed with pure oxygen, which was a prerequisite for keeping patients alive. Despite great efforts to reduce the danger, the gas continued to maim and kill scores of people. By the 1970s, anesthetists had discovered new classes of anesthetic gases that were much safer, giving them the opportunity to give up their reliance on ethylene.

. . .

$\mathcal{A}$FTER MONTHS of digging, Spiller took what he had discovered and, early in 2001, began to weave it together with what he had learned from the team about the Oracle. His efforts resulted in two papers coauthored with de Boer and Hale. The longer of the two reports—appearing in the *Journal of Toxicology,* the official publication of the American Academy of Clinical Toxicology, the nation's most prominent group devoted to acquiring practical knowledge about poisons and their treatment—laid out what the authors called a multidisciplinary defense of the gaseous-vent theory. Spiller, the lead author, first reviewed how the ancient literature had consistently linked the Oracle's powers to a fissure, a spring, and gaseous fumes.

Spiller then argued that the Oracle's reported behavior resembled that of people under the influence of light doses of anesthetics in general and ethylene in particular. He noted that the Pythia's intoxication came in two distinct forms—benign trances in which she heard questions and gave visitors coherent, if cryptic, replies in verse or ordinary speech, and less frequent occasions in which she fell into violent frenzies. Both states, he remarked, were consistent with degrees of intoxication by ethylene and the early stages of anesthesia.

The Oracle's normal state, he said, seemed to correspond to what Davy, James, and their peers in the early days of gaseous experimentation had described. In each case, modern and ancient, faint whiffs of gas appeared to produce what the initiates claimed to be extraordinary revelations, what James called "an intense metaphysical illumination."

Spiller noted that the natural setting of the vent would most likely have precluded the strict regulation of the gas's flow and that the Oracle would therefore have had little control over the depth of anesthesia. "The likelihood of an adverse event is high," he wrote, considering that, over the centuries, many hundreds of women would have inhaled the poorly regulated gas. Spiller noted that Luckhardt and Carter in their pioneering

1923 paper reported that two of their twelve subjects experienced periods of excitement, confusion, and combative behavior. The implication was that dozens of oracular sessions over the ages might have gone bad.

The most detailed descriptions of the Oracle's sessions from the ancient world tended to be the ones that went awry. That tendency, Spiller noted, resembled modern medical literature in which case reports of difficulties and adverse events got published in greater detail than pedestrian cases. Spiller quoted Plutarch's story of the Oracle who was forced to prophesize for rich clients—her voice harsh, her actions nearly hysterical as she shrieked and threw herself down. That description, he said, jibed with the occasional effects of the early phases of anesthesia: confusion, agitation, delirium, and the loss of muscular coordination. In fact, it appeared that ethylene alone rather than some mix of gases could account for all the effects of the pneuma at Delphi, including the risk of death.

Spiller, in a different line of reasoning, commented on the sweet odor that would drift every so often from the *adyton*. The two were consistent. He added that the Oracle's vault would tend to concentrate the fumes around the priestess, giving her a more significant dose than visitors in the outer areas, who might only occasionally detect a faint whiff.

Spiller also noted that medical doctors who used the gas for anesthetizing patients had done so with doses that were up to 80 percent ethylene (and 20 percent pure oxygen), which produced full insensibility to pain. However, long practice showed that administering as little as 20 percent ethylene in some cases had proved sufficient for surgery. In the case of the Oracle, Spiller concluded, a light dose of less than 20 percent would probably have been sufficient for letting her remain conscious while significantly altering her state of mind.

He suggested that another clue in the proposed links between ancient Delphi and the modern operating room was the fifth-century Athenian image of the Oracle in the midst of prophecy. During an age when Greek artists usually rendered human forms in erect postures, Spiller noted, she was depicted as slumped over, as a mildly anesthetized woman might appear.

A final parallel involved amnesia. Luckhardt and Carter reported that many patients forgot their experiences under the influence of ethylene, with such memory lapses typical of the first stage of anesthesia. So too the Pythia. Spiller noted that the ancient texts suggested that the Oracle tended to forget her utterances and other events that might occur in the course of her mantic sessions.

In conclusion, Spiller and his coauthors said, the many lines of evidence suggested that the Oracle's inhalation of ethylene or a mixture of ethylene and ethane was "the probable cause" of her rapturous trance.

O F COURSE, that was just a hypothesis. In contrast, the heart of science is experimentation and observation, testing and close scrutiny of results to see how well theories actually fit the facts. As William Gilbert put it some four centuries ago at the start of the scientific revolution, "In the discovery of secret things and in the investigation of hidden causes, stronger reasons are obtained from sure experiments and demonstrated arguments than from probable conjectures." Gilbert's call for "sure experiments" played to the heroic image of science, a sort of inevitable unraveling of nature's mysteries. But in truth, as the history of science demonstrates, the process is often murky, ambiguous, and frustrating. Many—perhaps most—experiments end in failure.

Aware of the challenge and uncertainties, Spiller embarked on a test. His goal was to move their conclusions from the realm of "the probable cause" closer to what they could reasonably describe as "the likely cause" or even "*the* cause." He wanted to narrow the knowledge gap and increase confidence in the theory beyond what de Boer and the rest of the team had been able to accomplish in the previous two decades. As with all experiments, it was a gamble.

A sketchy plan started to develop. Spiller would find a volunteer to breathe the gas in an appropriate setting and carefully observe the results.

Among his questions: Could enough gas flow up from a vent in a small room to intoxicate a subject, a setup radically different from the leakproof breathing masks once used in operating rooms? How would the person feel? Would the subject experience nothing, feel mystic ecstasies? How easy or hard would it be for the subject to talk if she got really high? Could a person outside the subject's immediate area smell the ethylene? How far away might the odor travel? And the ultimate question, though a positive answer seemed unlikely: Would the subject feel any prophetic impulses or experience any predictive visions?

In short, he wanted to know how plausible their theory was in its details and to see if the particulars of an experiment would confirm their ideas or throw them into doubt. Of course, Spiller mused, it went without saying that his oracle would have to be a woman, a mature woman, someone who knew something of the world if not the bliss of communing with Apollo.

After consulting with Hale about how large the simulated *adyton* should be, Spiller realized that he had the perfect site right at hand—his garden shed. Set next to a small woods, it was large enough to comfortably hold a volunteer in a realistic setting but small enough to keep the gas fairly concentrated at least for a minute or so before it leaked out. Moreover, the shed was far enough from his home to avoid the danger that household flames and sparks might accidentally ignite the highly flammable gas. Finally, Spiller had equipped his shed with two thick metal cables that, like tent ropes, held it down. He had added them as a precaution against high winds, the region having survived a few tornadoes. But since the anchors for the cables ran two feet into the ground, the wires also had the unintended effect of electrically grounding the shed, lessening the chance that stray buildups of static electricity might ignite the vapors and cause a violent explosion.

He ordered the ethylene. Typically, it came in forms that were anywhere from 98.00 to 99.99 percent pure. The usual contaminants, he discovered, could include small amounts of methane, ethane, propane, acetylene, propylene, carbon dioxide, hydrogen, oxygen, nitrogen, and sulfur. The tank Spiller got was the highest possible grade, virtually taintless and costing about twice the normal price. He figured his oracle deserved the best.

Rather unexpectedly, late in the summer of 2002, he found his volunteer in the Louisville suburb of Lanesville, Indiana, where he lived with his wife and five children. He recruited her after he had published the two papers and while he was making general preparations for the experiment. As it turned out, Dionysus aided the process. Just as Portuguese red wine had played a role in the project's inception, now a liberal decanting of homemade beer helped relax both the would-be experimenter and the subject.

It happened on a Saturday evening in August just after Spiller came back from a family vacation. He and his oldest daughter, Sarah, went over to a neighbor's house to thank them for taking care of their dog. Sarah was a friend of Meg Capshew, whom she knew from school. It was Meg's older brother Ben who had taken care of the dog, and Spiller needed to pay him.

Maureen, a smart, confident woman with an easy smile and no shortage of cordiality, welcomed them in. Spiller sat down at the dining room table to chat. The dining room of the Capshew residence no doubt served as the scene of many a fine meal, but it seconded nicely as an exhibition space for the achievements of home brew, its walls lined with signs and glasses and vats and bottle after bottle of homemade beer and wine. The Capshews took pride in the paraphernalia. Maureen was vice president of FOSSILS, Fermenters of Special Southern Indiana Libations Society. Her husband, Bob, had long officiated at LAGERS, the Louisville Area Grain Extract Research Society. The main focus of both clubs was making and drinking beer. At the start, some years earlier, participants had taken polite sips at parties. But the quality had improved dramatically over the years as members gained experience. Several of them, including Maureen and Bob, had toured breweries in Europe, traveling by bus from Belgium, to the Netherlands, to Germany, to the Czech Republic, sampling their way across the Continent and learning more about the intricacies of the art. The Capshews now prided themselves on their Belgian ale.

So when Bob and Maureen offered Spiller a home brew, he gladly accepted. And another. After all, he had just survived an all-day drive in the family vehicle. Good neighbors were extending themselves. It was a warm summer evening and the beer was refreshingly cool.

As Spiller and the Capshews chatted, the conversation inevitably turned to what the director of the Kentucky Regional Poison Center was up to these days. He told of his new project with university professors who were studying how the Oracle of Delphi got high. Spiller mentioned the gas thesis and the scientific papers and how he was now thinking of trying to re-create the *adyton*. He mentioned that he had already obtained a tank of the intoxicating gas, ethylene.

Maureen and Bob listened with rapt attention. Not only was the topic intrinsically interesting, but their son Ben was studying Latin in high school and developing an interest in Greek and Roman antiquity. Ben had heard about the Oracles in Latin class.

Imagine, Spiller said, breathing in whiffs of ethylene to try to achieve the kind of euphoria that helped the Oracle commune with Apollo thousands of years ago.

Wow, said Maureen and Bob.

Before he knew it, Spiller found himself popping the question. Recruiting for the experiment had been the last thing on his mind as he unwound from vacation. But the moment seemed right.

Maureen thought about it, imaging herself as the high priestess at the temple of Apollo.

Sure, why not? It will be an educational experience for Ben and the rest of the family, a real science project, not just something cooked up by a teacher or the state science board. It will help Ben better understand what the Oracles were all about.

They drank a toast.

Afterward, her kids said they supported her decision, and some of their friends said she was cool for doing the experiment.

But at one point Meg got worried. She asked if the gas was addictive.

It might be, Maureen replied. I guess we'll know if I start hanging out in Rick Spiller's garden shed all the time.

*T*HE DOORWAY was low enough to smack foreheads, so Spiller had to crouch down and show special care as he conducted a major cleanup and rearrangement of the shed's contents. On the floor of the mock *adyton,* Spiller laid a thin hose, ran its end through a cement block, and arranged some rocks around it for a touch of authenticity. It was meant to look, at least a little bit, like a natural fissure. Whatever the setup's artistic merits, the end of the hose was indisputably ready to act as a gaseous vent. He then buried the rest of the hose under some loose gravel and ran it out of the shed. To complete the picture, he moved a lawn chair inside, placing it near the vent.

Our oracle, he thought, deserves more than a tripod.

A translucent panel at the shed's back let in some daylight. Even with the doors closed, he figured, Maureen would have no need for a flashlight or an electric bulb. Spiller was glad of that—one fewer fire hazard.

Another neighbor, Dave Levdansky, a genius with things mechanical, helped Spiller set up the hose and the ethylene tank, including a gauge that showed how full it was. From vent to tank, all told, the hose ran about twenty feet. They carefully inspected its length for kinks or holes.

The test fell on a Saturday. All was quiet in Lanesville, with many neighbors still away on vacation. If the setting was surreal—a model of suburban America, with a garden shed serving as the holy of holies—they were nonetheless making a rather bold, unpretentious bid at trying to replicate a Greek rite that no one to their knowledge had performed for nearly two thousand years. In a small way, what they were doing could be viewed as historic.

Right at ten a.m., the prearranged time, Maureen showed up with Meg and Ben. A small crowd milled about during the final preparations. The day was perfect—bright sunshine, moderate temperatures, and virtually no wind. That helped. It seemed like Apollo's endorsement. Maureen sat down in the shed, ready to go. It was dim compared to the bright outdoors, a bit like a crypt. Spiller closed the doors. It grew darker.

Dave cranked back on the valve and the ethylene began to flow.

Maureen heard the hiss and tried to steady her breathing—in and out, in and out. She relaxed. It was nothing. In truth, it was sort of fun. Who ever got to play Oracle?

The smell was uniquely sweet, a perfumy kind of fruitlike odor.

She felt a tingling in her hands and feet, almost a numbness. Her head grew light and she could feel herself becoming giddy.

How do you feel? Spiller called.

Maureen laughed. The water's fine. Come on in.

The plan, such as it was, had no real provisions for last-minute volunteers. But it was clear after a while that things were going smoothly and it seemed like the right thing to do.

Dave Levdansky entered the shed, bringing in another lawn chair.

Finally, Spiller went in too. By the time he did, the lead experimenter had been monitoring the situation for a half hour or so—long enough to reassure himself that things were safe. Maureen was not about to lapse into unconsciousness or have some kind of violent reaction. And he had already checked repeatedly to see how far from the shed the ethylene could be detected. He caught the odor up to twenty-five feet away, making the ancient scenario seem quite plausible. At Delphi, his test suggested, visitors outside the *adyton* had a good chance of smelling the gas.

Oooh, this feels good, Spiller thought as he started to breathe deeply. This is very pleasant.

He couldn't believe he was sucking gas, the director of the Kentucky Regional Poison Center, the man who studied huffers, a national expert who ran programs that discouraged kids from messing around with drugs. It was so unlikely, so incongruous. Here he was doing a street thing, though as a scholar, Spiller reminded himself, a scholar. He was going to be clinical and skeptical and objective. He knew this stuff cold as a scientist and was not about to be swayed by subjectivity.

Then he giggled.

It caught, and the three of them started giggling and laughing and slapping their legs, sitting in their makeshift *adyton,* rocking on their lawn chairs, switching positions, jabbering happily, oblivious of most everything but their own bliss.

Spiller, wanting to see how much gas and time remained for the experiment, got up to check the gauge. Unsteady on his feet, he opened the shed doors and proceeded to slam his head into the low doorway.

Whoa, he said. The response was pure habit. He felt no pain.

Dave Levdansky got up and did exactly the same thing, smacking his forehead.

Maureen watched in disbelief.

I'm not moving, she thought. I'm fine right where I am.

Eventually, she did wander out to see what was happening. Spiller and Dave were stumbling down a hill, wandering around like drunken sailors.

The experiment was clearly over. Forty-five minutes after turning on the gas, the experimenters judged that the ethylene was nearly gone. So was their composure. There was no question that what had started out as a solemn enterprise had ended up resembling a drunken party. In a minute or so, her head cleared, and Maureen felt as if she was back to normal. The experiment was a success, though silly beyond imagining. By dint of audacity, they had all become Oracles, or at least modern versions of them. Though, as they talked, they agreed that their recollections of the experience were already starting to fade.

.　　.　　.

*H*ALE FOUND himself increasingly distracted and busy with his own projects, especially his book on the Athenian navy. In addition, off Greece in the Aegean, with a different set of scholars, he began hunting for the lost fleets of the Persian Wars, seeking to bring triremes back to life and retrieve some of the vast treasure of arms and armor believed to have gone down with the ancient warships. The rower had turned his avocation into expert knowledge that he brought to bear on a range of scholarly endeavors. Hale's crush of civic and academic obligations meant something had to give. His choice was to devote less time to the Oracle.

One of his last contributions during this period was to help write an article for *Scientific American,* his third for the magazine. Hale was the lead author, followed by de Boer, Chanton, and Spiller. It was the only time all four men appeared in print together. Hale worked hard not only on the text but on the illustrations, which in vivid cutaways showed how the faults at Delphi criss-crossed beneath the temple. In the article, the scientists wrote that the main lesson they took away from their collaboration was not the truism that modern science could illuminate old mysteries. Rather, it was how much science stood to gain if it approached problems with the same kind of interdisciplinary fervor that the Greeks themselves had displayed. In their own case, the rewards had been considerable.

*T*HE FRENCH seethed but said little. Finally, a few articles appeared that scorned the discovery. One quoted scientists from the French National Center for Scientific Research, the preeminent organization of its kind.

A geologist there conceded the possible existence of fractured limestones at Delphi but said he doubted they could continuously produce gas in concentrations sufficient to intoxicate people. He also cast doubt on gases explaining how pilgrims could detect a strange, sweet odor wafting from the *adyton,* as Plutarch reported. Near volcanoes, he said, people might whiff egglike odors but could never smell fumes arising from cracks in the earth.

Jean-Paul Toutain, a gas chemist at the French center, expressed acerbic disbelief about the whole thesis. "Jelle de Boer measured only 'traces' of gases that could be found only with difficulty in the water," he said. "That does not prove that these gases passed to the air. Besides, with such weak concentrations, the Pythia would have felt nothing at all!"

$\mathcal{D}$E BOER still had passion for the inquiry and confidence in the team's work. He felt the French were grasping at straws, nervously trying to avoid the embarrassment of having overlooked the answer to one of history's great riddles for more than a century. Their barbs were caricatures of the truth, he argued. The team's research suggested that the gas flow at Delphi could have been stronger in the past and then weakened, as Plutarch implied in speaking of the pneuma's variability. Sampling the water and the travertine had proved only the correctness of the principal, not the actual gas concentrations in antiquity.

Even without the French criticism, de Boer had long pondered the question of how weak emissions of potent gases at the temple might have become stronger. And now, though having studied Delphi for more than two decades, though still teaching at Wesleyan and approaching retirement age, he pursued the question.

After much research, he concluded that the authorities at the temple of Apollo had likely set up a mechanism in the *adyton* that let meager flows of ethylene build up over time, concentrating them enough so that their release was sufficient to aid the divine frenzy. He suspected that the arrangement was especially important in the Oracle's latter days as the faults beneath the temple closed because of earthquakes or became clogged with travertine, diminishing the flow of gases. In 2002, as Spiller performed his private experiment and the French voiced public contempt, de Boer investigated the issue with his usual energy.

His hunch centered on the odd limestone block that the French had found in the *adyton* and that Holland, the American archaeologist, had identified as a conduit for clouds of potent, drug-laden smoke. De Boer had developed an alternative hypothesis that he felt not only explained the facts better but tied the team's set of ethylene inferences and evidence into a persuasive whole. In many ways, it represented the culmination of his intellectual journey.

As Holland had proposed, de Boer saw the block as a central part of the *adyton*'s foundation. But instead of visualizing it as resting over a large subbasement where the priestess burned hemp or other mind-altering plants, he argued that it sat atop the fissured bedrock and spring, where it acted as a funnel to collect the gases.

Like Holland, he imagined a layered stone assemblage. First came the block, then a base for the two eagles, then the conical omphalos. So too, he saw all three penetrated by holes that when aligned made a conduit leading into the *adyton.* The shaft, smaller at the top than the bottom, would have acted like a bottle to collect lungfuls of gas.

In a new twist, de Boer visualized a small cap that would have sat atop the omphalos, keeping the gases collecting and building up below. The Oracle would have removed the cap to release the pent-up flow of ethylene and other gases, doing so once a month on Apollo's special day when earnest supplicants came for the god's advice.

Once released, the gases, slightly lighter than air, would have drifted upward, filling the *adyton.* He assumed that semidarkness was necessary to interact with the god of light—a precaution that also would have limited the danger of explosions if gas concentrations became too high. Some gas would rise to the low ceiling (if the sanctum had a roof) and from there occasionally waft into the visitor's area, where petitioners every so often would have gotten a whiff of the sweet fragrance.

De Boer was the first to admit that his thesis was tentative and the clues sketchy. Not only was it based on a number of inferences and assumptions, but one of the central pieces of evidence—the omphalos— had disappeared from a place of honor in the Delphi museum long ago, so he had no way to study it for signs that might have strengthened his case. De Boer wanted to confirm its antiquity and—just possibly—see if some of the surface materials might have retained traces of the intoxicating gases. He felt the riddle would probably remain unsolved unless the omphalos reappeared sometime in the future. Still, de Boer was loath to give up. He sought and found other evidence to bolster his case.

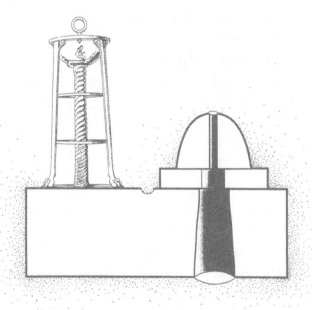

De Boer, the team leader, envisioned the odd limestone block from the Oracle's chamber acting as a reservoir to concentrate weak flows of ethylene, the main intoxicating gas. The vapors would rise into the Oracle's sanctum through conjoined holes in the block and a hollow omphalos.

In doing so he focused on the wider mystery of the existence of the omphalos. What made it so special? How did it come to symbolize the center of the earth, the umbilicus of the cosmos? Perhaps it represented the legacy of a primitive stone fetish, as some scholars argued. But the ancient literature hinted at other meanings that seemed to support the thesis. De Boer discovered that the term *omphalos* was often used interchangeably with another Greek word, *stoma,* meaning "mouth," reinforcing the idea that the Greeks saw the conical stone as penetrated by a hole. Apollo's holy breath, it was said, rose out of a stoma.

Ancient art echoed the linkage. Its images at times associated the mystic pneuma with the conic stone, implying that the vapors had so wafted into the *adyton.* De Boer found a striking picture of an ancient Greek vase dated to the fifth century BCE—the same period as when the Athenian artist drew the prophesizing Oracle. It had been uncovered at Spina, an ancient trading emporium on the Adriatic where Greeks and Etruscans had lived together and where merchants had imported vast quantities of Greek goods. The vase showed Apollo and Artemis, brother and sister, standing on either side of a small conic stone. From its center rose wavy lines apparently meant to signify fumes. To de Boer, it seemed to represent the pneuma rising from the omphalos. And the gods were beckoning, eager to give humans a glimpse of what it meant to be part of the divine family.

SEVEN

Mystic Clue

O NE DAY TOWARD the end of a visit to Delphi, after exploring the rugged site with the scientists and sharing many meals, I asked de Boer how he felt about the discovery, thinking he would warm to the subject. After all, the finding was a hit. He and his teammates had given lectures around the globe, published papers in top journals, granted many interviews, and even appeared in television documentaries. He was obviously proud of what he had done. Moreover, it seemed to me that no other aspect of his career had achieved such wide recognition. His investigations of the Oracle were in fact some kind of culminating event in his professional life.

Remarkably, he said the discovery was no big deal and that its admirers tended to emphasize its sensational aspects over its substance. De Boer immediately backpedaled, saying his comments probably sounded arrogant or like the crankiness of a cold Dutchman. But then he continued. The enthusiasts always tended to emphasize the drug angle, he said, always referred to how the Oracle was like a kid sniffing glue or a teen getting high on lighter fluid. That missed the point, de Boer said. He added that the narrowness of the standard interpretation left him quite disappointed.

So was he serious in disavowing what seemed like the central finding of the investigation? In polite society, of course, people often use speech not just to reveal thoughts but to mislead, and with that in mind I considered some possible explanations. I wondered about false modesty but judged it inconsistent with his personality. Then too, I thought, maybe de Boer was trying to distance himself from the perception that he was seeking popular approval, which can be frowned on in scholarly circles. But he struck me as too headstrong for that. Or perhaps, I reasoned, de Boer was defensive about the drug angle because the team's work might be seen as some kind of tacit approval for getting high. But that seemed unlikely. It seemed as improbable as a lawyer worrying about taking on a troubled client.

Ultimately, I judged that de Boer was speaking his mind. That impression grew over the months and years. He proved to be a rare thing—a scientist who saw his work in a modest light and who, more important, saw it as addressing serious issues of philosophy. De Boer's view resonated with questions that had lingered in the back of my mind ever since I studied as an undergraduate with a man named David Hull, who then taught philosophy at the University of Wisconsin. He challenged a basic tenet of modern science—that the march of progress would reveal a seamless web of knowledge in which investigators linked one theory and discipline to another, mapping out networks of intellectual ties and ultimately reducing the complexities of life to simple laws of physics. In contrast, he argued that close investigation showed that no such thing was possible.

Hull's critique, while fascinating, struck me as radical and unlikely to make headway. It seemed like centuries of science had succeeded in showing that the universe was, in essence, a giant machine that researchers were rapidly breaking down into increasingly small bits and explaining very nicely in the language of mathematics. Over time, I noted with some surprise that Hull's star rose quite high, his work widely admired and he himself eventually serving as president of the Philosophy of Science Association, his field's top post.

Now, intrigued by de Boer's comments about the Oracle, I dug back into the philosophy of science and discovered that the geologist's comments put him at the forefront of a furious international debate, one that Hull had foreshadowed decades earlier. It pitted staunch defenders of expansive science against those who argued that—in its current state of development, and perhaps forever—it failed to explain some of the world's most important features and possibilities, including all manner of things psychic and spiritual.

With something of a shock, I saw that the fume discovery threw the debate into high relief, illustrating its issues with remarkable clarity. It turned out that de Boer and the other men had similar views. Drawing not on books and academic disputes but their own experiences in the world of physical inquiry, they had come to see the limitations of reduction and in some cases to consider the existence of shadowy worlds beyond the reach of contemporary science. Their reflections might have deserved no more consideration than those of Myers and Dempsey, Freud and Dodds, except for the fume discovery's philosophical import. It gave the discussion new depth.

THE DICTIONARY calls metaphysics the branch of philosophy that deals with first principles and the problems of ultimate reality. It is rare in college curricula and often considered the highest form of philosophy. Even so, like the air we breathe, its questions involve the most basic things around us, including time, space, causation, being, substance, and identity. *Metaphysics* literally means after or beyond physics. But that definition is misleading because it turns out that science in general—despite its popular image as solid, factual, and no-nonsense—is full of metaphysics and empirically unprovable assumptions about the nature of reality. Whole books explore such beliefs. One is that nature is uniform. Another is that the universe is composed of particles moving according to laws that mathematics can fully describe. By definition, the metaphysics of science are too elementary to be explained in terms of science. In that narrow sense, metaphysics goes beyond physics. It is more basic.

Most fundamentally, de Boer and his colleagues questioned the heavy metaphysical responsibilities that contemporary science had thrust onto a foundation of the scientific process known as reduction. It is the general approach by which the men had made their discovery at Delphi. The scientists, like some scholars, valued its practical accomplishments but doubted its billing as the foremost path to true knowledge.

Reduction is the process by which scientists find points of investigative entry into natural systems that would otherwise be impenetrably complex. During reduction, scientists break nature into its constituent parts, moving down through the complex hierarchy of matter to focus on levels where interactions are more fundamental and mechanisms easier to understand. Ultimately, reduction seeks to shed weight, to dispense with irrelevancies in the effort to expose nature's sinews.

It is, indisputably, an engine of great progress. Reduction found that most elements in the universe arise in exploding stars, that many ruinous diseases stem from germs, that earthquakes begin as simple breaks in bedrock, that displays of lightning spring from the rapid flow of subatomic particles, and that the color of human eyes is determined by genes that pass heritable traits from one generation to the next. Such examples number in the thousands.

All that is pretty straightforward. Where reduction gets divisive is when its supporters claim that its realm includes not just physics and the other sciences but enormous swaths of metaphysical territory as well, as they have done intermittently in the course of the twentieth century and with increasing bravado in recent decades to the point that their assertions are now frequently seen as the conventional wisdom. The result is that the celebrated process has given birth to a contentious worldview.

Its champions claim that reduction's many successes show that the nature of ultimate reality is completely physical, that nothing exists beyond elemental forces and physical objects and their properties. This metaphysical leap is sometimes known as reductive naturalism. By whatever name, it is an act of faith rooted in materialism. Another *ism* it echoes is scientism, the belief that the investigative methods of the natural sciences should be applied to all fields of inquiry.

Reductive naturalism has many detractors inside and outside the sciences, apparently more as its popularity has grown. Some are known as holists, others as emergentists. One charge is that shattering the world into increasingly small bits can produce a narrow kind of materialism that advertises itself as addressing the major questions in life but ultimately sidesteps them and replaces them with endless bouts of skeptical inquiry and what religious critics fault as empty secularism.

Popular literature echoes the charge. Dan Brown in his bestseller *Angels and Demons* has the pope's chamberlain deride the mechanistic grinding of scientific inquiry. Its action, the cleric says, "has left us in a world without wonder. Our sunsets have been reduced to wavelengths and frequencies. The complexities of the universe have been shredded into mathematical equations."

The dispute can be strident and the issues knotty. But its metaphysical nub is fairly straightforward: Reductionists tend to see complex systems as the sum of their parts. Holists see them as greater, contending that novelties, unique properties, and nonmaterial qualities emerge at higher levels of organization.

Water is a good example. The molecule is composed of two atoms of hydrogen and one of oxygen and by itself exhibits few distinctive traits. But put trillions of them together and remarkable things start to happen—dripping, sloshing, rippling, splashing, sparkling, and freezing, which under the right conditions can produce a blizzard of snowflakes, each one unique. Other conditions can spawn any number of hurricanes, each one deadly in its own unique way. In other words, water in bulk exhibits qualities far beyond those of the molecule itself. Its properties and behaviors transcend its parts. Examples of emergence can run to very high levels of complexity where the novel properties become quite exotic and unpredictable, as with the most intricate emergent phenomena of all, life and human consciousness. Some analysts call emergence the god principle. But its transcendent qualities require no mysticism. Consider information. It can exist independently of any particular physical medium—as writing in a book, pulses in a computer, or chemicals in a brain. But the data, while rooted in physical objects, can have higher properties, at times much higher. It can, for instance, convey the subtleties of a Bach sonata, a Shakespeare sonnet, or a Rembrandt portrait. It starts in but ultimately transcends the material world.

Reductionists admit to the emergence of complex properties but some take a metaphysical leap to insist that they are entirely material in nature and—in theory if not yet in practice—completely attributable to aspects of matter. As evidence, they point to forms of scientific analysis that can make headway going in the direction opposite of reduction, from the bottom up, following the footsteps of physical emergence but seeking to put it on a solid foundation of rational analysis. Of late, several new fields have blazed this path. Chaos theory, complexity theory, and their little cousin, emergence theory, investigate how simple rules in theory can produce blindingly intricate structures, such as ant colonies, human brains, and city neighborhoods. Advocates say the work is accelerating and likely to produce breakthroughs in explaining the universe.

But so far, success in predicting emergent properties has been uneven at best. And little or no progress has been made against such tricky problems as snowflakes or life's complexities or—hardest of all—human consciousness. Skeptics see the new fields as no more than rallying metaphors. Historians see the upward scientific push as ignorant of the century of difficulties that dogged philosophers trying to forge a logic of emergence. Holists argue that the vast majority of life's complexities are irreducible to basic physical properties and will forever lie beyond science and materialist metaphysics. No computer algorithm, they say, will mimic a Bach, Shakespeare, or Rembrandt. Reduction, they say, can go from the complex to the elementary but its reverse can only rarely go from the elementary to the complex. The difficulty is that the whole is generally greater than the sum of its parts, especially at higher levels of organization.

Right or wrong, enlightening or not, the reductive impulse is quite old, if not its new metaphysics. The ancient Greeks sought to reduce the fundamentals of nature to just four elements—earth, air, fire, and water. Many thinkers of the ancient world saw the apparent multiplicity of nature as superficial. They held that the blur of perception hid a reality not of many things but of a few.

Criticism of excessive reduction is also quite old. The Oracle herself is reputed to have questioned the impulse on at least one occasion, during an inquiry about a boat. If, she asked a visitor, all the planks of a boat were replaced over time, would it still be the same boat? The owner of the vessel—shunning the reductive impulse—would probably say yes, even if during its long history of repairs he occasionally substituted pine planks for oak ones, or even if he eventually replaced all the original material. The boat was clearly more than the sum of its parts, more than the planks. Its heart and soul had to do with subtle relationships among the planks, with unique associations, with ties and organizing principles that gave the boat its characteristic shape, appearance, and abilities.

Today, the front lines of reduction involve not planks but thousands of elementary units such as chromosomes, photons, molecules, neurons, atoms, cells, proteins, monomers, quarks, chloroplasts, mesons, neutrons, membranes, X-rays, nuclei, gluons, prions, and ribosomes. Amazingly, most are invisible. The discovery of increasing numbers of these invisible units lies behind the vibrancy of modern science and one of its defining characteristics—specialization. Today, methods and nomenclature can be so different from one field to the next that specialists can have a hard time understanding one another.

In modern reduction, scientists work through a hierarchy of disciplines in their effort to wrestle phenomena down to more basic levels of understanding. One way to draw up the hierarchy and its subject matter goes like this:

paleontology	past life
ecology	living populations
anthropology	humanoid history
sociology	human social behavior
psychology	minds
biology	bodies
physiology	organs
cytology	cells
microbiology	germs
virology	viruses
genetics	genes
biochemistry	life molecules
chemistry	atoms, elements, compounds
physics	subatomic particles, elementary forces

The list is incomplete. Several disciplines fall outside its neat progression because they tend to be interdisciplinary or draw on several branches of primary science. For instance, geology can employ the principles of physics, chemistry, and biology. Astronomy draws on chemistry and physics.

The ultimate goal of physical reduction is to move down through this kind of hierarchy in search of simpler, more powerful explanations. Physics is at the bottom because it studies matter and energy at their most fundamental levels, finding the origin of much causation in the collisions of tiny particles of which much of the universe is apparently made. The downward push is ubiquitous. For instance, it recently went from psychology to biology in discovering that at least some forms of schizophrenia seem to arise from a specific gene. It went from biology to chemistry in finding that the diverse proteins of the human body are built from just twenty amino acids. And it went from chemistry to physics in learning that the ninety or so basic elements of nature are made of combinations of just three subatomic particles—electrons, protons, and neutrons. One of reduction's most fascinating and often disturbing frontiers is modern neuroscience. It seeks to turn mind into matter, often challenging the traditional view of what it means to be human, reducing ideas and feelings to the intricate biochemistry of firing neurons, to the whirl of a complex machine. In the future, scientists expect wide progress. Physicists talk about finding a Theory of Everything—jokingly known as TOE—one grand equation that might fit on a T-shirt yet explain the universe and its diverse phenomena, including why a person smiles.

Of late, scientists have characterized this kind of advance as accelerating. Edward O. Wilson, the distinguished Harvard biologist, in his book *Consilience: The Unity of Knowledge,* predicts that feats of reduction will soon expand to include many areas of human endeavor far beyond the traditional scope of the sciences, including not only religion but art, culture, ethics, and—most important because of its centrality to the rest—the mind. "All tangible phenomena, from the birth of stars to the workings of social institutions, are based on material processes that are ultimately reducible, however long and tortuous the sequences, to the laws of physics," he asserted. The ultimate goal of science, Wilson added, is to sail on a "Magellanic voyage that eventually encircles the whole of reality."

To be sure, specialists have no monopoly on the reductionist agenda. Its influence is seen in the wide hope for wonder cures and magic bullets to fight disease, even among people wholly unfamiliar with the reductionist idea. In the United States, it became law in 1980 when the Supreme Court ruled that man-made life could be patented, in effect saying that no distinction exists between living and nonliving things, between life and atoms. A few knowledgeable critics railed against the decision as an unjustified break with centuries of Western tradition.

Reduction has a swashbuckling image that arises in part because of its reputation for doing in old theories. For instance, large flows of electrons replaced Zeus, the father of lightning. Molecules of hydrogen and oxygen triumphed over the ancient notion of water as a primary element. Psychological models of delusion surrounding eccentric old women did in witches. And so on.

Centuries of scientific advance have produced much praise for reduction, especially the practical benefits. But many humanists have come to see its philosophical and metaphysical extremes as analogous to a wrecking crew methodically smashing its way through the Louvre. Among other things, they fear the assault will sow an unwavering skepticism that rejects not only humanistic beliefs but much of the commonsense world, including such things as modern art and cocktail parties. The fear is not unfounded.

Strict reductionists hold that the process defines reality and that all else is mirage—that the more fundamental objects in nature are more real than, say, parts of the material world that confront the human senses. Sir Arthur Eddington, a famous British astronomer, championed this view in what became known as the Two Table paradox. The table that he saw with his eyes, Eddington wrote, was an illusion. More real was the one science described as mostly empty space populated by swarms of tiny electrons, their nature and behavior well known and precisely measured. "Modern physics has by delicate test and remorseless logic assured me that my second scientific table is the only one which is really there," he said in a popular book, dismissing all else as feints of "the Alchemist mind." His kind of dismissive attitude is summed up in the popular reductionist phrase "nothing but," as in life is nothing but a series of chemical reactions.

Scientific liberals counter that reduction simply illuminates a slice of an enormously complex universe that is largely unexplored and perhaps opaque in some cases to human understanding. To them, it marks the beginning of the unknown, like the edge of a map.

A main charge leveled by philosophers and many scientists themselves focuses on what reductive naturalism tends to leave out—the big, messy, complex issues of life, things like truth, human values, justice, courage, moral goodness, purpose, love, history, political revolution, beauty, passion, ethics, intellectual integrity, consciousness, and what the Oracle of Delphi might have called the boat issue. Critics say that even discovering all there is to know about individual bits at the bottom of the reductionist pile often fails to reveal how complexity can emerge and how the system functions as a whole, despite Wilson's hopes to the contrary. Carbon atoms reveal little of diamonds, water molecules little of wetness, bricks little of a cathedral. As economists put it, every complex economy is more (or sometimes less) than the sum of its parts.

Recently, Michael P. Lynch, a young American philosopher, has argued persuasively that reductive naturalism harbors a contradiction that undoes its claim to being the exclusive means of obtaining reliable knowledge. He says reductionism cannot define truth, a nonmaterial quality, and that the reductionists therefore cannot claim that their worldview is the one true path to understanding. If truth matters, he says, pressing home his point, reductive naturalism must be false.

John C. Polkinghorne, a theoretical physicist turned Anglican priest, makes a similar point in noting how the process threatens to obliterate all logic. Reductionism, he says, "is suicidal. Not only does it relegate our experiences of beauty, moral obligation, and religious encounter to the epiphenomenal scrap-heap. It also destroys rationality. Thought is replaced by electro-chemical events. Two such events cannot confront each other in rational discourse. They are neither right nor wrong. They simply happen."

At their boldest, critics allege that the perceived triumphs of reduction are producing a spiritual crisis in Western civilization. The unconstrained

237

method, they say, works like acid to eat away at the foundations of the good and the worthy, replacing them with an empty doctrine that rejects all morality. "Reductionism today is a mask for nihilism," said Viktor E. Frankl of the University of Vienna. The challenge, he added, is "how to maintain, or restore, a unified concept of man in the face of the scattered data, facts and findings as they are furnished by a thoroughly compartmentalized science."

THE EFFORTS of de Boer and company ended in the triumphal grounding of the Oracle's nebulosity in an intoxicating molecule, ethylene. As such, it was an impressive case of reduction, as clear as any in the history of science. A complex phenomenon turned out to be rooted in a simple mechanism. It was, arguably, the reduction of religion to chemistry or, perhaps more plausibly, the reduction of psychology to chemistry. However described, the finding suggested that the Oracle's otherworldly visions resulted from nothing more mysterious than the chemical excitation of her neural circuits. In short, the high priestess got high.

The standard view of the discovery portrayed it as eliminating the Oracle's spiritual and mystic side. Moreover, the deconstruction went beyond the humbling of the priestess a century earlier when the French failed to find any evidence of a vaporous cleft. The discovery of the intoxicating fumes, after all, was a positive development, not a negative one. It carried more weight.

Reductionists now claimed that the team had unearthed proof that her divine marriage was a delusion, her merging with all time and space a hallucination, if not an outright lie. The priestess, like Maureen Capshew, came under the influence of a potent drug, nothing more and nothing less. All the old wonders and explanations associated with the Oracle seemed to collapse under the blow, much as science had earlier dethroned

Zeus as the father of lightning. It was reductive naturalism applied to antiquity, a banishing of all hints of otherworldliness for the idea that the Oracle's ultimate reality was completely physical in nature, that nothing in her world existed beyond objects and their properties, beyond wisps of ethylene and bouts of rapturous intoxication.

This view resurrected the importance of temple priests as surrogate visionaries. The Oracles—instead of being viewed as able women or, more recently, as fools or charlatans after the French excavations cast doubt on the truthfulness of the Delphic enterprise—could now be seen as so narcotized as to be constitutionally unable to have said anything meaningful to supplicants. They could utter only gibberish. Thus, the new interpretation held that politically savvy priests who knew how to frame written oracles in ambiguous verse played a crucial role in interpreting the confused blather, viewing it like a Rorschach test, seeing their own intuitions and predispositions in the prattle, rather than anything of objective consequence. In this view, the befuddled statements of the Oracles gave the temple authorities an opportunity to frame debates and ultimately gave legitimacy to any successful interpretations. Wrong ones, as usual in Greek prophecy, were dismissed as failures to comprehend the divine.

Scholarly and popular accounts of the team's discoveries often took this perspective and conveyed it in a derisive manner, as if temple authorities had been caught red-handed. An editorial in a medical journal concluded that the high priestess "was as much a glue sniffer as a guru," adding that "what was seen in Ancient Greece as prophecy would today be seen as a social problem." A different article said the scientists investigating Apollo's holy sanctuary had discovered "the source of its power—laughing gas!" That description, of course, misidentified the intoxicant.

The British press was particularly unkind. The *Sunday Times* drew on de Boer's London talk as an opportunity to do a breezy, tongue-in-cheek satire. The fantasy posited a world in which the Oracle was losing market share to the more aggressive Ceefax service. The main problem? "All lines to Apollo are engaged. Please try later." The lampoon held that when a supplicant finally got through, the Oracle would breathe ethylene fumes and proceed to engage in wild and incoherent talk. An example? "I predict that Greece will never be part of a single European currency system."

THE TEAM—most especially de Boer, who had investigated Delphi for decades and long meditated on the work's implications—found the reductionist view to be unconvincing. First, it wrongly put renewed emphasis on the priests. Recent scholarship held that the Oracles actually said what they were reported to have said and dismissed as sexist and unsupported the old idea that Oracles were incoherent babblers or mere figureheads. So any credible interpretation of the ethylene discovery had to deal with intoxicated Oracles, not ones addled to the point of incoherence. It had to take Plutarch's "inspired maidens" at face value. It had to view Clea as a smart, accomplished woman, not a druggie in a narcotized daze.

So what did the ethylene do? Not much, according to de Boer. He faulted reductionist views of the discovery that dwelled on the narcotic angle to the exclusion of the bigger picture, as if drugs alone could explain a sisterhood of mystics that over the course of twelve centuries helped shape and sustain one of the world's great civilizations. He held that the team's real discovery said nothing about the Oracles as drugged zombies and everything about their breathing the pneuma as one of many stimuli to a deeply religious state of mind. The ancient writers got it right, he declared, while the French had erred in thinking there was no vapor at all. Now the question was how the pneuma worked with other factors to inspire the Oracles, de Boer argued, suggesting the answer was rich in subtle phenomena and behaviors, many perhaps irreducible to physical objects and properties. He held that the team's findings, if examined dispassionately, in fact showed that reduction with ethylene did little to explain or diminish the Oracle's possibilities, even otherworldly ones.

Most notably, he argued that the team's discoveries said nothing about a range of oracular feats that were indisputably real. For instance, the chemical stimulus in no way explained the Oracle's cultural and religious power, her role as a font of knowledge, her liberation of hundreds of slaves, her encouragement of personal morality, her influence in helping the Greeks invent themselves, or—by extension—whether she really had psychic powers. Even if her prognostications were judged to have no basis in literal foreknowledge, it gave no explanation for how she reflected the underlying currents of ancient Greek society and how her utterances stood for ages as monuments of wisdom. It said nothing of how the priestess inspired Socrates or functioned as a social mirror, revealing the subconscious fears and hopes of those who sought her guidance, or of how she often worked as a catalyst, letting kings and commoners act on their dreams. In futility, the situation was like attributing masterworks of twentieth-century literature to the fact that major authors indulged in heavy drinking.

Science succeeds by focusing on questions that admit answers, by limiting itself to empirical realms. It ignores God and spirit. At Delphi, the challenge included explaining not only the behavior of individuals but the influence of the Oracle on a society that began much of what we judge to be Western civilization.

The moral of the story was that reductive naturalism could come up short as a means of explanation, both at Delphi and elsewhere. It could go from the complex to the elementary but not necessarily the other way around. Moreover, its downward advance tended to be very narrow, while the reverse analysis typically got lost in the wide, confusing landscape of the real world. In that sense, reductive naturalism harbored a major asymmetry, working fairly well in one direction but hardly at all in the other. Critics of reduction had long made that point, but the discovery at Delphi illustrated the challenge in a vivid new way, driving home the difficulty. Clearly, the ethylene alone could not explain the enduring spectacle of the Oracle. Delphi showed that the whole really was larger than the sum of its parts, as the holists had argued all along.

The successful reduction at Delphi, though revealing how the Oracle got high, and thus important for history and archaeology, clearly left intact many previous views and facts, explanations and questions. While the rhetoric of reduction often claimed a take-no-prisoners kind of aggressiveness that eliminated rivals, the truth was that the process in this case did little to undo the status quo. De Boer argued that it merely closed the circle on the historical understanding of the Oracle, resurrecting a view that predated the French excavations: the priestess had inhaled the pneuma, as the ancient Greeks reported. True, the reduction disclosed the real nature of the vapor. But it did little or nothing to dispel the surrounding layers of mystery.

The finding suggested that science—the most powerful institution of our day, a discipline rooted in the illuminating power of human reason—sheds a very strong but narrow light that can leave many intriguing questions and possibilities lurking in the shadows, including ones often associated with mysticism. It did not prove them, of course. That would take the development of models and theories that could be tested against observations. But, contrary to the claims of reductive naturalists, the finding did not rule them out, either.

This new appreciation of limitations perhaps mirrored the views of many working scientists. Perhaps the elders who made reductive pronouncements and proselytized on behalf of materialism constituted a vocal minority. After all, many scientists believe in God, not to mention poems and cocktail parties.

RICK SPILLER SAW no particular advantage in viewing the Oracle through the lens of reductive naturalism. From his own experience, he judged that the ethylene high was insufficiently strong to knock the Oracle out of commission and throw all responsibility for advising supplicants onto the shoulders of the temple priests. The physiological effect was much gentler than that, most certainly so at Delphi with its variable mix of light gases compared to the steady flow of extremely pure gas in his own experiment. Even then, what he experienced himself was not incapacitation but inebriation and exhilaration. It felt like a round of strong drinks, removing inhibitions, stirring the subconscious, increasing spontaneity. As for the Oracle, it seemed to Spiller that the discovery of ethylene intoxication took nothing from her cultural or religious side, nothing from her long history. The high was not an end in itself but a starting point, a stimulus.

His own inhalation of ethylene had demonstrated just how powerfully and readily the gas could act as a catalyst for transforming the Oracle's mental state. During the experiment, he had gone from cool investigator to reeling participant in a flash, despite his intention of keeping an objective air. In recent history, others seem to have experienced a similar transformation. Inhalation gave Davy "a highly pleasurable thrilling" and James a "tremendously exciting sense of an intense metaphysical illumination."

What a person experienced while breathing ethylene, Spiller concluded, depended a lot on his or her expectations. If a woman in ancient Greece came to the intoxication with a background of serious religious training, a feeling of devotion, a reverence for the gods, a preparation by fasting and ritual purification, and a belief in the nearness of Apollo, her experience might well have seemed like the heavens were opening. In her ecstasy, she might have said things that were wise and even profound.

The power of expectation, Spiller felt, became clear if you stripped away the chemical stimulation and looked at the sway of strong religious belief in its own right. An example was the Pentecostals, pious Christians who yearned for the presence of the Holy Ghost. They were so ready for spiritual intoxication that they needed no trigger, no physical catalyst, to experience possession and to speak in tongues. An artificial stimulus, it seemed to Spiller, could only intensify that kind of spiritual longing. A tingling in the hands and feet, a series of strange mental and physical sensations, a sense of disembodied euphoria, could combine to make divinity seem all the closer.

On the other hand, a lack of expectation could leave the experience devoid of any religious meaning whatsoever. The huffers and glue sniffers of his own studies were not seers or visionaries but druggies. Quite obviously, none had been hailed for divine wisdom. Just as the team's insights at Delphi said nothing about many aspects of the Oracle that were indisputably real, so too the ancient stimulation, if applied to modern situations, failed to produce Delphic behavior. There was no spiritual cause and effect. Contrary to the extreme reductionists, the religious environment at Delphi and the attitude of the Oracles and pilgrims turned out to be far more important than the vapor.

JEFF CHANTON WAS so meager a reductionist that he saw the team's work at Delphi as reinforcing the respectability of pure mysticism. He viewed the Oracle, and primitive religions in general, as potentially closer to the real order of the universe than modern religious orthodoxies. Science might try to plumb mysticism, he argued, but never grasp its truths.

WHILE NO FAN of reductive naturalism, John Hale had little enthusiasm for occult possibilities. By temperament and training, he was perhaps the most skeptical of the four men, deeply knowledgeable about ancient cultures and religions as well as their failures and delusions. Even so, from his own life, he told a fascinating story that illustrated how easily the Greeks could have concluded—rightly or wrongly—that the Oracle enjoyed all kinds of psychic powers.

The incident occurred in 1993. He was home reading the newspaper before going to work. That year's Kentucky Derby was a few weeks away and the papers were full of speculation on which horse might win.

Suddenly, Hale heard a voice.

Sea Hero, it rumbled.

Startled, he looked around but saw no one. He was alone. Yet the booming voice had resonated deeply in the space around him, naming one of the prospective horses, seeming to predict a winner.

Hale got excited but remained skeptical. At the time he was deep into his studies of Phormio, the forgotten sea hero of ancient Greece, and he assumed that his mind was simply playing tricks on him, producing a kind of auditory hallucination that reflected his passionate interest in the Greek admiral. After all, he had gone to Greece a few months earlier to study Phormio, and his mind was full of the man. So the possibility of some kind of self-induced illusion did not seem out of the question. Besides, in terms of the derby, Sea Hero was a long shot. The favorite was Prairie Bayou, an accomplished gelding.

Hale told students and friends about the experience, making light of it, depicting it as a hallucination. He became the object of some derision after a radio talk show at the University of Louisville mentioned the incident and said the professor planned to put money on the young stallion. Barbs became more pointed as Sea Hero stumbled in races leading up to the derby. To Hale's chagrin, the long shot was getting longer.

It was a beautiful spring day, Saturday, May 1, 1993, when Hale and his friends went to Churchill Downs. The track was dry and fast. But the odds on Sea Hero were an unlucky 13–1.

Early in the day, Hale put $10 on Sea Hero to win—a modest sum for a man supposedly in possession of inside information. He then went to the other races. Late in the day, at the approach of the tenth race, the derby, Hale reconsidered his stance. Where, he asked himself, was his conviction? Sure, maybe it was a bogus hunch. But what if it was the real thing, a genuine case of psychic premonition? Earlier that year while in

Greece, he had not only studied Phormio but gone to Delphi for the first time and experienced something of its grandeur. What if prophecy was real? What if the Oracle had actually peered into the future? And what if he had experienced something of that gift?

The crowd at Churchill Downs was singing "My Old Kentucky Home" as Hale raced to the betting window and, with seconds to spare, put all his remaining money on Sea Hero. It wasn't much—just $20 and some change. But he felt he had done the right thing, even though the odds had lengthened since his bet earlier in the day.

The field of the 119th Kentucky Derby was crowded with nineteen horses. In the starting lineup, Sea Hero had drawn the sixth spot, not too far from the rail. His placement was considered respectable. The race started with the usual rush for position. Sea Hero was hard to see, mostly lost in the middle. The anticipated leaders dominated the pounding throng, accompanied by loud cheers.

That's what I get for being so foolish, Hale rued. Embarrassed, he stole a sideways glance at his friends, many of whom had put money on Sea Hero. They looked gloomy.

Then, as the horses came into the last turn, there was a jostling among the leaders and a gap suddenly opened on the rail, a place where the derby is rarely won but often lost. The crowd fell silent as Sea Hero shot through the gap. In the final stretch, he drew clear of the thundering herd and crossed the finish line more than two lengths ahead of his closest rival, Prairie Bayou.

Hale and his friends went wild. The impossible had happened. Hale took home $560. Ever practical, despite his experience with a disembodied voice, he used the money to pave his driveway and form a small extension next to his great-grandfather's garage. It was a parking space for visitors. He dubbed it Sea Hero Drive and set up a little street sign there to commemorate the surprise win, to remind him of the extraordinary experience. A decade later, sitting on his front porch on a spring day just after the derby, recalling the tale while in sight of Sea Hero Drive, Hale waxed philosophic. The name Sea Hero had rung a bell for an understandable reason, and it was surely just a coincidence that the horse had gone on to win the derby.

But he came to accept the sincerity of those who served Apollo and reported mystic phenomena surrounding the Oracle. Such signs and visions were seemingly real, Hale concluded, whether received in a normal state while reading the newspaper or in an altered state while inhaling potent gases from a rocky fissure.

JELLE DE BOER attributed much of his open-mindedness to Java. Dutch attitudes toward life were typically forged in the iron bands of Calvinism, with little room for metaphysical dabbling, much less the occult. But the Indonesians lived in a sea of superstition, spirit worship, and animism, augmented by the teachings of Hinduism, Buddhism, and Islam, all of which had active traditions of mysticism. As a child, de Boer absorbed much of that atmosphere and witnessed what his family came to regard as an Indonesian curse in action when a friend of his father's suddenly fell ill and died.

In the privacy of his Connecticut home, de Boer would talk quietly of an invisible hand that guided him in the days and months after his escape from the Japanese prison camp, articulating an entirely unscientific view of providence. He said there was more to life than recognized by the scientific establishment, more to reality than textbooks would allow, more than ethylene behind the Oracle.

Not that he had lost enthusiasm for science. De Boer, while skeptical of the sweeping philosophical claims of reductive naturalism, had devoted his professional life to the process of reduction in one form or another, to seeking out simple explanations for nature's complexities. He did so in unraveling how shifting plates had formed Europe, how the Gulf of Corinth had developed, and how a volatile gas had intoxicated the Oracle.

He loved the process but realized that it missed a lot. Unlike Wilson, he made few metaphysical assumptions about how far it could go, even while embracing its power to illuminate the world.

De Boer recalled that when he was a college student in the Netherlands, his mother had once come to Utrecht looking for him urgently, worried that he was in serious trouble. She found him in jail. He had been arrested while trying to skirt an angry mob that had ransacked a Dutch Communist newspaper. No one knew where he was, de Boer said. But his mother, a woman who had suffered much from long imprisonments, somehow knew where to find him.

As for the Oracles, he said it seemed likely that more than one had psychic gifts but highly unlikely that, down through the ages, they all did. Much of the visionary power of temple authorities (including the Oracles) must have come from the treasures of information that flowed into Delphi as pilgrims from around the world flocked to Apollo's rocky sanctuary for spiritual guidance and remained there to discuss their cities, farms, and lives, de Boer argued. But he also maintained that some of the priestesses almost certainly had psychic gifts as well—perhaps enough to have occasionally tipped the balance of human history.

De Boer, increasingly happy to question establishment views as he neared retirement, faulted how the scientific world tended to dismiss psychic claims as unworthy of study. He called it arrogant. The intensity and long history of the condescension, he said, had slowed research on the topic and led many people—especially scientists—to feel ashamed about discussing the possibility of extrasensory perception even when their own experiences tended to lend it credence. He personally felt no sense of intimidation. With the Oracle, de Boer argued, the team had only scratched the surface. Their finding was a first step. Like Myers and other founders of the Society for Psychical Research, he held that future ages might uncover new realms of science that explained how the Oracle in fact achieved much of what the ancients described. There was much to do.

Epilogue

IT WAS MORE than three millennia ago that the Oracle began speaking on behalf of the gods. For much of that time, she enjoyed a reputation that was literally stellar, joined as she was to Apollo and the wonders of the firmament. But then, as the light of Greek civilization faded, her image fell into various states of disrepair that left her stained, demonized, lost, mocked, romanticized, and, after the French excavations, pitied and at times ridiculed.

In a way, the four scientists brought her back to life. Gone were images of the waif, the fool, the knave. In the aftermath of the team's find, she regained respectability as an intelligent woman and came back as—if nothing else—a serious historical figure. As the old claims took on new substance, so did the Oracle's air of mystery and spirituality, perhaps even some of her repute for navigating all time and space, for exploring the hidden powers of the mind. It was as if smart, sophisticated Clea had come back to preside over the sanctuary and wander the surrounding hills.

Be sensitive to the lessons of liberality, she seemed to be saying. Cherish your science but understand it as a finite guide to the immensities of time and space. It's not a religion, not a worldview. Will it save you? Can it explain my insights and actions? With Delphi, do not let knowledge of the vapors blind you to other truths, other vistas. Look far. Dance with the world rather than trying to explain it away. Consider the boat, not just the planks. Seize knowledge. Ask hard questions. But know, too, that your intellect is a small window and that its views can be surprisingly incomplete. Feel deeply. Revere truth in all its forms.

Yes, she seemed to be saying. You have discovered one of my secrets. I have others.

Chronology

2300	European Bronze Age begins.
1600	Delphi settled in late Bronze Age. Mycenaean civilization rises on Greek mainland.
c. 1200	Trojan war fought.
1100	Greek Dark Age begins, virtually all towns in ruins.
c. 1000–800	Cult of Apollo arrives at Delphi.
900	Greek Dark Age ends. First city-states form.
776	First known victor in the Olympic Games. Scholars mark the date as the beginning of the archaic era of ancient Greece.
c. 750–725	Homer's *Iliad* and *Odyssey* undergo standardization and refinement.
750–600	Delphi's fame spreads as cities of mainland Greece send out settlers to Italy, Sicily, the Black Sea, North Africa, and eventually France and Spain. The colonists send back tributes to Delphi, thanking Apollo for his guidance and blessings.
700	Hesiod active.
c. 650	First Greek coins.
600	Greeks found colony at Massalia—in time known as Marseilles, France. The colonists, like many cities, states, and other colonists, eventually build a treasury at Delphi.
595	Sacred war begins on behalf of Delphi against Crisa, a city that was taxing pilgrims and depriving Apollo's sanctuary of tribute.
594	Solon of Athens appointed to reform laws with mandate to defuse the growing tensions between rich and poor.
590–550	Delphi undergoes period of intense construction, including twelve treasuries and a stadium eventually able to seat seven thousand spectators.
585	Start of Greek rationalist philosophy.

582	Pythian Games begin at Delphi, the program similar to the athletic competition at Olympia but including singing and musical contests.
560	In Anatolia, Croesus becomes king of Lydia and proceeds to subdue the nearby Greek Colonies.
c. 550	Croesus tests seven oracles and declares Delphi the winner.
548	Temple of Apollo at Delphi burns down, prompting the authorities to solicit rebuilding funds from the whole Greek world.
546	Persians defeat Croesus and annex Lydia.
525	Aeschylus, first Greek tragic dramatist, born. Persians conquer Egypt.
c. 518	Pindar, foremost lyric poet of Greece, born.
508	A political revolution turns Athens into one of history's first democracies.
498	Pindar's earliest extant poem.
c. 496	Sophocles, second of three great tragic dramatists, born.
490	Persian invasion of Greece defeated at Marathon.
c. 485	Herodotus, father of history, born. Euripides, third of the great tragic Greek dramatists, born.
c. 483	Athenians find new veins of silver in their mines, letting them greatly expand their navy.
480	Persians under king Xerxes invade Greece as many city-states ally to counter the threat. At the isle of Salamis, outnumbered Greek triremes defeat the Persian armada in a bloody rout. Scholars mark this upset as the end of archaic era of ancient Greece and the start of the classical era.
479	Greeks expel the land forces of Xerxes.
479–475	Greek city-states send Delphi war booty and rich offerings to thank Apollo for their deliverance from the Persians.
469	Socrates, moral philosopher, born in Athens.
461	Pericles becomes leader of Athens, beginning an enlightened age.
447	Athenians begin work on the Parthenon.
c. 455	Aristophanes, comic playwright, born. He satirizes most divination but not the Oracle.
c. 440	Athenian potter renders a portrait of the Oracle.
438	Parthenon dedicated.
431	Sparta and allies declare war on Athens, starting the long decades of the Peloponnesian war.
430–23	Plague strikes Athens.
429	Pericles steps down as leader of Athens.
c. 429	Plato born.

Chronology

414	Athenians lay siege to Syracuse in Sicily, suffer humiliating defeat.
413	Sparta destroys Athenian fleet and army.
404	Athens surrenders to Sparta, ending the Peloponnesian war.
399	Socrates dies, drinking hemlock after being convicted of corrupting youth.
384	Aristotle born.
373	Earthquake destroys the temple of Apollo at Delphi.
356	Alexander the Great born.
356	War erupts over control of Delphi, with soldiers melting down some of its greatest treasures.
347	Plato dies.
343	Aristotle becomes tutor of Alexander.
336	Philip II, king of Macedonia, dies and is succeeded by his son, Alexander the Great.
335	Aristotle settles in Athens and founds the Lyceum.
323	Alexander the Great dies. Scholars mark his death as the end of the classical era of ancient Greece and the start of the Hellenistic era.
332	Aristotle dies.
279	Celts invade Greece and try to take Delphi.
146	Rome destroys Corinth and consolidates its hold on Greece, making it a Roman province.
90	Diodorus of Sicily born. The historian wrote that Delphi was founded after goats wandered into a cleft in the side of Mount Parnassus and became intoxicated.
c. 64	Strabo born. The geographer said the Oracle communed with Apollo by means of a divine pneuma that arose from a craggy vent.

CE

39	Lucan born, eventually pens a fiery melodrama describing how the Oracle foresees the future.
48–122	Delphi has a renaissance under sympathetic Roman emperors.
c. 50	Plutarch born.
66	Emperor Nero tours Greece and visits Delphi, eager to play in the Pythian Games (where no one was allowed to leave the stadium during his unnerving performance in the singing contest) as well as to consult the famous Oracle.
90	Plutarch arrives at Delphi, long serving as high priest.
c. 120	Plutarch dies.

c. 120	Pausanias born. The travel writer said the Kassotis spring at Delphi sank into the ground and inspired the Oracles, implying that a branch reemerged in the temple's *adyton*.
312	Roman emperor Constantine's conversion to Christianity lessens the influence of Delphi and other pagan shrines.
361–363	Julian the Apostate tries to reverse the decline of pagan religions, including the worship of Apollo at Delphi and the consulting of the god's Oracle.
391–392	Theodosius, a Christian emperor, issues decrees that forbid all forms of pagan worship, authorize the destruction of pagan buildings, and recommend death for anyone who carries out sacrifices and divinatory practices.
410	Visigoths capture Rome.
1436	Cyriac of Ancona, a scholar of the Italian Renaissance, travels to Greece to look for ancient sites and discovers hints of ancient Delphi.
1453	Constantinople falls to the Turks and Greece becomes part of the Ottoman Empire, starting centuries of oppression of the Greek people.
c. 1510	Michelangelo paints the ceiling of the Sistine Chapel with a fresco showing the Delphic Oracle as one of the seers who foretold the coming of Christ.
1676	George Wheeler, an English traveler, goes to Greece and rediscovers evidence of the buried ruins of Delphi under the ramshackle village of Kastri.
1821	Greece starts war of independence from Turkey that lasts until 1829.
1861	The French begin preliminary excavations at Kastri in search of ancient Delphi.
1882	The Society for Psychical Research founded in England, stirring interest in the alleged powers of the Oracle.
1889	The Greek government offers American archaeologists the right to unearth the sanctuary of Apollo at Delphi.
1891	A burlesque opera—*Apollo; or, The Oracle of Delphi*—plays in Vienna and New York City.
1891	John Collier, a British artist, paints *Priestess of Delphi*, a large portrait of the Oracle in which vapors rise from a craggy fissure to envelop her.
1891	Greek government awards France the monopoly to level the town of Kastri and excavate the ancient sanctuary of Apollo at Delphi.
1892	The French begin an archaeological dig at Delphi under a show of guns to subdue angry villagers.
1893	An archaic marble statue comes to light close to the treasury of the Athenians.
1894	French archaeologists focus on unearthing the temple.
1898	Excavators find an inscription in honor of Aristotle and his nephew Callis-

thenes for their ancient work in assembling a list of victors at the Pythian Games.

1904   Adolph Paul Oppé, a young British historian, publishes a paper saying the French have found no cave or fissure under the temple.

1927   Fernand Courby, an archaeologist, reveals that French excavators have identified the *adyton,* the Oracle's sanctum, but no chasm or vapors.

1950   Pierre Amandry, a French archaeologist who helped lead the Delphi excavations, declares that the region has no active volcanism and that the ground is thus incapable of producing intoxicating vapors.

1980–1981   Jelle de Boer, a geologist at Wesleyan University, goes to Greece and discovers an east-west fault outside Delphi that appears to run under the temple of Apollo.

1995   In Portugal, de Boer meets John Hale, an archaeologist at the University of Louisville, and the two decide to join forces to study the possibility that fumes once rose along the Delphi fault into the temple of Apollo.

1996   De Boer and Hale travel to Delphi and discover that the temple lies over thick beds of bituminous limestone, a likely source of intoxicating gases.

1997   At a London science meeting, de Boer unveils the team's geologic theory of gas formation at Delphi and how the Oracle got high.

1998   De Boer, while exploring the hills above Delphi, finds evidence of a north-south fault that runs toward the sanctuary of Apollo and bisects the east-west fault. From the temple's foundation and nearby retaining wall, de Boer and Hale take samples of travertine, a rocky crust that forms around springs, hoping to find traces of ancient gases trapped in its pores.

1999   Jeff Chanton, a chemist and team member at Florida State University, travels to Greece to take water samples and investigate whether gases still rise along the faults that cross beneath the temple.

2000   Henry Spiller, a medical toxicologist in Louisville, studies whether the Delphi gases can account for the Oracle's state of divine intoxication.

2001   De Boer, Hale, and Chanton publish the team's first comprehensive description of its geologic findings.

2002   Spiller does an experiment in which a volunteer oracle inhales ethylene gas to see its effects and whether bystanders can detect its sweet odor.

2003   Hale, de Boer, Chanton, and Spiller detail their overall findings in *Scientific American,* describing not only Delphi's unusual geology but its potent gases and their intoxicating effects.

Notes

This book is based mainly on interviews conducted between 2002 and 2005 with the scientists who made the fume discovery as well as reviews of their publications, letters, maps, diagrams, photographs, sketches, draft reports, notes, and e-mail correspondence. It also draws on reporting from Greece. In March 2003, I joined de Boer and Hale at Delphi and Thermopylae, and in July 2003 traveled with my family to Delphi, Thermopylae, and Zakynthos. Additionally, in May 2003, I went to Louisville and its suburbs to visit Hale, Spiller, the Capshews, and the garden shed where the oracle experiment took place. Last but not least, throughout my reporting I made trips to Connecticut to visit de Boer at his home and Wesleyan. In telling the history of the fume discovery, I have occasionally included dialogue among team members or, more rarely, an individual's thoughts. I have refrained from using quotation marks to signal that these are paraphrases rather than verbatim renderings. In addition to such material and recollections, I drew on the following sources.

PROLOGUE

3 *when I read one of the team's reports:* It was the first comprehensive paper—J. Z. de Boer, J. R. Hale, and J. Chanton, "New Evidence for the Geological Origins of the Ancient Delphic Oracle (Greece)," *Geology* 29, no. 8 (August 2001): 707–710. As sometimes happens, my interest resulted in an article, William J. Broad, "For Delphic Oracle, Fumes and Visions," *New York Times,* March 19, 2002, p. F1.

4 *Freud argued that extrasensory abilities:* He wrote a number of papers on such topics, including "Psychoanalysis and Telepathy" (1921), "Dreams and Telepathy" (1922), and "Dreams and the Occult" (1933). See George Devereux, ed., *Psychoanalysis and the Occult* (New York: International Universities Press, 1970). In his biography of Freud, Ernest Jones ascribed Freud's interest in the occult to the aberrancy of genius. See Ernest Jones, *The Life and Work of Sigmund Freud* (New York: Basic Books, 1957), vol. 3, pp. 375–407.

6 *wrote about the 1993 dive:* William J. Broad, *The Universe Below: Discovering the Secrets of the Deep Sea* (New York: Simon & Schuster, 1997), pp. 15–17, 94–150.

6 *sought to subsume religion:* See George Johnson, "Science and Religion: Bridging the Great Divide," *New York Times,* June 30, 1998, p. F4, and "True Believers: Science and Religion Cross Their Line in the Sand," *New York Times,* July 12, 1998, sec. 4, p. 1. Also see his book *Fire in the Mind: Science, Faith, and the Search for Order* (New York: Knopf, 1995).

6 *trace this development:* Corey S. Powell, *God in the Equation: How Einstein Became the Prophet of the New Religious Era* (New York: Free Press, Simon & Schuster, 2002).

6 *a small industry:* For a description, see Neil deGrasse Tyson, "Holy Wars, an Astrophysicist Ponders the God Question," *Skeptical Inquirer* 25, no. 5 (September–October 2001): pp. 24–27.

7 *Leon Lederman in* The God Particle *and Francis Crick in* The Astonishing Hypothesis: Leon Lederman, *The God Particle: If the Universe Is the Answer, What Is the Question?* (Boston: Houghton Mifflin, 1993), and Francis Crick, *The Astonishing Hypothesis: The Scientific Search for the Soul* (New York: Scribner's, 1994).

7 *unconventional arms:* Judith Miller, Stephen Engelberg, and William Broad, *Germs: Biological Weapons and America's Secret War* (New York: Simon & Schuster, 2001).

ONE: CENTER OF THE UNIVERSE

9 *but one description:* Mary Beard, *The Parthenon* (Cambridge, Mass.: Harvard University Press, 2003), p. 23.

10 *missing from any list of authors:* Among the lost authors are such unfamiliar names as Alcetas, Apelles, and Melisseus. See H. W. Parke and D. E. W. Wormell, *The Delphic Oracle,* vol. 2, *The Oracular Responses* (Oxford: Blackwell, 1956), p. xvi.

10 *a near riot of declarations:* There is no complete record of all the questions and answers. The numbers come from what scholars here gleaned from the extant literature. See Joseph Fontenrose, *The Delphic Oracle: Its Responses and Operations with a Catalogue of Responses* (Berkeley: University of California Press, 1978), p. 240; Parke and Wormell, *The Delphic Oracle,* vol. 2, p. 238.

10 *set up a throne:* Pausanias. *IV: Description of Greece, Books VIII.22-X.* W. H. S. Jones, trans. (Cambridge, Mass.: Loeb Classical Library, 2000), p. 511.

10 *imagery could throb:* See Lisa Maurizio, "The Voice at the Center of the World: The Pythias' Ambiguity and Authority," in Andre Lardinois and Laura McClure, eds., *Making Silence Speak: Women's Voices in Greek Literature and Society* (Princeton, N.J.: Princeton University Press, 2001), pp. 46–50.

11 *made them politically and militarily unassailable:* See Nassos Papalexandrou, *The Visual Poetics of*

Power: Warriors, Youths, and Tripods in Early Greece (Lanham, Md.: Lexington Books, 2005), pp. 9–52.

12   *We view this as myth:* Parke and Wormell, *The Delphic Oracle,* vol. 2, pp. 65–66.

12   *has a speaker mount the stage:* Maureen C. Howard, *Sophocles' Oedipus Rex* (New Haven, Conn.: Yale–New Haven Teachers Institute, 2004), www.yale.edu/ynhti/curiculum/units/1984/2/84.02.03.x.html.

12   *a code of extreme male chauvinism:* See H. D. F. Kitto, *The Greeks* (London: Penguin, 1951), pp. 219–236. Of course, the kind of repression of women that occurred in Athens had exceptions, especially so in Sparta, where the women, if not coequals in all things, achieved much freedom, respect, and fame for their athletic prowess.

12–13   *sang the virtues of hating women:* Plutarch. *Moralia,* vol. 5. Frank Cole Babbitt, trans. (Cambridge, Mass.: Loeb Classical Library, 1999), p. 311; Philipp Vandenberg, *The Mystery of the Oracles: World-Famous Archaeologists Reveal the Best-Kept Secrets of Antiquity* (New York: Macmillan, 1982), p. 135.

13   *woman petitioners seldom:* Frederick Poulsen, *Delphi* (London: Gyldendal, 1920), p. 23.

13   *two on call and one as a backup:* Plutarch, *Moralia,* p. 375.

14   *a fluid, pragmatic, polytheistic faith:* Walter Burkert, *Greek Religion* (Cambridge, Mass.: Harvard University Press, 2001), pp. 8, 111.

14   *suspicion of godlessness:* Ibid., p. 111.

14   *could never exert monopolistic control:* M. I. Finley, *The Ancient Greeks* (New York: Penguin, 1991), p. 50.

14   *many earthly rivals:* For a good overview of Greek divination and prophecy, despite the book's somewhat misleading title, see Robert Flaceliere, *Greek Oracles* (London: Elek, 1976). See also W. R. Halliday, *Greek Divination: A Study of its Methods and Principles* (1913; Whitefish, Mont.: Kessinger, 2003).

14   *priests studied curls of smoke:* Flaceliere, *Greek Oracles,* pp. 12–14.

15   *laid siege to the city of Syracuse:* J. B. Bury and Russell Meiggs, *A History of Greece* (London: Macmillan, 1978), p. 302.

15   *A sneeze, twitch, or shudder:* Flaceliere, *Greek Oracles,* p. 11.

15   *The spiritual elite claimed not only special gifts:* For an overview, see E. R. Dodds, "Telepathy and Clairvoyance in Classical Antiquity," in Anonymous, *Greek Poetry and Life: Essays Presented to Gilbert Murray on His Seventieth Birthday, January 2, 1936* (Freeport, N.Y.: Books for Libraries Press, 1967), pp. 364–385.

16   *Stoics held that a man:* Flaceliere, *Greek Oracles,* p. 79.

16   *thousands of statues and paintings:* Poulsen, *Delphi,* gives an excellent tour of Delphi's monuments, past and present, pp. 58–326, as does Vincent Scully, *The Earth, the Temple, and the Gods: Greek Sacred Architecture* (New Haven, Conn.: Yale University Press, 1979), pp. 108–115.

18   *a height of nearly sixty feet:* Pausanias, *IV,* p. 449; Poulsen, *Delphi,* 56.

18   *bore such inscriptions:* Plutarch, *Moralia,* p. 205; T. Dempsey, *The Delphic Oracle: Its Early History, Influence, and Fall* (Oxford: Blackwell, 1918), pp. 141–142.

18   *Its layout differed:* Ioanna K. Konstantinou, *Delphi: The Oracle and Its Role in the Political and Social Life of the Ancient Greeks* (Athens: Hannibal, n.d.), pp. 36–37.

18   *support the findings of psychic research:* Vandenberg, *The Mystery of the Oracles,* pp. 139–140; Dempsey, *The Delphic Oracle,* pp. 71–72.

19   *"knows the end supreme":* Dempsey, *The Delphic Oracle,* pp. 61–62.

19   *Only at Delphi did women:* Vanghelis Pendazos and Maria Sarla, *Delphi* (Athens: Yiannikos-Kaldis, 1984), pp. 15–16; H. W. Parke, *Greek Oracles* (London: Hutchinson University Library, 1967), pp. 30–32.

19   *whiffs of a strange, sweet odor:* Plutarch, *Moralia,* p. 495.

19   *"do not enter" or "inaccessible":* Walter Burkert, *Babylon, Memphis, Persepolis: Eastern Contexts of Greek Culture* (Cambridge, Mass.: Harvard University Press, 2004), p. 90.

21   *Ancient descriptions of Delphi's founding:* Diodorus Siculus. *The Library of History, Books XV.20–XVI.65.* Charles L. Sherman, trans. (Cambridge, Mass.: Loeb Classical Library, 1952), pp. 309–313.

21   *they made a tripod:* Far from simple utilitarian objects, tripods in ancient Greece were important symbols of power and social status that came to be used in many ceremonial functions beyond Delphi. They were given as awards in athletic contests and as gifts to the gods in religious ceremonies. Delphi drew on this legacy and helped give the tripod important new weightiness as a symbol of wisdom, divinatory power, and political unassailability. See Papalexandrou, *The Visual Poetics of Power,* pp. 9–52, 189–209.

21   *the reports of Diodorus and Plutarch:* Plutarch, *Moralia,* pp. 475, 485; Poulsen, *Delphi,* p. 14; Parke, *Greek Oracles,* p. 77; H. W. Parke and D. E. W. Wormell, *The Delphic Oracle,* vol. 1, *The History* (Oxford: Blackwell, 1956), pp. 20, 24.

21   *Archaeological evidence indicates:* Poulsen, *Delphi,* pp. 58–62. For a more recent view, see Christopher Mee and Antony Spawforth, *Greece: An Oxford Archaeological Guide* (New York: Oxford University Press, 2001), pp. 302–314.

22   *said to derive:* Ibid., p. 14; Pendazos and Sarla, *Delphi,* p. 9; Peter Hoyle, *Delphi* (London: Cassell & Company, 1967), p. 44.

22   *The Greeks deified springs:* Flaceliere, *Greek Oracles,* pp. 7, 14.

22   *a prerequisite to prophetic rites:* Ibid., p. 7, 14, 15, 29–30.

23   *keep the cleft hidden from view:* Neville Lewis, *Delphi and the Sacred Way* (London: Michael Haag, 1987), pp. 145–146.

23   *gods that foreshadowed the Olympians:* Burkert, *Greek Religion,* pp. 43–46.

24   *the mother of all living things:* Flaceliere, *Greek Oracles,* p. 7.

Notes

24 *patron deities came and went:* Pausanias, *IV,* p. 393.

24 *none had much cultural impact:* Some scholars argue that authorities at Delphi made up a long legacy of resident gods in order to try to establish the site's preeminence over its ancient rival, Dodona. Located in northwestern Greece, sheltered in a cold, windswept mountain valley reachable by a single high pass, Dodona possessed a grove of sacred oak trees though which Zeus spoke to pilgrims. The father of the gods, wielder of thunderbolts, answered questions in an uncharacteristically subtle way: by rustling leaves, the meanings of which his sibyls interpreted. Despite its remote location, the leaf oracle was a favorite. The adjoining theater could seat thousands of spectators. For the site, see Vandenberg, *The Mystery of the Oracles,* pp. 36, 21–38, and for the idea that Delphi claimed a false legacy, see Catherine Morgan, *Athletes and Oracles* (New York: Cambridge University Press, 1997), pp. 148–149. This interpretation is now becoming standard. See Simon Hornblower and Antony Spawforth, editors, *The Oxford Classical Dictionary* (New York: Oxford University Press, 2003), p. 445.

25 *wielded growing influence and renown:* Parke, *Greek Oracles,* pp. 33–43.

25 *In legend, young Apollo:* Hesiod. *Homerica Hymns, Homerica.* Hugh G. Evelyn-White, trans. (Cambridge, Mass.: Loeb Classical Library, 2002), p. 345.

27 *the idyll already had a resident:* Lucan. *The Civil War.* J. D. Duff, trans. (Cambridge, Mass.: Loeb Classical Library, 1997), p. 245.

27 *gave Delphi its other name:* Hesiod, *Homerica,* p. 351.

27 *came to be known as the Pythia:* Pausanias, *Description of Greece,* p. 401; Poulsen, *Delphi,* p. 6.

27 *earliest reference to the Oracle:* Homer. *Odyssey.* E. V. Rieu, trans. (Baltimore: Penguin, 1967), p. 124; Parke, *Greek Oracles,* pp. 16–19.

27 *"the treasures in rocky Pytho":* Homer. *Iliad.* W. H. D. Rouse, trans. (New York: New American Library, n.d.), p. 110; Poulsen, *Delphi,* p. 21.

28 *evaluate them as spurious:* Legends and folk tales are especially understandable, since the early Greeks drew few distinctions between history and a good story. If some of the Oracle's pronouncements were invented, scholars judge that others were exaggerated or otherwise altered, at times as apologia, most always to highlight the Oracle's powers. The simplest method was to credit her with predicting events that had already occurred. On the other hand, most accounts that have come down to us are judged authentic or grounded in fact and constitute, by far, the most interesting parts of the Delphic corpus. Two leading Delphi scholars conclude in their two-volume book that most of the Oracle's responses were rooted in factual history, by my count, 325 of her 615 responses. See Parke and Wormell, *The Delphic Oracle,* vol. 1, p. vii, vol. 2, pp. xviii–xix. Each chapter of vol. 2 has sections that delineate which oracles the authors judge as real or fictitious.

28 *the goddess Cyrene at the reins:* Pausanias, *IV,* p. 453.

28 *sent twenty statues of Apollo:* Ibid., p. 457; Parke and Wormell, *The Delphic Oracle,* vol. 1, p. 386.

28 *said to have sent out two eagles:* Plutarch, *Moralia,* p. 351.

28 *in the exact center of the Greek world:* Parke and Wormell, *The Delphic Oracle,* vol. 1, p. 1.

28 *Greek cosmology pictured the stars:* G. E. R. Lloyd, *Early Greek Science: Thales to Aristotle* (New York: Norton, 1970), p. 95.

28 *A striking fifth-century relief:* For the Piraeus relief and other examples, see Leicester B. Holland, "The Mantic Mechanism at Delphi," *American Journal of Archaeology* 37 (1933): pp. 206–207.

31 *known for its rough inhabitants:* F. A. Wright, *Lemprière's Classical Dictionary of Proper Names Mentioned in Ancient Authors* (London: Routledge & Kegan Paul, 1949), p. 626.

31 *"People say that Echecrates":* Diodorus Siculus, *The Library of History,* p. 313.

31 *An unwritten rule:* Burkert, *Greek Religion,* p. 98.

31 *"the chosen one from all the women":* Euripides. *Ten Plays.* Paul Roche, trans. (New York: Signet, 1998), p. 150.

32 *a plausible theory:* Parke and Wormell, *The Delphic Oracle,* vol. 1, pp. 35–36.

32 *rich in worldly benefits:* Steven J. Simon, "The Functions of Priestesses in Greek Society," *Classical Bulletin* 67 (1991): pp. 9–13.

32 *her own official residence:* Parke and Wormell, *The Delphic Oracle,* vol. 1, p. 44.

33 *"You are sinning too by ruthlessness":* Euripides, *Ten Plays,* p. 150.

33 *He dedicated his collection of essays:* Plutarch, *Moralia,* pp. 5–7, 85.

33 *as Plutarch took pains to note:* Hoyle, *Delphi,* p. 34.

33 *"It is impossible for the unlettered man":* Plutarch, *Moralia,* p. 321.

34 *the only surviving image:* John R. Hale, Jelle Zeilinga de Boer, Jeffrey P. Chanton, and Henry A. Spiller, "Questioning the Delphic Oracle," *Scientific American,* August 2003, p. 68.

35–36 *in nearby waters named Castalia:* Pausanias, *IV,* p. 413; Parke and Wormell, *The Delphic Oracle,* vol. 1, p. 30.

36 *"But come, you Delphians":* Euripides, *Ten Plays,* p. 107–108.

36 *emerged in the sanctuary:* Experts differ on exactly where the Kassotis emerged in ancient times, with some saying its location changed over the centuries. For a recent view, see Elena C. Partida, *The Treasuries at Delphi: An Architectural Study* (Jonsered, Sweden: Paul Åströms Förlag, 2000), pp. 264–271. For an earlier interpretation, see Parke, *Greek Oracles,* pp. 75–76.

36 *Oracle drank its sacred waters:* Hoyle, *Delphi,* p. 35.

36 *The authority of Zeus was invoked:* Vandenberg, *The Mystery of Oracles,* p. 136; Hoyle, *Delphi,* p. 45.

38 *an esteemed visitor representing an important city-state:* Poulsen, *Delphi,* p. 23; Parke and Wormell, *The Delphic Oracle,* vol. 1, p. 31.

38 *paying a nominal fee:* Flaceliere, *Greek Oracles,* pp. 39–40.

38 *Goats held a special place of honor:* Diodorus Siculus, *The Library of History,* p. 309.

38 *priests doused the animal with sacred water:* Parke and Wormell, *The Delphic Oracle,* vol. 1, p. 31; Parke, *Greek Oracles,* pp. 76–77.

38 *"Outside the temple":* Euripides, *Ten Plays,* p. 118.

38 *Disaster could strike:* Vandenberg, *The Mystery of the Oracles,* p. 145.

38 *"She went down into the Oracle unwillingly":* Plutarch, *Moralia,* p. 499.

39 *would read a petitioner's mind:* Hoyle, *Delphi,* p. 38; Dempsey, *The Delphic Oracle,* p. 68; Parke and Wormell, *The Delphic Oracle,* vol. 1, p. 34.

39 *would turn inward:* Poulsen, *Delphi,* p. 9.

39 *Peter Hoyle, a Delphi scholar:* Hoyle, *Delphi,* p. 38.

39 *scholars have battled for decades:* Hornblower and Spawforth, *The Oxford Classical Dictionary,* p. 445.

40 *women have lately argued:* For references to the controversy and a feminist reading of it, see Maurizio, "The Voice at the Center of the World," pp. 38–39. As Maurizio sums up her argument, "Simply put, the Pythias did compose and deliver Delphic oracles. The Pythias did speak. There is no evidence to the contrary."

40 *pilgrims could still get divine guidance:* Parke and Wormell, *The Delphic Oracle,* vol. 1, pp. 17–19.

40 *his devotees joined him in orgiastic rites:* Carl Kerényi, *Dionysos: Archetypal Image of Indestructible Life* (Princeton, N.J.: Princeton University Press, 1996), pp. 204–237.

40 *when such worship began:* Some scholars put his arrival before 582 BCE. See Poulsen, *Delphi,* p. 18.

41 *where the two gods cohabited:* Scully, *The Earth, the Temple, and the Gods,* pp. 115–117.

41 *Dionysus as Apollo's alter ego:* Letter, Elena C. Partida, curator of the Ephorate of Antiquities at Delphi, to author, May 4, 2005. "It's one of these 'fortunate' cases," she wrote, "where literary tradition and mythology are verified by archaeological finds."

41 *young women honored Dionysus:* Hoyle, *Delphi,* pp. 91–95.

41 *pledged to keep their activities secret:* Kerényi, *Dionysos,* pp. 214–225.

42 *"Up there in the snow":* Poulsen, *Delphi,* p. 19.

42 *A Greek amphora of the sixth century:* John Camp and Elizabeth Fisher, *The World of the Ancient Greeks* (London: Thames & Hudson, 2002), pp. 150–151. For the development of the role of the satyr, see Hornblower and Spawforth, *The Oxford Classical Dictionary,* p. 1361.

42 *rites culminated in screams and shouts:* Kerényi, *Dionysos,* p. 222.

42 *Carl Kerényi:* Ibid., p. 221.

42 *occasionally ended in chaos:* Ibid., p. 220.

42 *deeply entwined:* Parke and Wormell, *The Delphic Oracle,* vol. 1, pp. 11–13.

42 *make images of him:* Fontenrose, *The Delphic Oracle,* p. 260.

43 *"leave undisturbed what may not be told":* Plutarch, *Moralia,* p. 85.

43 *questions were typically mundane:* Vandenberg, *The Mystery of the Oracles,* p. 21; see also Morgan, *Athletes and Oracles,* p. 160.

43 *the most serious matters of state:* Morgan, *Athletes and Oracles,* p. 160. Moreover, the questions tended to be religious in character and not mere attempts to gauge the future for practical gain, as Parke and Wormell have noted. The Pythia's job was to tell of the divine aspect in coming events. Thus, a petitioner might ask what course of action would be the most virtuous or, if the step had already been decided, what would be the best way of attaining the goal. Parke and Wormell, *The Delphic Oracle,* vol. 1, p. 2.

44 *treated the prophetess of Delphi:* Morgan, *Athletes and Oracles,* pp. 150, 160.

44 *took their meals with the kings:* Ibid., pp. 170–171; Herodotus. *The Histories.* Aubrey de Sélincourt, trans. (Baltimore: Penguin, 1966), p. 379; Parke and Wormell, *The Delphic Oracle,* vol. 1, p. 84.

44 *crises and social instability:* Bury and Meiggs, *A History of Greece,* pp. 93–95. In its early days, Sparta was said to be the worst governed of Greece's many states. See Herodotus, *The Histories,* p. 37; Morgan, *Athletes and Oracles,* p. 170.

44 *the polis would achieve greatness:* Parke and Wormell, *The Delphic Oracle,* vol. 1, p. 89.

44 *"There are two roads":* Ibid., p. 87.

45 *Sparta became quite wealthy:* Bury and Meiggs, *A History of Greece,* pp. 95–96.

45 *"Love of money and nothing else":* Parke and Wormell, *The Delphic Oracle,* vol. 1, p. 88.

45 *retained archaic iron bars:* Ibid., p. 88; Bury and Meiggs, *A History of Greece,* p. 96.

45 *much political unrest:* Parke and Wormell, *The Delphic Oracle,* vol. 1, p. 88.

46 *"Many of the Athenians":* Ibid., p. 111.

46 *resisted calls for revolutionary steps:* Bury and Meiggs, *A History of Greece,* pp. 121–123.

46 *wove deference to Apollo:* Parke and Wormell, *The Delphic Oracle,* vol. 1, pp. 110–111.

46 *A celestial rite:* Parke and Wormell, *The Delphic Oracle,* vol. 1, p. 84; W. H. Parke, "The Deposing of Spartan Kings," *Classical Quarterly* 39, no. 3–4 (1945): pp. 106–112.

47 *A tale of uncertain date:* Parke and Wormell, *The Delphic Oracle,* vol. 1, p. 382.

48 *Apollo's preference:* Frederic W. H. Myers, *Essays, Classical* (London: Macmillan, 1911), pp. 46–47.

48 *echoed the feelings of the Delphians:* Parke and Wormell, *The Delphic Oracle,* vol. 1, p. 420.

48 *hundreds and perhaps thousands of slaves:* Hoyle, *Delphi,* p. 123.

48 *All refer to acts of manumission:* Krontira, *Getting to Know Apollo's Sanctuary,* p. 123.

48 *Oracle made herself available:* Fontenrose, *The Delphic Oracle,* p. 411.

49 *the most pious approach:* Xenophon, *Memorabilia, Oeconomicus, Symposium, Apology.* E. C.

Marchant and O. J. Todd, trans. (Cambridge, Mass.: Loeb Classical Library, 2002), pp. 45, 307.

49 *administration was judged too important:* Parke and Wormell, *The Delphic Oracle,* vol. 1, pp. 100–102.

49 *comprised twenty-four representatives:* Camp and Fisher, *The World of the Ancient Greeks,* p. 162.

49 *A silver one showed Apollo:* Ibid., p. 69.

49 *It was a remarkable claim:* For a discussion, see Papalexandrou, *The Visual Poetics of Power,* p. 40.

49 *"all days and all nights":* Parke and Wormell, *The Delphic Oracle,* vol. 1, p. 104. See also Hornblower and Spawforth, *The Oxford Classical Dictionary,* p. 1361.

50 *formally declared a center of pan-Hellenic worship:* Hoyle, *Delphi,* p. 89.

50 *vied for honors in singing and music:* Camp and Fisher, *The World of the Ancient Greeks,* p. 158; Pausanias, *IV,* pp. 403–407.

50 *thousands of people could disembark:* Hoyle, *Delphi,* p. 26.

50 *feel greater goodwill:* Poulsen, *Delphi,* p. 31.

51 *led the rebuilding effort:* Hoyle, *Delphi,* pp. 108–109.

51 *Another visitor was Solon:* Herodotus, *The Histories,* p. 23.

52 *As Herodotus tells us:* Ibid., p. 30. See also Vandenberg for modern descriptions of the various oracles.

52 *by way of dreams:* After fasting and other preparations, pilgrims went to sleep in a large hall. As they awakened, a priest would rush up to ask questions about any dreams and later analyze their meaning for hints of future events. Because pilgrims were able to verify personally the source of the inspiration, if not the interpretation, they put great faith in the sleep method. See Vandenberg, *The Mystery of the Oracles,* pp. 228–233; W. H. S. Jones, Pausanias, *I. Description of Greece, Books I and II* (Cambridge, Mass.: Loeb Classical Library, 1998), pp. 183–187.

52 *last oracle was the spookiest:* A supplicant would spend a few days praying and making sacrifices. On the appointed night, bathed and anointed with oil, dressed in a linen tunic girded with ribbons, he would drink from two springs: of Forgetfulness, to clear his mind, and of Memory, to recall the imminent revelation. In the darkness of the cave, the pilgrim was lowered into a hole to commune with the dead Trophonius and receive the prophecy. The priests kept the details secret. Vandenberg, *The Mystery of the Oracles,* pp. 236–243.

52 *"paralyzed with terror":* Pausanias, *IV,* pp. 347–355.

53 *"I count the grains of sand":* Herodotus, *The Histories,* p. 30.

53 *showered gifts on Delphi:* Ibid., pp. 31–32.

54 *believe the king died:* Vandenberg, *The Mystery of the Oracles,* p. 183.

54 *the hoard was uncovered accidentally:* Ibid., p. 176.

54 *the oracular test was a fiction:* Parke and Wormell, *The Delphic Oracle,* vol. 1, pp. 135–136. Other scholars see the test as real and cite it as a possible example of the Oracle's paranormal powers—in this case clairvoyance, also known as second sight or remote viewing. See Dempsey, *The Delphic Oracle,* p. 71; Myers, *Essays, Classical,* p. 41. Though skeptics dismiss such claims, the Pentagon and Central Intelligence Agency have considered them real enough to spend much time and money evaluating remote viewing as a possible new means of spying. See, for example, Joseph McMoneagle, *The Stargate Chronicles: Memoirs of a Psychic Spy* (Charlottesville, Va.: Hampton Roads Publishing, 2002).

54 *simple and straightforward:* Morgan, *Athletes and Oracles,* pp. 156–158.

56 *"pouring sweat":* Herodotus, *The Histories,* p. 178. I rely on this new translation of Herodotus for the whole epic. See pp. 178–237. For details on the war, see Barry Strauss, *The Battle of Salamis: The Naval Encounter That Saved Greece—and Western Civilization* (New York: Simon & Schuster, 2004).

61 *Xerxes and his forces withdrew:* The war was a defining moment in Greek history, as well as a claimed wonder of oracular accomplishment, so it is worth asking how well Herodotus's portrayals stand up. He was born around 480 BCE, the year Xerxes invaded Greece, and grew up hearing about the great events. Later, he had the opportunity to interview survivors and consult many records. By his late thirties, Herodotus had written much of his *Histories* and read parts aloud in Athens, winning acclaim while giving voice to what would become the first continuous prose narrative extant in Western literature. Modern scholars tend to see him as taking the first, tentative steps toward writing true history, eager to see things for himself, usually careful to present conflicting versions of events, candidly informing the reader when reports seem fabulous or incredible. See Herodotus, *The Histories,* translated by Walter Blanco and Jennifer Tolbert Roberts (New York: Norton, 1992), pp. 318–422. Overall on the war, he is judged as fairly accurate on the action (though inflating the number of Persian soldiers and ships). See Bury and Meiggs, *A History of Greece,* p. 169, and Strauss, *The Battle of Salamis,* p. 6. On the declarations of the Pythia, he is seen as more right than wrong. Parke and Wormell conclude that Herodotus erred on the prophecy of the Spartan king. All the evidence, they say, suggests that the Spartans made up the prediction to rationalize the devastating loss of Leonidas. But elsewhere he excelled. The prophecy of the winds they judge authentic and typical of the day, as was the ferocity of the storm. They also find credible the two oracles to the Athenians—of utter defeat and the wooden wall. No forger, they judge, would have been audacious enough to have had Zeus change his mind about one of the most decisive events of Greek history. They speculate that perhaps the Athenian delegation came to Delphi looking for approval of the naval plan of Themistocles,

and on hearing the Oracle's bleak prediction asked for a reconsideration that would further its execution. But they offer no evidence to back up this thesis. See Parke and Wormell, *The Delphic Oracle*, vol. 1, pp. 166–171. In 1959, an archaeologist from Princeton University discovered an ancient stone slab that was interpreted as showing that Themistocles had bribed the Oracle to make the wooden-walls prophecy. But many scholars judge the slab a forgery. See Vandenberg, *The Mystery of the Oracles*, pp. 189–208. Finally, for a new appreciation of the accuracy of Herodotus on a completely different matter, see Carol Andrews, *Egyptian Mummies* (Cambridge, Mass.: Harvard University Press, 2004), pp. 12–15.

62 *erected a column:* See Poulsen, *Delphi*, pp. 200–203. For the interpretation of unassailability, see Papalexandrou, *The Visual Poetics of Power*, pp. 9–52.

62 *forecast the city's renewed greatness:* Parke and Wormell, *The Delphic Oracle*, vol. 1, p. 185, vol. 2, pp. 53–54.

63 *a turning point that guided his inquiries:* Parke and Wormell take the Pythia's declaration as genuine and occurring fairly early in the career of Socrates, perhaps when he was around thirty-five. Since he died at seventy, that would mean the Oracle's declaration influenced him for some thirty-five years. Given the importance of his life, the two scholars rank the Oracle's inspiration of Socrates as her greatest contribution to Western thought. See Parke and Wormell, *The Delphic Oracle*, vol. 1, pp. 402–403.

63 *"The wisest of you men":* Edith Hamilton and Huntington Cairns, eds., *The Collected Dialogues of Plato* (Princeton, N.J.: Princeton University Press, 1973), p. 9.

63 *the philosopher's query:* Xenophon, *Memorabilia*, pp. 287–289.

63 *the Oracle was an essential guide:* Hamilton and Cairns, *The Collected Dialogues of Plato*, p. 491. For a detailed discussion of the evidence, see E. R. Dodds, *The Greeks and the Irrational* (Berkeley: University of California Press, 1963), pp. 64–101.

64 *"fetched from Delphi":* Hamilton and Cairns, *The Collected Dialogues of Plato*, p. 1339.

64 *a stela to the philosopher:* Flaceliere, *Greek Oracles*, p. 77.

65 *the most direct contact:* Poulsen, *Delphi*, p. 29; Parke and Wormell, *The Delphic Oracle*, vol. 1, p. 406.

65 *passion was for understanding nature:* Marjorie Grene, *A Portrait of Aristotle* (Chicago: Phoenix Books, University of Chicago Press, 1967), pp. 245–247.

66 *a cure for plague:* Parke and Wormell, *The Delphic Oracle*, vol. 2, pp. 76, 77, 104.

66 *marched on Delphi:* Ibid., vol. 1, pp. 254–259.

66 *Cicero . . . visited Greece:* Plutarch, *Lives, VII*, Bernadotte Perrin, trans. (Cambridge, Mass.: Loeb Classical Library, 1994), p. 93.

67 *no tradition of ecstatic prophecy:* Parke and Wormell, *The Delphic Oracle*, vol. 1, p. 22.

67 *no one bothered to describe her particulars:* Another interpretation is that the vapors never existed. In antiquity, only late writers such as Diodorus, Lucan, Plutarch, and Pausa-

nias mention the pneuma and its action, whereas early ones such as Homer and Herodotus are silent on the mystic current. One modern school attributes the silence to incomplete writing about commonly known phenomena, possibly compounded by the limited nature of the extant literature, while skeptics ask if the early absence means the vapors were a late invention. For an early skeptic who plays an important role in chapter 2, see A. P. Oppé, "The Chasm at Delphi," *Journal of Hellenic Studies* 24 (1904): pp. 214–240. For a later overview, see Parke and Wormell, *The Delphic Oracle*, vol. 1, pp. 19–24. The skeptics were strongly influenced by the French failure to find any evidence of the chasm and vapors. Now, with the discovery by the American team, it seems possible that the scholarly consensus will swing back to seeing the glass as half full rather than half empty.

67   *how goats on Mount Parnassus:* Diodorus Siculus, *The Library of History*, p. 311.

67   *"inspires a divine frenzy":* Strabo, *Geography, Books 8–9* Horace Leonard Jones, trans. (Cambridge, Mass.: Loeb Classical Library, 2001), p. 353.

67   *Lucan wrote a melodrama:* Lucan, *The Civil War*, pp. 243–257.

68   *used the lower waters for libations:* Parke and Wormell, *The Delphic Oracle*, vol. 1, p. 27.

68   *"There is, in fact, profound peace":* Plutarch, *Moralia*, pp. 337–339.

69   *"The prophetic current and breath":* Ibid., pp. 469–471.

69   *"The power of the spirit":* Ibid., p. 501.

70   *a headquarters of heathen belief:* Parke and Wormell, *The Delphic Oracle*, vol. 1, pp. 288–289.

70   *physically violated her:* Hoyle, *Delphi*, p. 42.

70   *"The fountain of Castalia is silent":* Clement of Alexandria, *Exhortation to the Heathen*, chapter 2, "The absurdity and impiety of the heathen mysteries and fables about the birth and death of their gods." The book can be found at www.newadvent.org.

70   *exempt from taxation:* Dempsey, *The Delphic Oracle*, p. 180.

71   *"Tell the king":* Hoyle, *Delphi*, p. 142.

TWO: DOUBTERS

73   *"My boy":* Lord Amberley (John Russell), "Experiences of Spiritualism," *Fortnightly Review* 21 (January 1874): p. 83.

74   *Its aim was to investigate:* For a society overview, see G. N. M. Tyrrell, *The Personality of Man: New Facts and Their Significance* (London: Penguin, 1954), pp. 44–51.

74   *its presidents included:* Others were Henri-Louis Bergson, the French philosopher and Nobel laureate; Sir William Crookes, the British chemist and discoverer of the element thallium; Sir Alister Hardy, the Oxford zoologist: Sir Oliver Lodge, the physicist and radio pioneer; and Charles Richet, the French physiologist and Nobel laureate. It took some courage for these men—especially the scientists—to explore

the spiritualist world. After all, the sciences of the day were racing toward a narrow kind of philosophical materialism.

75 *a member called for a detailed examination:* W. S. Lach-Szybma, "Correspondence," *Journal of the Society for Psychical Research* 1 (February 1885): pp. 284–285.

75 *Myers acted as its guiding hand:* For a biographical sketch of Myers, see Susy Smith, "Preface," in F. W. H. Myers, *Human Personality and Its Survival of Bodily Death* (Charlottesville, Va.: Hampton Roads Publishing, 2001), pp. xvii–xxv.

75 *coined the term* telepathy: Tyrrell, *The Personality of Man,* p. 57.

75 *coined the term* supernormal: Ibid., p. 52; see also Arthur Koestler, *The Roots of Coincidence* (London: Hutchinson, 1972), p. 32.

76 *a variety of classical topics:* Myers, *Essays, Classical.*

76 *he zeroed in on:* With typical integrity, Myers cited it not as an example of clear success but instead of the difficulties that scholars face in evaluating sketchy evidence. He noted that second sight, or clairvoyance, could be a modern explanation for the Oracle's success in knowing what the king was doing that day. But his rigor kept him skeptical. "It is obvious," he remarked, "that the documents before us are far from enabling us to prove even this hypothesis." See ibid., p. 41.

76 *"a true comprehension":* Ibid., pp. vii–viii.

76 *He pointed to issues of the* Proceedings: The *Proceedings* studies are summarized in Myers, *Human Personality,* pp. 127–166.

77 *Cyriac of Ancona:* Hoyle, *Delphi,* p. 145.

78 *Inscribed on one slab:* Vandenberg, *The Mystery of the Oracles,* p. 101.

78 *The main activity:* Hoyle, *Delphi,* p. 150.

78 *a show of force:* Ibid., p. 153.

78 *a more conciliatory approach:* Pierre Amandry, "Fouilles de Delphes et raisins de Corinthe," in Olivier Picard and Evangelos Pentazos, eds., *La redécouverte de Delphes* (Paris: De Boccard, École française d'Athènes, 1992), pp. 77–128.

78 *influenced the cautious Greeks:* Ibid., pp. 112–113.

78 *Athens offered the excavation rights:* Hoyle, *Delphi,* p. 155.

79 *fewer than one hundred homes:* Poulsen, *Delphi,* p. 46.

79 *"Any considerable delay":* Amandry, "Fouilles de Delphes," p. 105.

79 *"should not be allowed to escape":* Ibid., p. 107.

80 *just twenty-five thousand dollars:* Anonymous, "Art Notes," *New York Times,* April 27, 1890, p. 12.

80 *"It would be strange indeed":* Anonymous, "Fame Won at Delphi," *New York Times,* September 21, 1891, p. 4.

81 *a new man arrived from Paris:* Vandenburg, *The Mystery of the Oracles,* p. 104.

81 *"full of mystery, grandeur and divine terror":* Hoyle, *Delphi,* p. 155.

81   *a half million francs:* Poulsen, *Delphi,* p. 46.

81   *the French Ministry of State Education:* Amandry, "Fouilles de Delphes," p. 114.

82   *"played America against France":* Anonymous, "Art Notes," *New York Times,* March 29, 1891, p. 12.

82   *"indifference and lack of energy":* Anonymous, "After the Kaiser's Visit," *New York Times,* July 19, 1891, p. 1.

82   *shivered with anticipation:* Professor Louis Dyer, a classicist at Harvard, stuck a note of happy expectation in one of the first accolades. "It was no ordinary sanctuary," he enthused in his new book. "To make excavations at Delphi will be a glorious task." See Louis Dyer, *Studies of the Gods in Greece at Certain Sanctuaries Recently Excavated* (London: Macmillan, 1891), p. 32.

83   *opened in May 1891:* Anonymous, "Theatrical Gossip," *New York Times,* April 30, 1891, p. 8.

83   *one of its great hits:* "Every performance," said the *Times,* "has been filled to overflowing." Anonymous, "Theatrical Gossip," *New York Times,* May 18, 1891, p. 8.

83   *The story centers on a beautiful young maiden:* Anonymous, "The Casino's New Operetta," *New York Times,* May 3, 1891, p. 13.

84   *"It is, of course, a light and airy plot":* Anonymous, "Another Comic Opera," *New York Times,* May 8, 1891, p. 4.

84   *People loved it:* The operetta drew not just local crowds but businessmen and governors descending on New York. On May 11, the National Association of Millers and its guests saw the show, taking up a thousand of the Casino's seats. "The mills of the gods grind slowly," an official told the crowd of executives, "which shows what high-toned people were in the business at that time." See Anonymous, "Millers in Convention," *New York Times,* May 12, 1891, p. 8.

84   *tear up her contract:* Parker Morell, *Lillian Russell: The Era of the Plush* (New York: Random House, 1940), pp. 106–108.

84   *exhibited at the Royal Academy:* Geoffrey Ashton, "Collier, John," *The Dictionary of Art* (New York: Grove Dictionaries, 1996), vol. 7, p. 569.

85   *an opportunity to indulge himself:* The reaction of London circles to Collier's depiction is unknown, but in our day his *Priestess of Delphi* has managed to achieve electronic immortality on the Internet, where many images of it can be found. The original, oil on canvas, resides at the Art Gallery of South Australia, Adelaide, Australia. Good reproductions abound. Once in Vienna, I was looking through an upscale magazine when I spotted an ad for a luxury spa. It showed a naked woman in a large bathtub, her eyes closed, one arm resting atop her head, a few flower petals scattered across the water and her breasts. A full glass of wine sat nearby. The wall behind her held but one piece of artwork, a perfect mood setter, nicely framed amid faux temple columns and a vine in full flower. It was a large print of Collier's Oracle.

86 *The military was called in:* Poulsen, *Delphi,* p. 46.

86 *Photographers with large box cameras:* See Gérard Réveillac, "Photographies de la Grande Fouille," in Picard and Pentazos, *La redécouverte de Delphes,* pp. 180–193.

86 *started low on the rocky slope:* Leda Krontira, *Getting to Know Apollo's Sanctuary at Delphi* (Athens: Ekdotike Athenon, 1996), p. 80.

87 *Twin marble statues:* Poulsen, *Delphi,* p. 90.

87 *a marble statue of Antinous:* Ibid., pp. 324–326.

87 *A photograph of its unearthing:* Anne Jacquemin, "En feuilletant le *Journal de la Grande Fouille,*" in Picard and Pentazos, *La redécouverte de Delphes,* p. 173.

87 *Delphi's inglorious end:* Rome's turn to Christianity had left many Greek temples preserved as Christian churches. But the allure of Apollo's sanctuary at Delphi was so great that it had been judged a potential threat to the new religion. So the emperor Arcadius, coming to power three decades after Julian, in 395 CE, had ordered it razed. Poulsen, *Delphi,* p. 150.

87 *"a great deception":* Hoyle, *Delphi,* p. 165.

87 *neither its location nor its form:* Manolis Andronicos, *Delphi* (Athens: Ekdotike Athenon, 1980), p. 19.

90 *"We were greatly disappointed":* Flaceliere, *Greek Oracles,* p. 43.

90 *water did well up:* Picard and Pentazos, *La redécouverte de Delphes,* p. 156.

90 *suggesting that Pausanias had been right:* Pausanias, a Greek born in Asia Minor around 120 CE, traveled widely throughout the Roman Empire and, responding to the market for travel books, wrote the ten-volume *Description of Greece.* He found Delphi a rich subject and gave long descriptions of its statues and treasures, building and pediments (as well as lamenting the artworks that had disappeared). In passing, he mentioned the Kassotis spring, the one just above the temple, and gave what appears to be a significant new fact. Pausanias said it "sinks under the ground, and inspires the women in the shrine of the god." His statement was consistent with Plutarch's saying the pneuma could arise in the company of running waters and seemed to suggest that the spring and vaporous cleft were located at the same location, beneath the *adyton.* See Pausanias, *IV,* p. 511.

90 *found a monument to Aristotle:* Poulsen, *Delphi,* p. 29.

91 *foreign critics, especially the Germans:* Ibid., p. 46–47.

91 *"The Chasm at Delphi":* Oppé, "The Chasm at Delphi."

91 *"failed to find a trace":* Ibid., p. 233.

92 *the impossibility of a vaporous cleft:* He began not only a century of demythologizing about the cleft but also a vein of fervent speculation as to how the ancients got it so wrong. "These stories do not grow out of nothing," he declared. The scholar proposed that over time the ancient authors had confused the fissure under the temple with the

nearby Castalian gorge, whose spring and majestic beauty had, he claimed, made it the founding area of inspiration, "the original feature which invested Delphi with a peculiarly sacred and oracular power." He offered little evidence to back up his claim. See ibid., p. 234.

92 *"stood immediately under the temple"*: Ibid., p. 233.

92 *"They could never have inspired"*: Ibid., p. 234.

92 *the temple region had no spring*: Ibid., p. 233.

93 *He toured the dig in 1907*: Poulsen, *Delphi*, p. v.

93 *"any bottomless abyss"*: Ibid., p. 24.

93 *"increased the ecstasy"*: Ibid., p. 40.

94 *the violent nature of the Delphic region*: Dempsey, *The Delphic Oracle*, pp. 59–60.

94 *"highly probable"*: Ibid., p. 60.

94 *"a mere sham"*: Ibid., p. 61.

94 *cited the test of Croesus*: Ibid., pp. 71–72.

95 *deeply immersed in telepathic experiments*: Murray would go so far as to demonstrate his own alleged powers to small groups. He would ask those present to write down, after he left the room, a subject or a description of an incident from literature or current events. Upon returning, he would state his impression of the subject and the audience would compare that to what it had written down, often finding a match or an uncanny likeness. See C. E. M. Hansel, *ESP and Parapsychology: A Critical Reevaluation* (Buffalo, N.Y.: Promethus, 1980), p. 36.

95 *the evidence for psychic powers*: Dodds, "Telepathy and Clairvoyance in Classical Antiquity," pp. 364–385.

95 *came to accept ancient and modern telepathy*: E. R. Dodds, *Missing Persons: An Autobiography* (Oxford: Oxford University Press, 1977), pp. 97–111.

96 *able to report a major find*: Fernand Courby, *Fouilles de Delphes*, tome 2, *Topographie et Architecture, la Terrasse du Temple* (Paris: De Boccard, 1927), pp. 47–70.

96 *described two areas*: In addition to the French volume, see Hoyle, *Delphi*, p. 164, and Poulsen, *Delphi*, pp. 150–151.

97 *nine feet wide and sixteen feet long*: Courby, *Fouilles de Delphes*, p. 69, and Parke and Wormell, *The Delphic Oracle*, vol. 1, p. 29. In time, excavations of other temples found similar constructions and gave added credibility to the existence and layout of Delphi's *adyton*. See Flaceliere, *Greek Oracles*, pp. 29–30.

97 *Courby expressed publicly*: Courby, *Fouilles de Delphes*, p. ii.

98 *judged to be the omphalos*: Ibid., pp. 70–80.

98 *debate centered on an intriguing block*: Holland, "The Mantic Mechanism at Delphi," p. 207.

99 *the block was part of an altar*: Ibid, p. 213.

99   *offered an alternative explanation:* Walter Miller, *Daedalus and Thespis,* vol. 1 (New York: Macmillan, 1929), p. 82.

100   *Visual evidence:* Holland, "The Mantic Mechanism," p. 208.

100   *"help in some way":* Miller, *Daedalus and Thespis,* p. 82.

100   *a long article of 1933:* Holland, "The Mantic Mechanism," pp. 201–214.

100   *leap of imagination:* As for the tripod, Holland agreed with Miller on its general placement but went further by suggesting that early in Delphi's history it had been raised up on a circular stone base. That, he said, like the square base, accounted for a smooth, circular region around the triangle of holes where no calcite deposits had formed. Ibid., p. 210.

102   Everyday Life in Ancient Times: National Geographic, *Everyday Life in Ancient Times: Highlights of the Beginnings of Western Civilization in Mesopotamia, Egypt, Greece, and Rome* (Washington, D.C.: National Geographic Society, 1951), p. 217.

102   *"No one could understand her incoherent ravings":* Ibid., p. 216.

103   La Mantique Apolliniene à Delphes: Pierre Amandry, *La Mantique Apolliniene à Delphes: Essai sur le founctionnement de l'Oracle* (Paris: De Boccard, 1950).

103   *took on the trappings:* Ibid., pp. 219–220.

104   *incapable of producing mind-altering vapors:* Ibid., pp. 196–230.

104   *dismissed Holland's thesis:* Ibid., pp. 220, 233.

104   *a disinformation campaign:* Ibid., p. 239.

104   *"It will be admitted with difficulty":* Ibid., p. 168.

105   *"As for the famous 'vapours'":* Dodds, *The Greeks and the Irrational,* p. 73.

105   *"There was no vapor and no chasm":* Fontenrose, *The Delphic Oracle,* pp. 196–197. Though I have worked from the paperback, the hardcover version was first published in 1978, according to its copyright page.

105   *"The excavators have found no cleft":* Saul Levin, *The Old Greek Oracles in Decline (Aufstieg und Niedergang der römischen Welt II,* no. 18, vol. 2, pp: 1599–1649. 1989), p. 1612.

105   *"emitted a gas with any intoxicating properties":* Parke and Wormell, *The Delphic Oracle,* vol. 1, p. 22.

106   *"Probably the majority of these women":* Ibid., p. 38.

106   *Nowhere in the new consensus:* Even old friends of the Oracle began to treat her as something of an embarrassment. Renée Haynes, the nom de plume of Mrs. Jerrard Tickell, a well-known member of the council of the British Society for Psychical Research, wrote a detailed history of extrasensory perception, *The Hidden Springs,* that came out in 1961 in Britain and the United States. She gave the Oracle little attention. Instead, the book dwelled on levitation in saints and telepathy in migrating eels and butterflies. See Renée Haynes, *The Hidden Springs: An Enquiry into Extra-Sensory Percep-*

tion (Boston: Little, Brown, 1973). This edition is an American revision of the 1961 book. A knowledgeable reviewer gently criticized her tiptoeing around Delphi, implying that Haynes had failed to acknowledge a colossus. "She has almost nothing to say about the Greeks of the classical period," huffed H. H. Price, a professor of logic at Oxford University and a past president of the society. He noted a brief reference to the priestess of Delphi and a few similar digressions, "and that is all." See H. H. Price, "The Hidden Springs," *Journal of the Society for Psychical Research* 41 (June 1961), pp. 93–97. In truth, the snub was no fault of the author's. Most everywhere, the investigation of the Oracle and her professed abilities, after nearly a century of fitful decline, had reached a new low.

THREE: INQUISITIVE MAN

108 *smoke often rose from the ruins:* Frank Press and Raymond Siever, *Understanding Earth* (New York: Freeman 1998), p. 116.

109 *failed to force the colonial government:* Jean Gelman Taylor, *Indonesia: Peoples and Histories* (New Haven, Conn.: Yale University Press, 2003), pp. 312–313.

111 *crammed himself into small Dutch submarines:* H. W. Menard, *Ocean of Truth: A Personal History of Global Tectonics* (Princeton, N.J.: Princeton University Press, 1986), pp. 120–123; see also Simon Winchester, *Krakatoa: The Day the World Exploded* (New York: HarperCollins, 2003), pp. 86–114.

112 *discovered ancient magnetic signatures:* Press and Siever, *Understanding Earth,* pp. 499–501.

112 *allowed tiny magnetic grains to align themselves:* For paleomagnetic studies, this volcanic process is more important than it might seem. Volcanoes are often thought of as rare, isolated events. But in fact, volcanism creates roughly 80 percent of the earth's crust, much of it volcanic basalts underlying the oceans and all of it magnetized. See Ibid., pp. 105, 500.

112 *learned to read the old alignments:* The tools of the paleogeographers included magnetometers for measuring distant magnetism (in rocks at the bottom of the sea, for instance) as well as drills and polarizing microscopes for examining magnetic grains up close.

112 *The art was difficult:* One of the difficulties was that the investigators had to develop methods to scrub signs of the earth's current magnetic field from old rocks undergoing analysis, a process that if done incorrectly could distort or destroy ancient evidence.

112 *illuminate the origins of lands:* He showed how paleomagnetic data (most gathered by the Utrecht group) indicated that this belt in past eons had moved independently of the main Eurasian landmass. The Italian peninsula, for instance, had rotated some forty

degrees counterclockwise. So had the Spanish peninsula. Where had they come from? Why did they rotate that way? How had the belt achieved its current position in the rocky collage of southern Europe? These were the kinds of questions he and his colleagues sought to answer. See Jelle de Boer, "Paleomagnetic Indications of Megatectonic Movements in the Tethys," *Journal of Geophysical Research* 70, no. 4 (February 15, 1965): pp. 931–944.

112 *weigh their significance:* One form of life he studied was ancestors of the nautiluses, which swarmed in certain warm seas millions of years ago. Their fossil shells, de Boer noted in one paper, lay strewn across not only the Alps but the Himalayas thousands of miles away. Ibid., p. 943.

113 *thousands of caves:* John Middleton and Tony Waltham, *The Underground Atlas* (New York: St. Martin's, 1986), pp. 69–83.

113 *spill out into the open:* Press and Siever, *Understanding Earth,* pp. 305–308.

114 *The shells of bygone animals:* Closely examine a polished stone monument or the walls of an elegant old building and you will often see tiny shells—spirals, ovals, swirls—all millions of years old. At Grand Central Station in New York City, people rush by these diminutive fossils, unaware of the panorama. One of my favorite areas is the stairway leading to Vanderbilt Avenue, its sides rich in ancient life.

115 *up to 40 percent of most rocks:* Press and Siever, *Understanding Earth,* pp. 296–297.

116 *The climax came at the end of the Cretaceous:* Ibid., p. 532.

116 *mountains rose across a vast belt:* Michael Dennis Higgins and Reynold Higgins, *A Geological Companion to Greece and the Aegean* (Ithaca, N.Y.: Cornell University Press, 1996), p. 16.

117 *among the most violent places on earth:* Ibid., p. 211.

118 *the mound destined to be called the Acropolis:* Ibid., pp. 29–30.

118 *too small for commercial exploitation:* Anonymous, "Greece," Country Analysis Briefs, Energy Information Administration, Department of Energy, Washington, D.C. August 2000.

119 *explored the Atlantic and Pacific:* His analysis of the rocky seabed south of Iceland revealed patterns of fossil magnetism that backed the idea that the seafloor there had slowly spread apart over the ages. It was a contribution to the new science of plate tectonics. The region he investigated marked the seam where the Old and New Worlds once joined and the place from which they were still drawing apart. See Jelle de Boer, Jean-Guy Schilling, and Dale C. Krause, "Magnetic Polarity of Pillow Basalts from Reykjanes Ridge," *Science* 166 (November 21, 1969): pp. 996–998.

121 *these violent upsets:* Christopher L. Liner, University of Tulsa, *Greek Seismology* (Tulsa: self-published, 1997), pp. 12–23.

121 *"overthrew the city":* Plutarch, *Moralia,* p. 479.

121 *conspiracy to promote nuclear power:* Encouraging nuclear power was the last thing team

members wanted to do. In fact, in its few months on the job, the team had concluded that most of the proposed sites were terrible choices, the bedrock highly unstable. Contrary to public perception the specialists were preparing to throw cold
water on many of the government's plans.

126   *Strong earthquakes hit Athens:* Anonymous, "Greek Quake Kills 15, Seriously Wounds 53
and Chips Parthenon," *New York Times,* February 26, 1981, p. A3; Associated Press,
"Quake Produced Cracks in Parthenon's Columns," *New York Times,* February 28, 1981,
p. A24.

127   *Poseidon struck again:* Associated Press, "Much of Greece Is Struck," *New York Times,*
March 5, 1981, p. A8.

127   *He decided to quit the team:* De Boer went home to Connecticut, wrote the National Science Foundation, a federal agency, and won funding for three years of basic research,
the kind of blue-sky investigation that hopes to discover fundamental truths about
nature on the assumption that new knowledge is a good thing and can lead to un-
foreseen advances. That grant paid for his continued investigations of Greece. Such
open-ended research has been under fire for decades from politicians who want pre-
dictable results, and according to critics, their pressure is weakening the foundations of scientific research. See William J. Broad, "U.S. Is Losing Its Dominance in the
Sciences," *New York Times,* May 3, 2004, p. A1.

FOUR: SLEUTHS

132   *his doctoral dissertation:* For a summary, see John R. Hale, "The Viking Longship," *Scientific American,* February 1998, pp. 46–53.

132   *The large Roman villa:* See Stephanie J. Maloney and John R. Hale, "The Villa of Torre de
Palma (Alto Alentejo)," *Journal of Roman Archaeology* 9 (1996): pp. 275–294.

132   *Hale directed a large team:* The villa had first come to light when farmhands plowing
fields unearthed a striking mosaic that depicted the nine muses, the goddesses who
presided over music, dancing, and the other liberal arts. Portuguese scholars made a
preliminary survey, finding that the mosaic came from the dining room of what was
clearly a large Roman estate. The Louisville team redoubled the effort.

132   *The team uncovered a complex:* The main house bore hints of luxury, including not only
numerous mosaics but a central atrium surrounded by columns. Hale and his team
assumed that the estate got its start as a land grant to a retired Roman officer. An altar in the villa featured Mars, the god of war, with his spear turned upside down and
the point in the ground—the warrior turned farmer. Many Roman coins were
found in the ruins. Among other things, the team documented that the ancient
villa was the largest ever found in Iberia, which in Roman times supported scores of

great estates. The villas thrived not through subsistence farming or local trade but the sale of wine, wheat, olive oil, and racehorses to distant markets. They were bastions of empire.

133   *researching a book:* His efforts eventually produced two books: Jelle Zeilinga de Boer and Donald Theodore Sanders, *Volcanoes in Human History: The Far-Reaching Effects of Major Eruptions* (Princeton, N.J.: Princeton University Press, 2002), and Jelle Zeilinga de Boer and Donald Theodore Sanders, *Earthquakes in Human History: The Far-Reaching Effects of Seismic Disruptions* (Princeton, N.J.: Princeton University Press, 2005).

135   *writing up his findings:* See John R. Hale, "The Lost Technology of Ancient Greek Rowing," *Scientific American,* May 1996, pp. 66–71.

135   *to learn about Phormio:* John R. Hale, "Phormio Crosses the T," *Quarterly Journal of Military History* 8, no. 4 (1996): pp. 38–41.

135   *cities on the south shore:* John Noble Wilford, "Scientists Unearth Urban Center More Ancient Than Plato," *New York Times,* December 2, 2003, p. F3, and Tom Gidwitz, "City of Poseidon," *Archaeology,* January–February 2004, pp. 40–47.

139   *volcanoes in the blue Aegean:* De Boer knew such issues intimately not only because of his studies for the reactor project and the science agency but because of the extensive research he had conducted for his volcano book. He realized that the Gulf of Corinth region—home to Delphi—had no volcanoes, in contrast to the Aegean. One chapter of his book focused on Santorini. Unlike most Aegean isles, it has no white beaches, its sands being black. Its central volcano exploded around 1650 BCE; the force was even more powerful than that of Krakatoa near Java. Many experts, including de Boer, judged that the upheaval helped destroy Minoan civilization on nearby Crete and, on the mainland, bolster the Mycenaeans, the ancestors of the ancient Greeks. See de Boer and Sanders, *Volcanoes in Human History,* pp. 47–73.

141   *"Le roc fissuré par l'action des eaux":* Courby, *Fouilles de Delphes,* p. 66.

145   *It was a page from the Courby tome:* Ibid., p. 46, figure 45.

155   *they built massive reefs:* Claudia C. Johnson, "The Rise and Fall of Rudist Reefs," *American Scientist,* March–April, 2002, pp. 148–153.

160   *it was another clue:* During this trip, the two also looked unsuccessfully for the lost island. The Isle de Chalcis had been located near the gulf's northern shore not far from Delphi. Hale had brought along his old map showing its location and lots of new ones that displayed only empty gulf waters in the region. Their plan was to comb the shoreline for a fault or some other physical clue that would help pinpoint where the island once lay. If lucky, they might even find signs of the sunken island. Hale planned to interview local fishermen and anyone else that might be around. But they had no luck. Most of the coast in the target area turned out to have been torn apart for a large harbor, the construction obliterating not only local rocks but

the area's topography. De Boer could find no evidence of a fault or other landscape feature that might point to the presence of a nearby isle. And Hale could find no one who knew of the mystery. The disappearance of the island might have shocked locals at the time of the earthquake but it seemed that subsequent generations had forgotten the episode.

163   *all but unknown to most geologists:* That is true especially of American geologists. By contrast, over the decades a few European geologists have shown interest in Delphi. See, for example, Pierre Birot, "Géomorphologie de la Région de Delphes," *Bulletin de Correspondance Hellénique,* vol. 83, no. 1 (1959-I), pp. 258–274, and Luigi Piccardi, "Active Faulting at Delphi, Greece: Seismotectonic Remarks and a Hypothesis for the Geologic Environment of Myth," *Geology* 28, no. 7 (2000): pp. 651–654.

FIVE: X MARKS THE SPOT

167   *de Boer wrote Rozina Kolonia:* Letter, Jelle Zeilinga de Boer to Rozina Kolonia, Archaeological Museum of Delphi, May 20, 1996.

168   *The rocky specimens:* "Proposal," September 21, 1996.

168   *decided to press ahead:* Letter, John R. Hale to Robert Bridges, American School of Classical Studies, October 3, 1996.

169   *the large size of the crisscross family:* For a discussion of some of the main intersecting faults, see Robert J. Twiss and Eldridge M. Moores, *Structural Geology* (New York: Freeman, 1992), pp. 81–84, 113–127. Most basically, they separate massive blocks that slip past one another to cause earthquakes. The motion is often uneven because the blocks typically run deep and, at different depths, experience different amounts of stress, temperature, pressure, and friction. To appreciate the unevenness, picture a massive sidewalk that runs for a distance of one hundred miles and extends down into the earth some five miles. Suddenly, it settles a bit. The chances of its movement being completely uniform are slim to nil. The strains that accumulate during the uneven descent are soon released along new breaks that run roughly perpendicular to the length of the sidewalk. The earth's largest perpendicular faults—hundreds to thousands of miles long—arise in rift zones where two plates pull slowly apart, often with molten rock oozing up in between them to form new planetary crust. The seam between the plates can extend for immense distances. The one running down the middle of the Atlantic, for instance, extends from above Greenland to below Patagonia. As plates spread away from this seam at uneven rates, huge stresses build up and produce gargantuan right-angle tears known as transform faults that let local sections of the plate slide freely past one another. For a history of the discovery of transform faults, see Menard, *Ocean of Truth,* pp. 238–255, 282.

169 *A 1985 report:* Jelle de Boer, draft manuscript, "Tectonic Characteristics of Normal Faults, and the Possible Origin of Cross-Grain Rift Zones (Corinth and Evvian) in Central Greece."

171 *a potentially strong piece of evidence:* For citations to some of the Delphi spring papers that de Boer read, see J. Z. de Boer and J. R. Hale, "The Geological Origins of the Oracle at Delphi, Greece," in W. J. McGuire, et al., eds, *The Archaeology of Geological Catastrophes* (London: Geological Society Special Publication no. 171, 2000), pp. 399–412.

172 *an area of major hydrocarbon leakage:* I. R. MacDonald et al., "Gas Hydrate That Breaches the Sea Floor on the Continental Slope of the Gulf of Mexico," *Geology,* August 1994, pp. 699–702.

173 *A temple of Apollo:* Hale had learned of Hierapolis after remembering an article about it he had read in the journal *Antiquity.* See T. M. Cross and S. Aaronson. "The Vapours of One Entrance to Hades," *Antiquity* 62 (1988): pp. 88–89. See also P. L. Hancock et al., "Creation and Destruction of Travertine Monumental Stone by Earthquake Faulting at Hierapolis, Turkey," in McGuire, *The Archaeology of Geological Catastrophes,* pp. 1–14.

173 *On the west coast at Claros:* Vandenberg, *The Mystery of the Oracles,* pp. 89–99.

173 *a site known as Didyma:* Ibid., pp. 63–88.

175 *went against the meeting's grain:* For an example, see Iain Stewart, "Preface," in McGuire, *The Archaeology of Geological Catastrophes,* p. viii.

175 *The news media loved it:* For instance, see Aisling Irwin, "Delphic Oracle Was Indeed a Gas, Geologist Says," *Vancouver Sun* (reprinted from the *London Daily Telegraph*), April 28, 1997, p. A1; Bob Holmes, "Did Ancient Gases Inspire Powers of Prophecy?" *New Scientist,* May 3, 1997, p. 1616.

175 *a major fault bisects the island:* For details of the geology, see Higgins and Higgins, *A Geological Companion,* pp. 104–105.

176 *described a site on Zakynthos:* Herodotus, *The Histories,* p. 307.

180 *According to a paper by Greek geologists:* M. D. Dermitzakis and P. Alafousou, "Geological Framework and Observed Oil Seeps of Zakynthos Island: Their Possible Influence on the Pollution of the Marine Environment," *Thalassographica* 10, no. 2 (1987): pp. 7–22.

180 *used them in face creams:* Ibid., pp. 16–17.

186 *The sanctuary at Delphi, they wrote:* Higgins and Higgins, *A Geological Companion,* pp. 80–81.

190 *De Boer got out his chisel and hammer:* The sampling eventually appeared on Dutch television, Jos Wassink, "Oracle on Gas," VPRD Noorderlicht, which aired April 18, 1998.

191 *They relaxed and talked:* "Oracle on Gas," VPRD Noorderlicht.

193 *revealed a gradient:* The travertine from the Kerna spring high atop the sanctuary turned out to hold just 0.13 parts per million methane, and no detectable ethane. By contrast, the temple sample had 2.82 parts per million methane, and 0.03 parts

per million ethane. It appeared that Apollo's home was relatively rich in hydro-carbons.

193 *revealed that the principle was correct:* See de Boer, Hale, and Chanton, "New Evidence for the Geological Origins of the Ancient Delphic Oracle."

193 *conditions that Chanton had been required to create:* In Florida, the geochemist had crushed the rocky samples into spheres the size of dimes, packed them into glass vials, re-moved the air, and added nitrogen, an inert gas that reacts very little with other substances. Finally, when the gas chromatograph was carefully calibrated and rechecked and its sensors were judged ready to go, he added phosphoric acid to dis-solve the rocks and release whatever gases their voids might have held. See ibid., p. 709.

198 *produced the lowest hydrocarbon readings of all:* For details, see de Boer and Hale, "New Evi-dence," p. 709.

198 *more abundant at the Kerna:* In an interview, de Boer noted that the Kerna sample, be-cause of the spring's rerouting, had to be drawn from a city holding tank—perhaps letting some of the gas escape as it sat around and lessening the water's concentra-tions. If so, the actual levels of the methane, ethane, and ethylene as they came out of the ground would have been even higher.

SIX: RAPTURE

202 *editor's death had delayed its publication:* For the editor's death, see Stewart, "Preface," in McGuire et al., *The Archaeology of Geological Catastrophes,* p. vii.

202 *preparing for* Geology: de Boer, Hale, and Chanton, "New Evidence for the Geological Origins of the Ancient Delphic Oracle."

204 *more than a million new inhalant abusers:* The National Institute on Drug Abuse gathers sta-tistics on such abuse and how to treat it. See http://www.nida.nih.gov. For a journal-istic view of the problem, see Shankra Vedantam, "Inhalant Abuse on the Rise Among Children," *Washington Post,* January 24, 2005, p. A6.

205 *found that it arises:* He learned about a world of agribusiness that sprays ethylene on fruits and vegetables to speed ripening. Commercial growers use it to ripen and loosen grapes, cherries, blueberries, dates, pears, bananas, apples, melons, mangoes, avocados, pineapples, papayas, and jujubes. Agribusiness relies on ethylene most heavily during the Northern Hemisphere's winter, when supply lines stretch south and growers have less opportunity to ripen crops naturally. See Frederick B. Abeles, *Ethylene in Plant Biology* (New York: Academic Press, 1973), p. 162. So too, chefs and homemakers know the trick. Tomatoes put in a bag ripen faster than those exposed

to air, and tomatoes enclosed with a ripe banana turn red even faster, in both cases because the naturally emitted gas becomes more concentrated, speeding maturation. On the flip side, both domestic and industrial food handlers try to remove as much ethylene as possible to help preserve fruits and vegetables. Growers store apples in bins flushed with carbon dioxide to prevent its accumulation. Spiller, in chatting with neighbors, discovered an inconspicuous world of household products meant to keep foods fresh. Evert-Fresh Green Bags look like clear plastic bags but are made of a mineral that soaks up the sweet gas, extending the shelf life of produce while reducing the loss of vitamins. ExtraLife Disks work the same way. Put in a refrigerator's crisper bin, they slow the rate of ripening and spoilage among fruits and vegetables.

205   *It acts as a hormone:* Ibid., pp. 153–196.

206   *first inhaled nitrous oxide in 1798:* David Knight, *Humphry Davy: Science and Power* (New York: Cambridge University Press, 1998), pp. 28–39.

206   *"extending from the chest to the extremities":* Sir Humphry Davy, *Researches, Chemical and Philosophical, Chiefly concerning Nitrous Oxide, or Dephlogisticated Nitrous Air, and Its Respiration* (New York: Johnson Reprint Corporation, 1972), pp. 289–290.

206   *"great extacy":* Ibid., p. 207.

206   *"appears capable of destroying physical pain":* Ibid., 329.

206   *Only decades later did physicians:* The word *anesthesia* seems to have entered the English language around this time, from the Greek word *anaisthesia,* "lack of sensation." For 1847 and 1848, the *Oxford English Dictionary* lists several examples for *anesthesia* and *anesthetic,* suggesting the rapid adoption of the new words. See *The Compact Edition of the Oxford English Dictionary* (New York: Oxford University Press, 1971), p. 301.

207   *the group's most celebrated members:* In November 1874, shortly after receiving Blood's pamphlet, James reviewed it for the *Atlantic Monthly,* finding it fascinating but flawed in contending that something as simple as a gas could foster cosmic enlightenment. James apparently wrote that before trying it himself. Anonymous, "Review of 'The Anaesthetic Revelation and the Gist of Philosophy,'" *Atlantic Monthly,* November 1874, pp. 627–629.

207   *"the keynote of the experience":* William James, "Subjective Effects of Nitrous Oxide," *Mind* 7 (1882): pp. 186–208.

208   *"One conclusion was forced upon my mind":* William James, *The Varieties of Religious Experience* (New York: Modern Library of Random House, 1929), pp. 378–379. In 1910, in his last published essay, James said nitrous oxide had given him confidence that curious individuals could combine the mystic and scientific approaches to life. He wrote that the illuminations had no deadening ties to grand philosophies or religious doctrines

and were inherently democratic, available to anyone with access to a whiff or two of the intoxicating gas. See Dmitri Tymoczko, "The Nitrous Oxide Philosopher," *Atlantic Monthly,* May 1996, pp. 93–101.

208–209   *Investigators traced the problem to gas leaks:* See Abeles, *Ethylene in Plant Biology,* pp. 3, 154.

209   *their writings hinted:* A. B. Luckhardt and J. B. Carter, "The Physiologic Effects of Ethylene," *Journal of the American Medical Association* 80, no. 11 (1923): pp. 765–770.

209   *"under the influence of the gas for all time":* Ibid., p. 768.

209   *On recovery, he talked excitedly:* Ibid., p. 769.

209–211   *observers found it necessary to hold him down:* Ibid., p. 769.

211   *A 1964 report:* J. G. Bourne, "Uptake, Elimination and Potency of the Inhalational Anesthetics," *Anesthesia* 19, no. 1 (January 1964): pp. 12–32.

211   *a tendency to explode:* For a review of the hazard when the anesthetic was still in wide use, see Isabella C. Herb, "The Present Status of Ethylene," *Journal of the American Medical Association* 101, no. 22 (November 25, 1933): pp. 1716–1720.

212   *two papers coauthored with de Boer and Hale:* H. A. Spiller, J. R. Hale, and J. Z. de Boer, "The Oracle at Delphi: A Multi-disciplinary Defense of the Gaseous Vent Theory," *Journal of Toxicology* 40 (2002): pp. 189–196; and H. A. Spiller, J. R. Hale, J. Z. de Boer, "Ancient Inhalers: The Oracle of Delphi," *Mithridata* (the newsletter of the Toxicological History Society) 12, no. 1 (January 2002): pp. 3–8.

215   *He ordered the ethylene:* Each year, the world's chemical industry makes and devours millions of tons of the gas. Producers form it mainly by cracking natural gas and often locate their factories near oil refineries. Why so much interest? Industrial chemists found over the decades that ethylene's reactive nature makes it an ideal petrochemical feedstock, a starting point for the manufacture of scores of other chemicals and goods. It is the basis of polyethylene—the world's most widely used plastic—as well as ethylene glycol (used in antifreeze), polyvinyl chloride (for plastic pipes), and ethanol (used in solvents and toiletries). Worldwide, it dominates the petrochemical industry. See Ludwig Kniel, Olaf Winter, and Karl Stork, *Ethylene: Keystone to the Petrochemical Industry* (New York: Marcel Dekker, 1980), pp. iii, 34–35.

221   *especially his book on the Athenian navy:* John R. Hale, ed., *Lords of the Sea: The Athenians and Their Navy in the Golden Age* (forthcoming).

221   *the lost fleets of the Persian Wars:* William J. Broad, "Off Greece, a Risky Hunt for Lost Fleets of Legend," *New York Times,* April 20, 2004, p. F1.

221   *an article for* Scientific American: Hale, Zeilinga de Boer, Chanton, and Spiller, "Questioning the Delphic Oracle."

221   *One quoted scientists:* Sophie Laurant, "Les vapeurs de la pythie: Un gaz souterrain inspirait-il ses visions?" *Science and Vie Junior,* August 2002, pp. 72–76.

224   *the first to admit:* Jelle Zeilinga de Boer, "Delphi's Small Omphalos: An Enigma," un-

published draft manuscript, May 12, 2002. The conic stone, after scholars had given it careful scrutiny and even debated its authenticity (some concluded that it had fallen into the *adyton* from the village atop the ruins), disappeared sometime after 1951. Detailed searches of the Delphi museum's collection and the sanctuary grounds, done in 1989 and 1999, failed to locate the ancient piece.

SEVEN: MYSTIC CLUE

228   *challenged a basic tenet of modern science:* Hull's main case study centered on the prospect that Mendelian genetics could be reduced to molecular genetics. For years, he sought to erect a theoretical structure for doing so but in the end argued that the endeavor was hopeless. David Hull, *Philosophy of Biological Science* (Englewood Cliffs, N.J.: Prentice-Hall, 1974), pp. 8–44.

229   *It pitted staunch defenders:* One of the most thoughtful is John C. Polkinghorne, a theoretical physicist turned theologian and Anglican priest. He has argued his case in a half dozen books, such as *Belief in God in an Age of Science* (New Haven, Conn.: Yale University Press, 2003). For some of his reduction arguments, see John Polkinghorne, *One World: The Interaction of Science and Theology* (Princeton, N.J.: Princeton University Press, 1987), pp. 86–98. He also has a long paper on reductionism in the *Interdisciplinary Encyclopedia of Religion and Science,* which can be found online at www.disf.org/en/Voci/104.asp. For a professional overview of reduction and its limitations, see Evandro Agazzi, ed., *The Problem of Reductionism in Science* (Boston: Kluwer Academic Publishers, 1991).

230   *Whole books:* See, for example, Edwin Arthur Burtt, *The Metaphysical Foundations of Modern Science* (Garden City, N.Y.: Doubleday, 1954). First published in 1924, it discusses the leap of faith that the founders of modern science made in reducing all nature to a system of mathematical equations.

231   *metaphysical leap:* For a discussion, see Michael P. Lynch, *True to Life: Why Truth Matters* (Cambridge, Mass.: MIT Press, 2004), p. 76. Also see E. Agazzi, "Introduction," pp. vii–xviii, and "Reduction as Negation of the Scientific Spirit," pp. 1–29, and H. Primas, "Reductionism: Palaver without Precedent," pp. 161–172, in Agazzi, *The Problem of Reductionism.*

231   *an act of faith rooted in materialism:* An unassuming but powerful expression of logic known as Occam's razor is often used to bolster aggressive reductionism and materialist points of view. William of Occam was a Franciscan monk and medieval English philosopher who, like Saint Francis, led a humble life centered on the belief that poverty was a path to God. His philosophy echoed his life. He espoused a minimalism that said the simplest explanation among competing theories is preferable and more likely to reflect reality. His rule, which became a guide of modern science, is

often called the principle of parsimony. With it, scientists choose the simplest hypothesis as most likely to be correct if no experiment can settle the matter. For instance, Occam's razor suggests that if you hear hoofbeats, think horses, not zebras. In other words, assume the correctness of the most likely explanation, not the most exotic. Occam's razor appeals to materialists skeptical of otherworldly claims. For instance, they say parapsychology is a pseudoscience that violates Occam's razor. The simplest explanation for its claims is not that human minds enjoy all kinds of extraordinary powers, they argue, but that wishful thinking makes humans gullible and easily fooled.

231   *"a world without wonder":* Dan Brown, *Angels and Demons* (New York: Pocket Star, 2000), p. 379.

232   *Examples of emergence:* For discussions of emergence in biology and its philosophical implications, see Ricard Solé and Brian Goodwin, *Signs of Life: How Complexity Pervades Biology* (New York: Basic Books, 2000) and Irun R. Cohen, *Tending Adam's Garden: Evolving the Cognitive Immune Self* (Boston: Elsevier, 2004).

232   *going in the direction opposite of reduction:* An early analysis of this type is known as synthesis. It led to laws that let physicists predict some aspects of how masses of particles will behave at different levels of organization, such as how water molecules at certain temperatures will turn from a liquid into a gas. See Edward O. Wilson, *Consilience: The Unity of Knowledge* (New York: Vintage, 1999), pp. 93–104.

232   *blazed this path:* See M. Mitchell Waldrop, *Complexity: The Emerging Science at the Edge of Order and Chaos* (New York: Simon & Schuster, 1993) and Steven Johnson, *Emergence: The Connected Lives of Ants, Brains, Cities, and Software* (New York: Scribner's, 2004).

232   *Skeptics see the new fields:* Wilson, *Consilience,* p. 97.

232   *Historians see the upward scientific push:* Achim Stephan, "Emergence—A Systematic View on Its Historical Facets," pp. 25–48, and Brian P. McLaughlin, "The Rise and Fall of British Emergentism," pp. 49–93, in Ansgar Beckermann, Hans Flohr, and Jaegwon Kim, eds., *Emergence or Reduction? Essays on the Prospects of Nonreductive Physicalism* (New York: Walter de Gruyter, 1992).

233   *saw the apparent multiplicity of nature as superficial:* See Kitto, *The Greeks,* pp. 177–180.

233   *reputed to have questioned the impulse:* Antoine Danchin, *The Delphic Boat: What Genomes Tell Us* (Cambridge, Mass.: Harvard University Press, 2002). Plutarch in his *Lives* suggests that the boat question was a standing problem among ancient philosophers, and it appears that the Oracle restated rather than invented the old puzzle.

234   *scientists work through a hierarchy of disciplines:* In addition to reduction and synthesis, scientists pursue many other strategies to comprehend nature, most notably integration. It tends to be relatively rare but can be quite powerful. Einstein's theory of general relativity won wide acclaim for its unexpected coupling of space, time, and matter.

235   *scientists expect wide progress:* Francis Crick, the codiscoverer of DNA's structure and an

outspoken reductionist, observed that "the ultimate aim of the modern movement in biology is in fact to explain all biology in terms of physics and chemistry." See F. H. C. Crick, *Of Molecules and Men* (Seattle: University of Washington Press, 1966), p. 10.

235 *predicts that feats of reduction:* Wilson, *Consilience,* pp. 291, 293. Many influential scientists hailed the book. Interestingly, the scientific backers of Wilson tended to be physicists, who deal with a spare world, and the detractors tended to be biologists, especially evolutionary biologists, who wrestle with extremely knotty problems. Perhaps the most prominent biological critic was Stephen Jay Gould, who, like Wilson, taught at Harvard. He spent his last days questioning Wilson's ideas. See *The Hedgehog, the Fox, and the Magister's Pox: Mending the Gap Between Science and the Humanities* (New York: Harmony, 2003). See also a review of Gould's book by Robert N. Proctor, "Conciliation, Gould's Last Discourse," *Science,* October 31, 2003, p. 785. For pointed criticism of Wilson by an evolutionary biologist, see H. Allen Orr, "The Big Picture: E. O. Wilson's New Book Is Ambitious, Vague, and Philosophically Naïve," *Boston Review,* October–November 1998, pp. 42–45.

236 *A few knowledgeable critics:* See Harold J. Morowitz, "Reducing Life to Physics," *New York Times,* June 23, 1980, p. A23.

236 *reputation for doing in old theories:* But few experts agree on how the process works. For a sampling of the vigorous debates on theory replacement via reduction, see Justin Schwartz, "Reduction, Elimination, and the Mental," *Philosophy of Science* 58, no. 2 (June 1991): pp. 203–220, and Colin Cheyne, "Reduction, Elimination, and Firewalking," *Philosophy of Science* 60, no. 2 (June 1993): pp. 349–357.

236 *championed this view:* Arthur Eddington, *The Nature of the Physical World* (Ann Arbor: University of Michigan Press, 1958), pp. xi–xv.

237 *despite Wilson's hopes to the contrary:* Wilson, *Consilience,* pp. 99–104.

237 *Carbon atoms reveal little of diamonds:* Daniel C. Dennett, a leading American philosopher of science, has coined the term "greedy reductionism" to denounce those forms that try to explain too much with too little. For instance, greedy reductionism would explain the workings of a Web browser by looking only at the whirl of electrons. See Daniel C. Dennett, *Darwin's Dangerous Idea: Evolution and the Meanings of Life* (New York: Simon & Schuster, 1995), pp. 82–83, 195, 394–396. Mary Midgley, a British philosopher, has called aspects of modern reduction "absurdly misleading." She notes the difficulty a reductionist faces in relying solely on a list of constituent atoms to identify a leaf. A botanist, she notes, would look beyond that to such things as the leaf's structure, the probable tree and woodland that it came from, the likely ecosystem, and so on. See Mary Midgley, "Do We Ever Really Act?" in Dai Rees and Steven Rose, eds., *The New Brain Sciences: Perils and Prospects* (New York: Cambridge University Press, 2004), p. 17.

237   *reductive naturalism harbors a contradiction:* Lynch, *True to Life,* pp. 75–100.

237   *threatens to obliterate all logic:* Polkinghorne, *One World,* p. 92.

238   *"a mask for nihilism":* Viktor E. Frankl, "Reductionism and Nihilism," in Arthur Koestler and J. R. Smythies, eds., *Beyond Reductionism: New Perspectives in the Life Sciences* (Boston: Beacon Press, 1969), pp. 396, 398.

239   *An editorial in a medical journal:* Anonymous, "A Whiff of the Future," *British Journal of Sports Medicine* 35 (October 2001): p. 285.

239   *"the source of its power":* Anonymous, "Oracle at Delphi," *Skylights,* Austrian Airlines, May–June 2004, p. 25.

239   *a breezy, tongue-in-cheek satire:* Anonymous, "Brief Lives," *Sunday Times* (London), May 4, 1997, style section, p. 12.

241   *said nothing about a range of oracular feats:* In fairness to the press, at least one article anticipated some of the team's views on the limitations of reductive naturalism in relation to the ethylene discovery. See Philip Ball, "Gassing with the Gods," *New Scientist,* September 1, 2001, pp. 40–42.

242   *This new appreciation of limitations:* Despite new tolerance brought on by my Delphi experience, I have to admit that I am still skeptical of many psychic claims. The world is full of fake psychics and faulty predictions. By contrast, modern science has an astonishingly successful record of acting like a highly reliable crystal ball that can peer far into the future and routinely outdo claimed feats of prophecy—forecasting the weather, warning of disease, even looking billions of years into the future to foresee our sun's final days. The magazine *Skeptical Inquirer,* which I have read for many years, is an excellent antidote to psychic credulousness. See, for example, Bryan Farah, "Blundered Predictions in 2004: A Sylvia Browne Review," *Skeptical Inquirer,* March–April 2005, pp. 8–9, and Anonymous, "Bin Laden Dead, Powell President? Psychic's Predictions for 2004 Missed Big Time," *Skeptical Inquirer,* March–April 2005, pp. 7–8.

245   *The favorite was Prairie Bayou:* Joseph Durso, "Awkward, Yes, but Prairie Bayou Is Poised as Favorite," *New York Times,* April 27, 1993, p. B11.

245   *as Sea Hero stumbled in races:* Joseph Durso, "Shift to Dirt Leaves Sea Hero in the Dust," *New York Times,* February 8, 1993, p. C9.

246   *more than two lengths ahead of his closest rival:* Joseph Durso, "3-Year-Old Gives 85-Year-Old His Derby Dream," *New York Times,* May 2, 1993, section 8, p. 1.

248   *almost certainly had psychic gifts: The Double Tongue,* a portrait of the recruitment and life of an Oracle by William Golding, the Nobel laureate, echoes de Boer's view that the perceptions of the priestess were both worldly and psychic. The book was Golding's last novel, unfinished at the time he died in 1993. See William Golding, *The Double Tongue: A Draft of a Novel* (New York: Farrar, Straus, and Giroux, 1995).

Selected Bibliography

Abeles, Frederick B. *Ethylene in Plant Biology* (New York: Academic Press, 1973).

Agazzi, Evandro, ed. *The Problem of Reductionism in Science* (Boston: Kluwer Academic Publishers, 1991).

———. "Reduction as Negation of the Scientific Spirit," in Evandro Agazzi, ed., *The Problem of Reductionism in Science* (Boston: Kluwer Academic Publishers, 1991), pp. 1–29.

Amandry, Pierre. *La Mantique Apolliniene à Delphes: Essai sure le founctionnement de l'Oracle* (Paris: De Boccard, 1950).

———. "Fouilles de Delphes et raisins de Corinthe," in Olivier Picard and Evangelos Pentazos, eds., *La redécouverte de Delphes* (Paris: De Boccard, École française d'Athènes, 1992), pp. 77–128.

Amberley, Lord (John Russell). "Experiences of Spiritualism," *The Fortnightly Review* 21 (January 1874): pp. 82–91.

Andronicos, Manolis. *Delphi* (Athens: Ekdotike Athenon, 1980).

Ashton, Geoffrey. "Collier, John," *The Dictionary of Art* (New York: Grove Dictionaries, 1996), Vol. 7, p. 569.

Ball, Philip. "Gassing with the Gods," *New Scientist,* September 1, 2001, pp. 40–42.

Beard, Mary. *The Parthenon* (Cambridge, Mass.: Harvard University Press, 2003).

Beckermann, Ansgar, Hans Flohr, and Jaegwon Kim, eds. *Emergence or Reduction? Essays on the Prospects of Nonreductive Physicalism* (New York: Walter de Gruyter, 1992).

Bickerman, E. J. *Chronology of the Ancient World* (London: Thames and Hudson, 1968).

Birot, Pierre. "Géomorphologie de la Région de Delphes," *Bulletin de Correspondance Hellénique* 83, no. 1 (1959): pp. 258–274.

Bourne, J. G. "Uptake, elimination and potency of the inhalational anesthetics," *Anesthesia* 19, no. 1 (January 1964): pp. 12–32.

Broad, William J. *The Universe Below: Discovering the Secrets of the Deep Sea* (New York: Simon & Schuster, 1997).

———. "For Delphic Oracle, Fumes and Visions," *New York Times,* March 19, 2002, p. F1.

———. "Off Greece, a Risky Hunt for Lost Fleets of Legend," *Times,* April 20, 2004, p. F1.

—————. "U.S. Is Losing Its Dominance in the Sciences," *New York Times,* May 3, 2004, p. A1.

Brown, Dan. *Angels and Demons* (New York: Pocket Star, 2000).

Burkert, Walter. *Greek Religion* (Cambridge, Mass.: Harvard University Press, 2001).

—————. *Babylon, Memphis, Persepolis: Eastern Contexts of Greek Culture* (Cambridge, Mass.: Harvard University Press, 2004).

Burtt, Edwin Arthur. *The Metaphysical Foundations of Modern Science* (Garden City, N.Y.: Doubleday, 1954).

Bury, J. B., and Russell Meiggs. *A History of Greece* (London: Macmillan, 1978).

Camp, John, and Elizabeth Fisher. *The World of the Ancient Greeks* (London: Thames and Hudson, 2002).

Cheyne, Colin. "Reduction, Elimination, and Firewalking," *Philosophy of Science* 60, no. 2 (June 1993): pp. 349–357.

Cohen, Irun R. *Tending Adam's Garden: Evolving the Cognitive Immune Self* (Boston: Elsevier, 2004).

Courby, Fernand. *Fouilles de Delphes, tome 2, Topographie et Architecture, La Terrasse du Temple* (Paris: De Boccard, 1927).

Crick, Francis. *Of Molecules and Men* (Seattle: University of Washington Press, 1966).

—————. *The Astonishing Hypothesis: The Scientific Search for the Soul* (New York: Scribner, 1994).

Danchin, Antoine. *The Delphic Boat: What Genomes Tell Us* (Cambridge, Mass.: Harvard University Press, 2002).

Davy, Sir Humphry. *Researches, Chemical and Philosophical, Chiefly Concerning Nitrous Oxide, or Dephlogisticated Nitrous Air, and Its Respiration* (New York: Johnson Reprint Corporation, 1972).

De Boer, Jelle. "Paleomagnetic Indications of Megatectonic Movements in the Tethys," *Journal of Geophysical Research* 70, no. 4 (February 15, 1965): pp. 931–944.

—————. "Delphi's Small Omphalos: An Enigma," unpublished draft manuscript, May 12, 2002.

—————, Jean-Guy Schilling, and Dale C. Krause. "Magnetic Polarity of Pillow Basalts from Reykjanes Ridge," *Science* 166 (Nov. 21, 1969): pp. 996–998.

—————, and J. R. Hale, "The Geological Origins of the Oracle at Delphi, Greece," in McGuire, W. J., et al., eds., *The Archaeology of Geological Catastrophes* (London: Geological Society, Special Publication no. 171, 2000), pp. 399–412.

—————, J. R. Hale, and J. Chanton. "New Evidence for the Geological Origins of the Ancient Delphic Oracle (Greece)," *Geology* 29, no. 8 (August 2001): pp. 707–710.

—————, and Donald Theodore Sanders. *Volcanoes in Human History: The Far-Reaching Effects of Major Eruptions* (Princeton, N.J.: Princeton University Press, 2002).

—————, and Donald Theodore Sanders. *Earthquakes in Human History: The Far-Reaching Effects of Seismic Disruptions* (Princeton, N.J.: Princeton University Press, 2005).

DeGrasse Tyson, Neil. "Holy Wars, An Astrophysicist Ponders the God Question," *Skeptical Inquirer* 25, no. 5 (September/October 2001): pp. 24–27.

Dempsey, T. *The Delphic Oracle: Its Early History, Influence, and Fall* (Oxford: Blackwell, 1918).

Dennett, Daniel C. *Darwin's Dangerous Idea: Evolution and the Meanings of Life* (New York: Simon & Schuster, 1995).

Devereux, George, ed. *Psychoanalysis and the Occult* (New York: International Universities Press, 1970).

Diodorus Siculus. *The Library of History, Books XV.20–XVI.65*. Charles L. Sherman, trans. (Cambridge, Mass.: Loeb Classical Library, 1952).

Dodds, E. R. "Telepathy and Clairvoyance in Classical Antiquity," in anonymous, *Greek Poetry and Life: Essays Presented to Gilbert Murray on his Seventieth Birthday, January 2, 1936* (Freeport, N.Y.: Books for Libraries Press, 1967).

———. *The Greeks and the Irrational* (Berkeley: University of California Press, 1963).

———. *Missing Persons: An Autobiography* (Oxford: Oxford University Press, 1977).

Dyer, Louis. *Studies of the Gods in Greece at Certain Sanctuaries Recently Excavated* (London: Macmillan, 1891).

Eddington, Arthur. *The Nature of the Physical World* (Ann Arbor: University of Michigan Press, 1958).

Euripides. *Ten Plays*. Paul Roche, trans. (New York: Signet, 1998).

Finley, M. I. *The Ancient Greeks* (New York: Penguin, 1991).

Flaceliere, Robert. *Greek Oracles* (London: Elek, 1976).

Fontenrose, Joseph. *The Delphic Oracle: Its Responses and Operations with a Catalogue of Responses* (Berkeley: University of California Press, 1978).

Frankl, Viktor E. "Reductionism and Nihilism," in Arthur Koestler and J. R. Smythies, eds., *Beyond Reductionism: New Perspectives in the Life Sciences* (Boston: Beacon Press, 1969).

Golding, William. *The Double Tongue: A Draft of a Novel* (New York: Farrar, Straus, and Giroux, 1995).

Gould, Stephen Jay. *The Hedgehog, the Fox, and the Magister's Pox: Mending the Gap Between Science and the Humanities* (New York: Harmony, 2003).

Grene, Marjorie. *A Portrait of Aristotle* (Chicago: University of Chicago Press, 1967).

Hale, John R. "The Lost Technology of Ancient Greek Rowing," *Scientific American,* May 1996, pp. 66–71.

———. "Phormio Crosses the T," *The Quarterly Journal of Military History* 8, no. 4 (1996): pp. 38–41.

———. "The Viking Longship," *Scientific American,* February 1998, pp. 46–53.

———, ed., *Lords of the Sea: The Athenians and their Navy in the Golden Age* (forthcoming).

———, Jelle Zeilinga de Boer, Jeffrey P. Chanton, and Henry A. Spiller. "Questioning the Delphic Oracle," *Scientific American,* August 2003, pp. 66–73.

Halliday, W. R. *Greek Divination: A Study of Its Methods and Principles* (Whitefish, Montana: Kessinger, 2003).

Hamilton, Edith, and Huntington Cairns, eds. *The Collected Dialogues of Plato* (Princeton, N.J.: Princeton University Press, 1973).

Hansel, C.E.M. *ESP and Parapsychology: A Critical Reevaluation* (Buffalo, N.Y.: Promethus, 1980).

Haynes, Renée. *The Hidden Springs: An Enquiry into Extra-Sensory Perception* (Boston: Little, Brown, 1973).

Herb, Isabella C. "The present status of ethylene," *Journal of the American Medical Association* 101, no. 22 (Nov. 25, 1933): pp. 1716–1720.

Herodotus. *The Histories.* Walter Blanco and Jennifer Tolbert Roberts, trans. (New York: Norton, 1992).

———. *The Histories.* Aubrey de Sélincourt, trans. (Baltimore: Penguin, 1966).

Hesiod. *Homerica Hymns, Homerica.* Hugh G. Evelyn-White, trans. (Cambridge, Mass.: Loeb Classical Library, 2002).

Higgins, Michael Denis, and Reynold Higgins. *A Geological Companion to Greece and the Aegean* (Ithaca: Cornell University Press, 1996).

Homer. *Iliad.* W. H. D. Rouse, trans. (New York: New American Library, n.d.)

———. *Odyssey.* E. V. Rieu, trans. (Baltimore: Penguin, 1967).

Howard, Maureen C. *Sophocles' Oedipus Rex* (New Haven, Conn.: Yale-New Haven Teachers Institute, 2004), www.yale.edu/ynhti/curriculum/units/1984/2/84.02.03.x.html.

Hoyle, Peter. *Delphi* (London: Cassell & Company, 1967).

Holland, Leicester B. "The Mantic Mechanism at Delphi," *American Journal of Archaeology* 37 (1933): pp. 201–214.

Hornblower, Simon, and Antony Spawforth, eds. *The Oxford Classical Dictionary* (New York: Oxford University Press, 2003).

Hull, David. *Philosophy of Biological Science* (Englewood Cliffs, N.J.: Prentice-Hall, 1974).

Jacquemin, Anne. "En feuilletant le *Journal de la Grande Fouille,*" in Olivier Picard and Evangelos Pentazos, eds., *La redécouverte de Delphes* (Paris: De Boccard, École française d'Athènes, 1992), p. 173.

James, William. "Subjective Effects of Nitrous Oxide," *Mind* 7 (1882): pp. 186–208.

———. *The Varieties of Religious Experience* (New York: Modern Library of Random House, 1929).

Johnson, Claudia C. "The Rise and Fall of Rudist Reefs," *American Scientist,* March–April, 2002, pp. 148–153.

Johnson, George. *Fire in the Mind: Science, Faith, and the Search for Order* (New York: Knopf, 1995).

———. "Science and Religion: Bridging the Great Divide," *New York Times,* June 30, 1998, p. F4.

———. "True Believers; Science and Religion Cross Their Line in the Sand," *New York Times,* July 12, 1998, sec. 4, p. 1.

Johnson, Steven. *Emergence: The Connected Lives of Ants, Brains, Cities and Software* (New York: Scribner, 2004).

Jones, Ernest. *The Life and Work of Sigmund Freud*: (New York: Basic Books, 1957).

Kerényi, Carl. *Dionysos: Archetypal Image of Indestructible Life* (Princeton, N.J.: Princeton University Press, 1996).

Kitto, H. D. F. *The Greeks* (London: Penguin, 1951).

Kniel, Ludwig, Olaf Winter, and Karl Stork. *Ethylene: Keystone to the Petrochemical Industry* (New York: Marcel Dekker, 1980).

Knight, David. *Humphry Davy: Science and Power* (New York: Cambridge University Press, 1998).

Koestler, Arthur. *The Roots of Coincidence* (London: Hutchinson, 1972).

————, and J. R. Smythies, eds. *Beyond Reductionism: New Perspectives in the Life Sciences* (Boston: Beacon Press, 1969).

Konstantinou, Ioanna K. *Delphi: The Oracle and Its Role in the Political and Social Life of the Ancient Greeks* (Athens: Hannibal, undated).

Krontira, Leda. *Getting to Know Apollo's Sanctuary at Delphi* (Athens: Ekdotike Athenon, 1996).

Lach-Szybma, W. S. "Correspondence," *Journal of the Society for Psychical Research 1* (February 1885): pp. 284–285.

Laurant, Sophie. "Les vapeurs de la pythie: Un gaz souterrain inspirait-il ses visions?" *Science & Vie Junior,* August 2002, pp. 72–76.

Lederman, Leon. *The God Particle: If the Universe Is the Answer, What Is the Question?* (Boston: Houghton Mifflin, 1993).

Levin, Saul. "The Old Greek Oracles in Decline," *Aufstieg und Niedergang der römischen Welt II,* no. 18, vol. 2, pp: 1599–1649.

Lewis, Neville. *Delphi and the Sacred Way* (London: Michael Haag, 1987).

Lloyd, G. E. R. *Early Greek Science: Thales to Aristotle* (New York: Norton, 1970).

Lucan. *The Civil War.* J. D. Duff, trans. (Cambridge, Mass.: Loeb Classical Library, 1997).

Luckhardt, A. B., and J. B. Carter, "The Physiologic Effects of Ethylene," *Journal of the American Medical Association 80,* no. 11 (1923): pp. 765–770.

Lynch, Michael P. *True to Life: Why Truth Matters* (Cambridge, Mass.: MIT Press, 2004).

MacDonald, I. R., et al. "Gas hydrate that breaches the sea floor on the continental slope of the Gulf of Mexico," *Geology,* August 1994, pp. 699–702.

Maurizio, Lisa. "The Voice at the Center of the World: The Pythias' Ambiguity and Authority," in Andre Lardinois and Laura McClure, eds., *Making Silence Speak: Women's Voices in Greek Literature and Society* (Princeton, N.J.: Princeton University Press, 2001).

McGuire, W. J., et al., eds. *The Archaeology of Geological Catastrophes* (London: Geological Society, Special Publication no. 171, 2000).

McMoneagle, Joseph. *The Stargate Chronicles: Memoirs of a Psychic Spy* (Charlottesville, Va.: Hampton Roads Publishing Company, 2002).

Mee, Christopher, and Antony Spawforth. *Greece: An Oxford Archaeological Guide* (New York: Oxford University Press, 2001).

Menard, H. W. *Ocean of Truth: A Personal History of Global Tectonics* (Princeton, N.J.: Princeton University Press, 1986).

Miller, Judith, Stephen Engelberg, and William Broad. *Germs: Biological Weapons and America's Secret War* (New York: Simon & Schuster, 2001).

Miller, Walter. *Daedalus and Thespis,* Vol. 1 (New York: MacMillan, 1929).

Morell, Parker. *Lillian Russell: The Era of the Plush* (New York: Random House, 1940).

Morgan, Catherine. *Athletes and Oracles* (New York: Cambridge University Press, 1997).

Morowitz, Harold J. "Reducing Life to Physics," *New York Times,* June 23, 1980, p. A23.

Myers, Frederic W. H. *Essays, Classical* (London: Macmillan, 1911).

———. *Human Personality and Its Survival of Bodily Death* (Charlottesville, Va.: Hampton Roads Publishing, 2001).

Oppé, A. P. "The Chasm at Delphi," *Journal of Hellenic Studies* 24 (1904): pp. 214–240.

Orr, H. Allen. "The Big Picture: E. O. Wilson's New Book Is Ambitious, Vague, and Philosophically Naïve," *Boston Review,* October/November 1998, pp. 42–45.

Papalexandrou, Nassos. *The Visual Poetics of Power: Warriors, Youths, and Tripods in Early Greece.* (Lanham, Md.: Lexington Books, 2005.)

Parke, H. W. "The Deposing of Spartan Kings," *Classical Quarterly* 39, no. 3–4 (1945): pp. 106–112.

———. *Greek Oracles* (London: Hutchinson University Library, 1967).

———, and D. E. W. Wormell. *The Delphic Oracle: Vol. 1, The History* (Oxford: Blackwell, 1956).

———, and D. E. W. Wormell. *The Delphic Oracle: Vol. 2, The Oracular Responses* (Oxford: Blackwell, 1956).

Partida, Elena C. *The Treasuries at Delphi: An Architectural Study* (Jonsered, Sweden: Paul Åströms Förlag, 2000).

———. Letter to author, May 4, 2005.

Pausanias. *I: Description of Greece, Books I and II.* W. H. S. Jones, trans. (Cambridge, Mass.: Loeb Classical Library, 1998).

———. *IV: Description of Greece, Books VIII.22–X.* W. H. S. Jones, trans. (Cambridge, Mass.: Loeb Classical Library, 2000).

Pendazos, Vanghelis, and Maria Sarla. *Delphi* (Athens: Yiannikos-Kaldis, 1984).

Picard, Olivier, and Evangelos Pentazos, eds. *La redécouverte de Delphes* (Paris: De Boccard, École française d' Athènes, 1992).

Piccardi, Luigi. "Active faulting at Delphi, Greece: Seismotectonic Remarks and a Hypothesis for the Geologic Environment of Myth," *Geology* 28, no. 7 (July 2000): pp. 651–654.

Plutarch. *Lives, VII.* Bernadotte Perrin, trans. (Cambridge, Mass.: Loeb Classical Library, 1994).

———. *Moralia* Vol. 5. Frank Cole Babbitt, trans. (Cambridge, Mass.: Loeb Classical Library, 1999).

Polkinghorne, John C. *One World: The Interaction of Science and Theology* (Princeton, N.J.: Princeton University Press, 1987).

———. *Belief in God in an Age of Science* (New Haven, Conn.: Yale University Press, 2003).

Poulsen, Frederick. *Delphi* (London: Gyldendal, 1920).

Powell, Corey S. *God in the Equation: How Einstein Became the Prophet of the New Religious Era* (New York: The Free Press, 2002).

Press, Frank, and Raymond Siever. *Understanding Earth* (New York: Freeman, 1998).

Price, H. H. "The Hidden Springs," *Journal of the Society for Psychical Research* 41 (June 1961): pp. 93–97.

Proctor, Robert N. "Conciliation, Gould's Last Discourse," *Science,* October 31, 2003, p. 785.

Rees, Dai, and Steven Rose, eds. *The New Brain Sciences: Perils and Prospects* (New York: Cambridge University Press, 2004).

Réveillac, Gérard. "Photographies de la Grande Fouille," in Olivier Picard and Evangelos Pentazos, eds., *La redécouverte de Delphes* (Paris: De Boccard, École française d'Athènes, 1992), pp. 180–193.

Schwartz, Justin. "Reduction, Elimination, and the Mental," *Philosophy of Science* 58, no. 2 (June 1991): pp. 203–220.

Scully, Vincent. *The Earth, the Temple, and the Gods: Greek Sacred Architecture* (New Haven, Conn.: Yale University Press, 1979).

Simon, Steven J. "The Functions of Priestesses in Greek Society," *Classical Bulletin* 67 (1991): pp. 9–13.

Solé, Ricard, and Brian Goodwin. *Signs of Life: How Complexity Pervades Biology* (New York: Basic Books, 2000).

Spiller, H. A., J. R. Hale, and J. Z. de Boer. "The Oracle at Delphi: a Multidisciplinary Defense of the Gaseous Vent Theory," *Journal of Toxicology* 40 (2002): pp. 189–196.

———. "Ancient Inhalers: The Oracle of Delphi," *Mithridata* (Newsletter of the Toxicological History Society) 12, no. 1 (January 2002): pp. 3–8.

Strabo. *Geography, Books 8–9.* Horace Leonard Jones, trans. (Cambridge, Mass.: Loeb Classical Library, 2001).

Strauss, Barry. *The Battle of Salamis: The Naval Encounter That Saved Greece—and Western Civilization* (New York: Simon & Schuster, 2004).

Taylor, Jean Gelman. *Indonesia: Peoples and Histories* (New Haven, Conn.: Yale University, 2003).

Twiss, Robert J., and Eldridge M. Moores. *Structural Geology* (New York: Freeman, 1992).

Tymoczko, Dmitri. "The Nitrous Oxide Philosopher," *The Atlantic Monthly,* May 1996, pp. 93–101.

Tyrrell, G. N. M. *The Personality of Man: New Facts and Their Significance* (London: Penguin, 1954).

Vandenberg, Philipp. *The Mystery of the Oracles: World-Famous Archaeologists Reveal the Best-Kept Secrets of Antiquity* (New York: Macmillan, 1982).

Waldrop, M. Mitchell. *Complexity: The Emerging Science at the Edge of Order and Chaos* (New York: Simon & Schuster, 1993).

Wilson, Edward O. *Consilence: The Unity of Knowledge* (New York: Vintage, 1999).

Winchester, Simon. *Krakatoa: The Day the World Exploded* (New York: HarperCollins, 2003).

Wright, F. A. *Lemprière's Classical Dictionary of Proper Names Mentioned in Ancient Authors* (London: Routledge & Kegan Paul, 1949).

Xenophon. *Memorabilia, Oeconomicus, Symposium, Apology.* E. C. Marchant and O. J. Todd, trans. (Cambridge, Mass.: Loeb Classical Library, 2002).

Glossary

acropolis The high point of a Greek city that typically would hold a shrine to its most important god. In classical Athens, the acropolis was the site of the **Parthenon**, a large temple dedicated to **Athena**, the city's patron goddess.

adyton A sacred place or the innermost shrine in a temple forbidden to the general public. *Adyton* in ancient Greek means "do not enter" or "inaccessible" and consisted of a separately defined space or inner room of great sanctity. At **Delphi** within the temple of **Apollo**, the French excavations left unclear the exact layout of the *adyton* as well as whether the inner sanctum had its own roof.

Aegean Sea An arm of the Mediterranean located between the Greek peninsula and **Anatolia.** It has more than three thousand islands. In antiquity, the islands served as stepping stones for the emerging civilizations of the Greek mainland.

Aeschylus (525–455 BCE) The first of three great tragic Greek dramatists. His play *Eumenides,* which depicts the triumph of law over violence, starts with the **Oracle** of **Delphi** giving a detailed recounting of her sanctuary's history and the arrival of bright **Apollo.**

Agamemnon The mythological king of **Mycenae** who **Homer** depicted as leading the Greeks against **Troy.**

Alexander the Great (356–323 BCE) A king of Macedonia who conquered much of the known world and spread Greek culture.

Amandry, Pierre A French archaeologist who worked on the excavations of **Delphi** between 1937 and 1949, penned a critique of **Delphi** analysts in 1950, and served as director of the French School of Archaeology in Athens from 1969 to 1981.

amphictyony A religious league of ancient Greek cities participating in the cult of a common deity. The amphictyony that oversaw **Apollo**'s sanctuary at **Delphi** became unusually large and powerful, a rare example of extensive teamwork among the normally fractious Greek states.

amphora A two-handled clay jar used in antiquity for the storage and transport of such things as wine, oil, and pitch.

Anatolia The Asian (as opposed to the European) part of modern day Turkey, also known as Asia Minor. It occupies the peninsula between the Black Sea, the Mediterranean, and the **Aegean.**

Apollo The Greek god of light, prophesy, poetry, music, and healing. As the god of spiritual healing, Apollo purified those guilty of murder or other grievous sins. For many centuries this son of **Zeus** was the most revered and influential member of the Greek **pantheon.**

archaic A period of Greek history and culture extending from 776 BCE (the first Olympic Games) to 480 BCE (when the Greeks defeated Persian invaders).

Aristophanes (*c.* 455–385 BCE) A comic playwright who satirized Athenian politics and culture during the city's golden age. He opposed **Athens'** war with **Sparta** (the **Peloponnesian War**) and earned lasting fame for his comedy *Lysistrata,* in which the women of Greece band together to deny their husbands sex until the war ends. His other plays include *The Frogs, The Clouds,* and *The Birds.*

Aristotle (384–322 BCE) A philosopher who studied with **Plato** and taught **Alexander the Great.** In contrast to Plato, Aristotle placed much value on knowledge gained from the senses and set the stage for what centuries later would become the scientific method.

Athena The patron goddess of **Athens,** as well as of wisdom, the arts, and peace and war.

Athens The most celebrated city of the ancient world, the seat of Greek art and drama, literature and philosophy. Named after its patron goddess, **Athena,** Athens basically invented the European idiom.

Attica The territory of the ancient city-state of **Athens.** Its plains, hills, and rocky coastlines formed a triangular promontory that extended into the **Aegean;** its overall size was similar to that of greater Los Angeles.

augur A seer or diviner, especially one who worked from omens. The augur's job in ancient Greece was to interpret signs in nature, such as the shape and condition of animal entrails, and to divine the future and whether the gods approved of planned military and political acts.

augury The art or practice of **divination,** usually from signs and omens.

BCE Before the Common Era is the term scholars use to designate BC, but without the religious connotations. In the Christian calendar, BC means Before Christ.

bedrock The solid rock underlying unconsolidated surface materials such as sand and soil.

bitumen Sticky, blackish mixes of **hydrocarbons** and other substances occurring naturally as tar or obtained by distillation from coal or petroleum. Bitumen—also called asphalt, tar, or pitch—is basically petroleum in solid or semisolid form.

Bronze Age The period in history after the Stone Age characterized by the development of bronze and its use, especially for weapons and tools. The specific dates of the Bronze Age vary from region to region because they are defined in terms of the technologies of particular cultures rather than a fixed time.

Byron, Lord (1788–1824) An English romantic poet and Greek enthusiast who condemned the British removal of ancient sculptures from the **Parthenon** for display in London. "Dull is the eye," he wrote in *Childe Harold's Pilgrimage,* "that will not weep to see thy walls defaced."

calcium carbonate A colorless or white crystalline compound that occurs naturally as chalk, **limestone,** and marble.

Castalia Named after a **naiad,** this spring flowed down a gorge a half mile east of the temple of **Apollo** at **Delphi.** The **Oracle** would bathe in its sacred waters as part of the ceremonial preparation for communing with Apollo.

CE Common Era is the term scholars use to designate AD, but without the religious connotations. AD stands for Anno Domini, or "in the year of our Lord."

clairvoyance A supposed power of mental perception in which a person sees objects or actions removed at a distance in space or time or otherwise concealed from view.

classical A period of Greek history and culture extending from 480 BCE (when the Greeks defeated Persian invaders) to 323 BCE (when **Alexander the Great** died).

Corinth Famous for its vices, rich from olive oil, foreign trade, and prostitution, this ancient Greek city lay west of **Athens** on the Isthmus of Corinth, the narrow stretch of land that joins mainland Greece to the **Peloponnese.** Its prostitutes worshipped Aphrodite, the goddess of love and beauty. In ancient times, bustling Corinth eclipsed **Athens** as a regional power but then saw its enterprising neighbor pull ahead.

Corinth, Gulf of A body of salty water, some 80 miles (130 kilometers) long and up to 20 miles (32 kilometers) wide, that divides central Greece. It opens in the west to the **Ionian Sea.** To its north lies **Delphi** and to the south the **Peloponnese.**

Courby, Fernand (1878–1932) A French archaeologist who in the 1920s helped describe the results of the excavations of ancient **Delphi.**

Cretaceous The geologic period from roughly 65 million to 145 million years ago, a time of warm, shallow seas. Flowering plants arose and the dinosaurs died out.

Croesus The last king of **Lydia,** ascending to the throne around 560 BCE. After ruling for about a decade, he initiated a test to discover the world's most accurate **oracle** and eventually declared **Delphi** the winner.

Delphi The sanctuary of **Apollo** with its large temple and nearby city were located on a southern flank of **Mount Parnassus** in central Greece just north of the **Gulf of Corinth** and a little more than one hundred miles northwest of **Athens.** Delphi was revered throughout the Greek world as the site of the most prestigious **Oracle** of **Apollo** as well as the **omphalos,** a conical stone that marked the sanctuary as the center of the universe. More than a religious site, Delphi also boasted a large theater and a stadium that could seat about seven thousand spectators. It hosted the **Pythian Games** of athletic, musical, and poetic competitions, all dedicated to the god Apollo.

Delphic Pertaining to **Delphi,** but also meaning obscure, ambiguous, or enigmatic, as in Delphic inscrutability.

Democritus (*c.* 460–370 BCE) A Greek philosopher who held that atoms of different sizes and shapes make up everything in nature, including the body and soul, life and mental activity.

Didyma An ancient Greek city in southwestern **Anatolia** whose centerpiece was a prominent temple and **oracle** of **Apollo.**

Diodorus A historian born in Sicily who flourished around 44 BCE and wrote histories of Egypt, **Persia,** Syria, Media, Rome, Carthage, and Greece, including an account of how the **Oracle** got her start.

Dionysus The Greek god of wine, music, and the arts, especially drama. His orgiastic cult celebrated the power of fertility and animal impulse, rebirth and renewal. At **Delphi,** Dionysus held a position almost equal to that of **Apollo.** His women followers were known as **maenads,** his male devotees as satyrs. Devoted to drink as a holy sacrament, they would pursue one another in a state of sexual excitement.

divination The supposed art of using **augury** or supernatural aid to foretell future events or reveal occult knowledge.

Dodds, Eric (1893–1979) A British scholar who was the Regius Professor of Greek at Oxford University between 1936 and 1960 and served as president of the British Society for Psychical Research between 1961 and 1963.

Doric A style of great simplicity in Greek architecture.

emergence In philosophy, the view that complex aspects of nature arise out of fundamental entities to which they cannot be reduced. For instance, emergence holds that human consciousness arises out of atoms in the brain but that its distinguishing characteristics cannot be explained solely in terms of the particles. A phenomenon known as *emergent* is usually unexpected and unpredictable from lower level descriptions. However, somewhat confusingly, the term *emergence* also refers to a new branch of science that seeks to follow this natural assendency and find simple developmental rules for complex structures, such as cities and ant colonies. The research strategy is similar to **reduction** except that the analytic push through the hierarchy of natural complexity is upward rather than downward.

emergentism In philosophy, the belief in nature's powers of **emergence,** in contrast with the scientific powers of **reduction.** It views nature as layered in domains of increasing complexity.

ethane A colorless, odorless, **hydrocarbon** gas. A constituent of natural gas, it is used as a fuel and a refrigerant.

ethylene A colorless, flammable, **hydrocarbon** gas that is derived from natural gas and petroleum. Ethylene is used as a feedstock in the petrochemical industry, as a fuel in welding and cutting metals, as a ripening agent for fruits, and as an anesthetic.

Etruscans The dominant people of pre-Roman Italy.

Euripides (*c.* 480s–407 BCE) The bad boy of Greek tragedy and the youngest of the three great tragic playwrights whose works survive, he is considered darker than **Aeschylus** or **Sophocles.** His most famous plays include *Medea, The Trojan Women, Electra,* and *The Bacchae.*

fault In geology, a straight or gently curved break in the earth's crust. When blocks of rock on either side of the fault shift suddenly and undergo displacement in relation to one another, they cause earthquakes.

fissure A narrow crack or cleft in a rock face, sometimes used as a synonym for a **fault** or fracture.

Gaia A Greek goddess personifying the earth who by some accounts was the founding deity at **Delphi.** In this history, **Apollo** took over the oracle of Gaia or the mouthpiece of other gods for his own use in the art of prophecy.

hellenistic A period of Greek history and culture extending from 323 BCE (when **Alexander the Great** died) to 146 BCE (when Greece became a Roman province). Some scholars extend the era into Roman times.

Hellenes The name that the ancient Greeks bestowed upon themselves, after Hellen, their eponymous ancestor.

Hellenic Relating to the **Hellenes.**

Herodotus (*c.* 480s–420s BCE) Born around the time **Xerxes** invaded Greece, he grew up hearing about the Persian wars and later interviewed survivors and consulted many records to learn their story. By his late thirties, Herodotus had written much of his *Histories,* the first continuous prose narrative extant in Western literature.

Hesiod An early Greek poet thought to have lived around 700 BCE. His works describe rural life, genealogies of the gods, and the origins of the world.

holism The philosophical view that the whole is greater than the sum of its parts and that its existence cannot be reduced to that of its constituents. For instance, human consciousness is more than the billions of atoms that make up the human brain. Contrasting viewpoints include **reductionism.**

Homer The ancient storyteller credited with the authorship of major Greek epic poems, including *Iliad,* about the Trojan war, and *Odyssey,* about the journey of Odysseus after the fall of **Troy.** Scholars debate whether Homer was the name given to one or more oral poets and exactly when his poems took shape and were written down.

Homolle, Théophile (1848–1925) An early French archaeologist who was named director of the French School of Archaeology at Athens in 1890 and led the successful French campaign to win the right to excavate ancient **Delphi.**

hydrocarbons Any of numerous compounds, such as benzene and **methane,** that are composed of hydrogen and carbon atoms.

Ionian Sea An arm of the Mediterranean located between western Greece and southern Italy and Sicily.

Julian (331–363 CE) A Roman emperor from 361 to 363 CE who declared a policy of religious tolerance, seeking to undo Christian domination and restore the pagan cults, especially those of ancient Greece.

Kassotis A spring in the sanctuary of **Apollo** at **Delphi** located near the temple. Its resident **naiad** possessed the power of prophetic inspiration, according to **Pausanias,** a travel writer. He implied that a branch of the Kassotis emerged in the temple's *adyton.*

Kastri The small Greek village that, in the late nineteenth century, consisted of perhaps one hundred homes and two hundred inhabitants living atop the ruins of the ancient sanctuary of **Apollo** at **Delphi.**

Korykian cave Gloomy and forbidding, with a narrow mouth and a large central chamber with stalagmites, the cave lies on the flanks of **Parnassus** about a four-hour climb from **Delphi.** In antiquity, male and female worshippers of **Dionysus** went there to engage in orgiastic rites.

kouros An ancient Greek statue of a youth.

libation A liquid offering poured as part of a religious ritual or ceremony.

limestone A sedimentary rock formed mainly of **calcium carbonate,** often from the remains of bygone sea creatures.

Lucan (39–65 CE) A Roman poet who described the procedures of the **Oracle** in his book, *The Civil War,* an account of Julius Caesar's conquest of the failing Roman republic.

Lycurgus The ancient Greek politician, perhaps legendary, perhaps real, said to have fashioned **Sparta**'s early laws.

Lydia An ancient kingdom of western **Anatolia** that sparkled with natural wealth. **Croesus** took its throne around 560 BCE and eventually lost it to Persian invaders.

maenad A female worshipper of the god **Dionysus.**

Marathon A plain in **Attica** some forty-two kilometers, or twenty-six miles, northeast of **Athens,** framed by mountains and the **Aegean.** There the outnumbered Greeks in 490 BCE defeated an invading Persian army. Afterward, a warrior ran to Athens to inform the citizens of the victory. The distance of that run provides the basis for the modern race.

metaphysics The branch of philosophy that investigates the nature of first principles and ultimate reality.

methane An odorless, colorless, flammable, **hydrocarbon** gas that is the major component of natural gas.

Mycenae An ancient city of the **Peloponnese** and a military stronghold that dominated much of southern Greece before the rise of **Sparta.** The period of Greek history from about 1600 BCE to 1100 BCE is called Mycenaean in recognition of the city's importance.

Myers, Frederic (1843–1901) A British scholar and principal founder of the Society for Psychical Research.

naiad In Greek mythology, a type of **nymph** who presides over brooks, springs, and fountains.

nymph A female nature deity.

Oedipus Mythical son of the king and queen of **Thebes.** An **oracle** foretold that he would kill his father, so Oedipus was sent away at birth to be put to death. Spared and eventually adopted by the king, he unknowingly killed his father and married his mother, fullfilling the prophecy.

Olympus The highest mountain in Greece, near the Aegean coast in the remote north. It rises 9,570 feet, or 2,911 meters.

omphalos A conical stone that marked **Delphi** as the spiritual heart of the ancient Greek world. The word means "navel" or "center." The Delphic authorities kept the omphalos in the *adyton* and put replicas of it around the sanctuary to remind pilgrims of the site's centrality and holiness.

oracle A spiritual person or agency considered to be a source of divine prophecy or wise counsel, often via a deity. The word—derived from the Latin verb *orare,* to speak—also refers to the message itself, often transmitted through a human. Many sites of antiquity gained renown for oracular wisdom. The most famous was the Oracle of **Apollo** at **Delphi,** who exerted influence throughout the Greek world.

paleomagnetism Old magnetization from the earth's magnetic field as recorded in ancient rocks.

Pangaea A supercontinent that coalesced some 300 million years ago and whose breakup, starting some 200 million years ago, produced the configuration of the existing continents.

pantheon The gods of a particular mythology considered collectively, sometimes as a family.

parapsychology The academic study of alleged psychic phenomena.

parapsychologist A student of **parapsychology.**

Parnassus A craggy mountain in central Greece located just north of the **Gulf of Corinth.** It towers over **Delphi.** The tallest of its jagged peaks rises 8,061 feet, or 2,457 meters. Carved of gray **limestone** and heavily forrested in its lower reaches,

Mount Parnassus is crisscrossed with caves, sinkholes, and **faults,** which cleave in some places to form breathtaking rock faces. It is one of the tallest mountains in Greece and only slightly shorter than **Mount Olympus.**

Parthenon A temple of **Athena** built during the time of **Pericles** on the **acropolis** of **Athens.** It replaced what the Persians had destroyed in their 480 BCE invasion. Work began in 447 and the temple was dedicated in 438 but not finished until 432. The Parthenon held a large gold and ivory statue of **Athena,** the patron goddess of **Athens.**

Pausanias (*c.* 120–180 CE) A Greek born in **Anatolia,** Pausanias traveled widely throughout the Roman Empire and wrote a ten-volume *Description of Greece.* The guidebook gave a tour of **Delphi**'s statues and treasures, buildings and pediments. He said the **Kassotis** spring, the one just above the temple, "sinks under the ground, and inspires the women in the shrine of the god," seeming to imply that a branch rose in the *adyton.* In the late nineteenth century, French excavators read Pausanias as a main guide to unearthing **Apollo**'s sanctuary.

Peloponnese A large peninsula in Greece south of the **Gulf of Corinth.** In ancient times, it was dominated first by **Mycenae** and then **Sparta.**

Peloponnesian War Fought from 431 to 404 BCE, it involved a test of wills between **Athens** and **Sparta** to dominate Greece. Sparta prevailed but failed to achieve political unification.

Pericles (*c.* 495–429 BCE) The leading politician of **Athens** during its golden age in the fifth century and a main patron behind many of the city-state's cultural achievements.

Persia The first real empire in Western history. By the fifth century BCE, it had come to control most of the eastern world—**Lydia,** Thrace, Macedonia, Egypt, Ionia, Mesopotamia, and many other lands stretching from the Balkans to the Himalayas. During this period, Persia set its sights on Greece as an impediment to its westward expansion.

Phormio An Athenian general and admiral whose exploits Thucydides recorded in his *History of the Peloponnesian War.* In the Battle of Naupactus in 429 BCE, at the mouth of the **Gulf of Corinth,** he defeated the Corinthian fleet, trapping it in a narrow strait and capturing twelve ships.

Pindar (*c.* 518–443 BCE) A famous Greek lyric poet born in **Thebes** who wrote a dozen Delphic odes.

plate In geology, one of a dozen or so segments of the earth's outer crust that move about as distinct units, propelled by churning currents in molten rock far below.

plate tectonics In geology, the general theory of plate formation, movement, interaction, and destruction. Its application seeks to explain such phenomena as volcanism, earthquakes, mountain building, and the fate of the continents.

Plato (*c.* 429–347 BCE) A student of **Socrates** and teacher of **Aristotle,** Plato held that knowledge gained through the senses is always confused and impure and that true knowledge comes from turning away from the world to inner contemplation. It is through Plato's writings that we learn much about Socrates.

Plutarch (*c.* 50–120 CE) A philosopher and biographer, he arrived at the sanctuary of **Apollo** at **Delphi** around 90 CE and long served as high priest. His essays on the **Oracle** are the most thorough and revealing in the extant literature.

pneuma In ancient Greek, wind or breath, spirit or soul, much as the Sanskrit word *prana* refers to both breath and vital spirit. At **Delphi,** the mysterious substance was said to be a gift of the god **Apollo** that inspired the **Oracle**'s divine madness, though accounts were vague on whether its nature was material, spiritual, or some combination of the two. In English, *pneuma* forms the root of such words as *pneumatics,* the study of the mechanical properties of air, and *pneumatology,* the study of spiritual beings and phenomena.

polis General name for a Greek city-state.

protein A basic material of life that is made of amino acids and is essential for the growth and repair of tissue.

Pythia A synonym for the high priestess of **Apollo** at **Delphi.**

Pythian Games Held in honor of **Apollo** every four years at his sanctuary in **Delphi,** the games featured competitions not only in athletics but music and poetry. The contests were one of four Panhellenic games of ancient Greece, including, most famously, those of Olympia, forerunner of the modern Olympic games. The Pythian Games ranked second in importance. They included not only single events but the pentathlon, a grueling competition of discus, javlin, jump, footrace, and wrestling.

python In Greek mythology, the monster that ruled **Delphi** before **Apollo** killed the beast and took control of the oracular site.

reduction The main research strategy in science since the start of the scientific revolution nearly four centuries ago. It is the process by which objects, concepts, theories, or even whole sciences are reduced to more basic ones. For instance, reduction holds that a bolt of lightning with its bright flashes and fiery tendrils is nothing more than a quick flow of subatomic particles known as electrons. Strict reductionists believe that complex systems are nothing but the sum of their parts.

reductionism An attitude that sees wholes solely in terms of their parts and scientific **reduction** as the one true story of the world. Akin to **reductive naturalism,** it finds contrasting points of view in such beliefs as **holism** and **emergentism.**

reductive naturalism A philosophical view arguing that **reduction**'s many successes over the centuries show that the nature of ultimate reality is completely physical and that nothing exists beyond elemental forces and physical objects and their properties.

remote viewing A procedure developed by **parapsychologists** at the Stanford Research Institute to perform **clairvoyance** under highly controlled conditions.

Salamis A Greek island half again as large as Manhattan that nestles along the southwestern coast of what in ancient Greece was **Attica.** In 480 BCE, when the Persians invaded, Salamis belonged to **Athens** and gave shelter to perhaps a hundred thousand of the city's fleeing inhabitants. Its narrow straits saw a Greek navy of some three hundred **triremes** defeat a Persian force more than twice as large.

sedimentary rock A rock formed by the slow accumulation and cementing together of mineral grains from marine sources and the erosion of older rocks.

sibyl A woman in antiquity who was reputed to possess personal powers of prophecy or **divination.**

Socrates (469–399 BCE) He never wrote a word but became the most famous philosopher of antiquity because of his deep investigations of morality. A consummate busybody, he questioned most everyone and everything. We know of his life mainly from the writings of **Plato, Aristophanes,** and **Xenophon,** who knew him personally, and **Aristotle,** who was born a generation later.

Solon A leading politician of **Athens** during the sixth century BCE who came to sympathize with the poor and helped the city-state reform its political rights and responsibilities, laying the foundations for its democratic success.

Sophocles (c. 496–406 BCE) The second of the three great tragic dramatists of ancient Greece. He wrote more than 120 plays and won more honors than any contemporary. In *Oedipus Rex,* he has a speaker emphasize the **Oracle**'s infallibility. Even so, his general theme was that man constantly misunderstands the gods, leading to mistaken action, misery, and death.

Sparta An ancient Greek city famous for its martial prowess that dominated the **Peloponnese** prior to the fourth century BCE and often vied with **Athens** for regional power, most famously during the **Peloponnesian War.**

spiritualism The belief that departed spirits can communicate with people by means of physical phenomena, such as rapping on tables, or through mediums who go into unusual mental states such as trances to communicate with the dead.

stela An upright stone or slab with an inscribed or sculptured surface, used as a monument or a commemorative tablet.

Stoics A sect of Greek philosophers that recommended strict discipline of the body, personal bravery, and indifference to pleasure or pain. The Stoics looked to logic and virtue for guidance in life.

Strabo (*c.* 64 BCE–25 CE) A geographer born in **Anatolia,** Strabo traveled widely throughout the ancient world and reported that the **Oracle**'s sanctum beneath the temple of **Apollo** bore a rocky opening "from which arises breath that inspires a divine frenzy."

sulfur A pale-yellow nonmetallic element occurring widely in nature both free and in such compounds as hydrogen sulfide and sulfuric acid.

Syracuse A city of ancient Sicily that Greek colonists from **Corinth** founded in the eighth century BCE.

Tethys A sea goddess of Greek mythology, the wife of Oceanus. She was seen as the mother of the world's main rivers, such as the Nile, and three thousand **nymph** daughters known as the Oceanids. Modern scientists bestowed her name on a vast body of water that, millions of years ago, separated the primordial continents of Eurasia and Africa and shrank over the eons to form the Mediterranean.

telepathy A supposed power of mental perception in which impressions of any kind are communicated from one mind to another independent of the known senses. Though sometimes called thought transference, it is seen as potentially more diverse, involving the transfer of thoughts, feelings, or images directly from the mind of one person to another.

Thebes A celebrated Greek city about seventy-five kilometers, or fifty miles, east of **Delphi** where **Pindar** was born. In 336 BCE, **Alexander the Great** leveled the city after it rebelled against him but spared Pindar's birthplace.

Thermopylae A narrow pass in northern Greece between high mountains and the Gulf of Evia. There, in 480 BCE, the Spartans set up a defensive line against Persian invaders. In Greek, the word *Thermopylae* means "the hot gates," a reference to hot springs and steaming pools that bubble up there along a line of young **faults.**

travertine A natural stone made of **calcium carbonate** that is usually precipitated from groundwater. Often creamy or light in color and quite porous, it is deposited around certain springs, lakes, and streams, as well as within caves in the form of stalactites and stalagmites.

tripod A three-legged chair on which the **Oracle** sat during prophetic sessions and a main symbol of **Delphi.** After mounting the tripod, **Strabo** wrote, the **Pythia** "inhales the vapor and prophesies."

trireme An ancient warship with three tiers of oars, up to two hundred rowers, and a bronze ram at the prow for sinking enemy ships. In addition, each trireme could carry soldiers who boarded enemy ships to wage hand-to-hand combat.

Trojans The people of ancient **Troy.**

Trojan War According to legend, the conflict began when Paris of **Troy** ran away with Helen of **Sparta,** and Greek warriors in hot pursuit proceeded to besiege the Anatolian city for ten years. Frustrated in battle, they devised a hollow horse to secrete warriors into the city, achieving victory and burning Troy to the ground. Some historians see the saga as a fusion of stories told by Greeks of the **Bronze Age** or Mycaenaean period, while others discern an actual conflict usually dated to around 1200 BCE.

Troy A legendary city of **Anatolia** and site of the **Trojan War,** which Homer described in the *Iliad.* Archaeologists have unearthed a city in western Turkey, strategically placed at the entrance to the Dardanelles, that appears to be Troy.

Xenophon (*c.* 430–355 BCE) A Greek soldier and historian who early in life, like other affluent young men around **Athens,** enjoyed the company of **Socrates.** Before joining mercenaries who ransacked **Persia,** he went to **Delphi** and famously asked the **Oracle** to what god he should sacrifice in order to ensure a safe return.

Xerxes Tall and handsome, the Persian "King of Kings" ascended to the throne in 486 BCE, making him a relative newcomer when he set out to avenge his father, Darius, by conquering the Greeks. In 480 BCE, he led an armada of more than one thousand **triremes** and an army of perhaps two hundred thousand men. Xerxes watched in shock as the badly outnumbered Greeks drew much blood at **Thermopylae** and soundly defeated his navy at **Salamis,** dashing his hopes of westward expansion. In 465, one of his aides murdered him in his sleep.

Zeus The father of the gods living atop **Mount Olympus** in northern Greece.

Acknowledgments

My debts are large because this book led me into unfamiliar territory where my own knowledge proved to be quite limited. The guides on whom I relied have my deep gratitude. Any errors of fact, interpretation, or omission are, of course, my own. But I am quite thankful knowing that their generosity has made this book much better than it otherwise would have been.

To begin at the beginning, my colleagues in the science department of *The New York Times* shared my excitement when I learned of the team's findings and worked hard to produce a beautifully illustrated article on the research for the Science Times section. Thanks to Cory Dean, Laura Chang, David Corcoran, Bill Marsh, John MacLeod, and Frank Ippolito. Over the years, *Times* colleagues discussed a variety of related topics, helping me develop ideas. Thanks especially to Gina Kolata, Jim Glanz, Joe Berger, and Emily Hager. I owe much to George Johnson for his writings on the relationship between science and religion and their long efforts to subsume one another. My science colleagues are known within the paper for their collegiality and open-mindedness. If some find this book too critical of the reductive status quo, I hope they will nonetheless see it as done in a spirit of honest inquiry.

In Greece, many thanks go to Elena Partida, an archaeologist in Delphi when we first met and now the site's Curator of the Ephorate of Antiquities. Over the years, her encouragement and constructive criticism have been an enormous help. Rozina Kolonia of the Museum of Delphi also provided valuable assistance. In Greece, I was fortunate to share many meals, adventures, and musings with a production company that was making a documentary about the team's research for the Discovery Channel. Thanks to Daphna Rubin, Monica Pinto, Dave Goulding, Pat French, and Victoria King. In Delphi, on more than one occasion, the courteous staff of the Hotel Xenia made work a pleasure, an observation that in my experience can be generalized to much of Greece. Thanks to Delphi merchants Vangelis Karambalis and Aristotelis Zhsimoy. I would also like to gratefully acknowledge the help of Adonis Photiades and Vassilis Papadopoulos at the Institute of Geology and Mineral Exploration, Dominique Mulliez and Kalliopi Christophi of the French School of Athens, Gabriella Vasdeki and Katerina Papatheophani of the Gennadius Library of the American School of Classical Studies in Athens, and Dimitrios Metaxas of the Greek Ministry of Culture. In Australia, Tracey Dall of the Art Gallery of South Australia, and in Paris, J. B. Chaulet of De Boccard publishers, provided timely assistance.

In the United States, thanks go to John Adams of California State University, Heidi Butler and Betty Eo of the Rush University Medical Center, Ann Cairns of the Geological Society of America, Bonnie Clendenning of the Archaeological Institute of America, Susan Collier of the New York Graphic Society, Theodossis Demetracopoulos and Andreas Stamatakis of the Greek Press Office in New York City, Kimberley Denney of DigitalGlobe, Daniel Lederman of Google Earth, Chris Liner of the University of Tulsa, and Lisa Maurizio of Bates College.

The professionals at the Larchmont Public Library in New York turned difficult requests into a seemingly unending flow of books and articles. Special thanks go to Frank Connelly, Nancy Donovan, Ellen Fentas, Liam Hegarty, and June Hesler. Thanks, too, to the Westchester County Library System, an author's dream come true. In Britain, the Society for Psychical Research and its computerized database proved an excellent window into more than a century of the organization's literature. Thanks also go to Mark Christel of the Vassar College libraries for a professional courtesy in the final days of the book's production. In the main, the dates and spellings I use here follow those of the *Oxford Classical Dictionary*, third edition, the standard scholarly reference. Finally, the modern literature on the Oracle played a significant role in my education. As the endnotes suggest, I relied especially heavily on Herbert William Parke, Greek scholar at Trinity College, Dublin. During the middle of the last century, almost singled-handedly, he did the hard work that helped turn an abstract force of the distant past into a historical reality that modern readers had some chance of understanding.

My deepest appreciation goes to the scientists and other individuals who lived the detective story. It was their opening up in interviews and putting up with follow-up questions, their sharing of all kinds of research materials, their patience during the process of fact checking, that made this book possible. They also made excellent suggestions for its improvement. Many thanks to Jeff Chanton, Rick and Susan Spiller, and Maureen, Bob, and Sarah Capshew.

Particular thanks go to Jelle de Boer and his wife Felicité. Time spent with them—at their home in Connecticut, at Wesleyan, in Delphi and elsewhere in Greece—was not only a constant education but a source of inspiration for me and my family. I will always remember their sense of dignity and integrity, and how they graciously opened their world to us. They spared no effort in tracking down materials, responding to questions, and recalling many details of their extraordinary lives. If a book can have a heart and soul, they are it.

Acknowledgments

I owe an unusual debt of gratitude to John Hale. His own fascination with de Boer and the Oracle led him to gather materials for a book. In the end, his treatise on the Athenian navy took precedence and he generously shared the materials he had gathered, including Delphi papers, maps, drawings, and rare books. Few authors have been so lucky. At my request, Hale also produced a detailed chronology of the various phases of the discovery and combed through years of e-mails for important narrative details. Moreover, his long meditation on Delphi and his deep knowledge of classical antiquity produced an encyclopedia of insights about the Oracle and her world that he freely shared with me, and that I often incorporated into this book. It was Hale, for instance, who first pointed out the Dionysian aspects of the temple of Apollo and the importance of the Oppé paper. As if that was not enough, Hale also made available his research assistant, Bess Reed. She helped me track down important papers and books, made copies of e-mails, and produced duplicates of Hale's Delphi slides. Words cannot express my gratitude.

A number of friends, colleagues, and family members aided the enterprise or made comments that proved valuable. Thanks especially to Cecil Bakalor for *Snow*, Susan Broad for a smart distinction, Peter Coleman for *Emergence*, Sophie Kent for French translations, David Wrobel for *Julian*, and the Metro North ladies (you know who you are) for garrulous encouragement. With skill and patience, Gregory Kent used his knowledge of computers to produce a great Web site.

I owe a special debt of thanks to friends and specialists in a variety of fields who read all or part of the manuscript, making a steady stream of suggestions that greatly improved the readability and accuracy of the text. Many thanks to Walter Blanco, Gene Cittadino, Michael Lynch, Jarl Mohn, Elena Partida, Stuart Wachs, and Mitch Waldrop. This brief acknowledgment gives insufficient weight to their often extensive comments and significant help on issues ranging from factual accuracy to narrative structure, sometimes over several drafts. If this book works, it has much to do with their generosity.

It was my agent, Peter Matson of Sterling Lord Literistic, who first asked me if the scientific discoveries about the Oracle of Delphi warranted a book. The repercussions of his question included years of stolen hours. Even so, it was worth it, Peter, if only for the philosophical voyage you helped set me on.

As for Ann Godoff at The Penguin Press, my editor, I can scarcely find words to express my gratitude. Her careful guidance through every stage of this book, from inception to artwork, leaves me breathless. She got the big picture as well as the microscopic details, usually conveying her insights with elegant simplicity (but at times, when needed, with a sledgehammer). Once, late in the editing process, I was astonished to see that she had gone back and compared part of what I had just submitted with an earlier draft, and suggested, correctly as it turned out, that the previous version was better. That's dedication.

Acknowledgments

Thank you, Ann, and thanks to all the people at Penguin for making this experience so personal and pleasurable. It was more like joining a family than interacting with a corporation. Particular thanks go to Liza Darnton, Claire Vaccaro, Jennifer Tait, Abigail Cleaves, and Jackie Aher for her wonderful illustrations.

Lastly, I owe the greatest debt to my own family. It was their love and support, understanding and interest, that gave this book its human foundations. I'll never forget seeing Delphi through the eyes of my children—Max, Izzi, and Julie—or watching how they fell in love with Greece and took such pride in suggesting improvements for the book. They also made important contributions in their own right, Julie taking the jacket photograph, Izzi developing ideas for the Web site, and Max scrutinizing the Chronology.

My wife, Tanya Mohn, aided all phases of the book's production, from parsing the philosophical issues to translating French and Greek phrases to shaping the manuscript to correcting my grammar to weighing subtitles to acquiring the book's artwork. My best friend and best critic, she often played a decisive role. Tanya also knew when to step back, graciously putting up with *the other woman*, as we call her, the one who came to visit and ended up staying—day after day, year after year. Tanya never grew resentful, or if she did, she never showed it. Instead, she constantly made the sacrifices that let me spend more time with the guest. Oracles and muses of all kinds are probably more important than we realize. I know little of such things. What I know for sure, and what I treasure, is that, without Tanya, this book would not be.

Index

Index

Index

Mount Parnassus, 18, 22–24, 27, 67, 77, *144,* 188, 298, 301, 302–3
  cleft in side of, 21, 22, 23, 69, 125
  de Boer at, 122, 123, 125
Murray, Gilbert, 94–95
Mycenaeans, 23, 27, 295, 301, 303, 307
Myers, Frederic W. H., 75–76, 94, 106, 229, 248, 302
mysticism, 1, 242, 244, 247
  in Greece, *see* Greek religion and mysticism
  spiritualism, 73–74, 75, 76, 84, 306
  see also extrasensory perception; prophecy and divination

naiads, 22, 36, 297, 301, 302
narcotics, 172, 205
National Geographic Society, 102
Nature, 193
New York Times, 80–81, 82, 84
Nietzsche, Friedrich, 41
nitrous oxide, 205, 206–8, 209, 211
Norton, Charles, 79, 80
nymphs 302, 306

occult, *see* mysticism
Odyssey (Homer), 27, 300
Oedipus, 12, 302
Oedipus Rex (Sophocles), 12, 305
Olympus, 23, 24, 25, 302, 307
omphalos, 28–30, *29, 30,* 36, *37,* 223, 224–25, 298, 302
  archaeological investigations and, 98
  Holland's ideas on, 100–101, 102
Oppé, Adolph Paul, 91–93, 94, 98, 101, 103, 104
Oracle of Delphi (Pythia), 1–2, 249–50
  adyton of, *see adyton* at Delphi
  ambiguous information given by, 16, 18, 54, 56, 239
  Apollo's union with, *11,* 30, 34–36, 243
  Apollo voiced through, 1, 10, 11, 19
  Aristotle and, 63, 65
  Athens and, 45–46
  Christianity and, 70–71
  cold weather and, 40, 172
  Collier's portrait of, *iv, vi,* 84–85, 102, 185
  colonies and, 27–28, 43
  Crisa and, 49–50
  Croesus and, 52–54, 76, 94, 95, 298
  cup with portrait of, 34, *35*
  debate over, 90–106, 130, 139, 140
  decline of, 68, 69
  Dionysus and, 42
  early communications of, 24
  flailing portrayal of, *11*
  in fourth century, 66
  governance guided by, 43, 44, 45–47, 66

  importance and status of, 2, 10–12, 14, 16, 18–19, 25, 27, 28, 49, 51, 55, 63, 240, 241, 242, 249
  innocence of, 30–31
  literature on, 9–11, 27, 39–40, 66–69, 76–77, 91–92, 93, 94, 105, 121, 136–37, 139, 213, 240; *see also* Plutarch
  Michelangelo's painting of, 3, *3,* 77
  moral influence of, 2, 47–48, 241
  mystic pneuma inhaled by, 19–21, 36, 67, 68, 69, 90, 91–94, 98, 104, 105–6, 121, 136–37, 213, 240, 247, 304; *see also* Delphi, fumes underneath; ethylene
  opera on, 83–84
  Persians and, 10, 53–62
  petitioners of, 36–40, 43–44, 66, 68
  Plato and, 63, 64
  psychic powers of, 1–2, 3–4, 6, 18, 20, 39, 94–95, 105, 106, 241, 244, 246, 247, 248
  as Pythia, 27, 304
  recorded answers of, 39–40, 239, 240
  reduction and, 233, 237, 238–42, 244
  rituals of, 34–36, 38–39, 67, 297
  silencing of, 71, 77, 150, 198
  slavery and, 48, 241
  Society for Psychical Research's interest in, 75, 76
  Socrates and, 63–64, 241
  Sparta and, 44–45, 46–47, 59–60
  tripod of, 21, *26,* 36, *37,* 49, 70, 81, *99,* 100, 101, 151, 159, 307
  wealth and, 48
  women chosen as, 13, 21, 30–34
oracles, 14, 32, 302
  alphabet, 15
  Croesus's test of, 52–53, 298
  men as, 19
  questions asked of, 43
Oropus, 52

paleomagnetism, 112, 119, 302
Pan, 14
Pangaea, *116,* 302
pantheon, 302
Papalexandrou, Nassos, 62
paranormal, 75
  see also extrasensory perception
parapsychology, 302
Parke, H. W., 32, 48, 105, 139
Parnassus, *see* Mount Parnassus
Parthenon, 9, 62, 82, 126, 295, 297, 303
Pausanias, 36, 50, 52, 77–78, 86, 90, 92, 139, 151, 301, 303
Peloponnese, 19, 23, 24, 25, 44, 60–61, 91, 122, 135, 297, 301, 303, 305
Peloponnesian War, 303, 305
Pericles, 303
Persia, 10, 53–62, 221, 303

Index

Illustration Credits

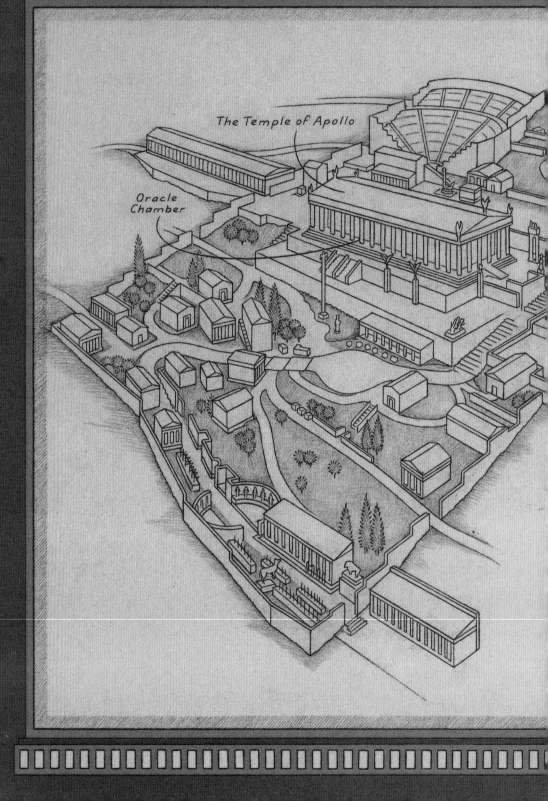

The Temple of Apollo

Oracle
Chamber